Latin American Media:
Guidance and Censorship

Latin American Media:
Guidance and Censorship

M A R V I N A L I S K Y

IOWA STATE UNIVERSITY PRESS / AMES

Composed and printed by
The Iowa State University Press
Ames, Iowa 50010

FIRST EDITION, 1981

Library of Congress Cataloging in Publication Data

Alisky, Marvin.
    Latin American media.

    Includes bibliographical references and index.
    1. Mass media—Censorship—Latin America.
I. Title.
P95.82.L29A4   302.2′3   81–5084
ISBN 0–8138–1525–8   AACR2

Contents

Preface

FOR more than thirty years I have followed the efforts of numerous reporters, broadcasters, editors, and publishers to chronicle the public life of Latin America with as little governmental direction as possible or at least with as few official restraints and demands on communication as political realities allowed. Some journalists have endured jail or exile for their principles. Others have grown wealthy accepting government bribes and subsidies to portray regimes in power in the most sympathetic light.

Latin American governments have ranged from mild and harsh right-wing dictatorships to authoritarian reformer regimes to Communist rule—with variations all along the political spectrum. Those Latin American republics with democratically chosen, representative governments and genuinely free mass media have always been in the minority. A majority of the Latin American nations for years relied on overt censorship to diminish political opponents and bolster the administration in power. But in recent decades several Latin American nations have provided a third category: countries with considerable government guidance of the media without direct censorship.

The thrust of this book, therefore, is to emphasize first those Latin American nations with controls over the media that are less obvious than censorship and that seemingly project the harmless image of routine regulatory entities and regulations required by the modern economies. These controls include distribution of paper, which periodicals need in order to publish, and broadcasting regulations for a region of the world in which radio has become the number one mass medium of communication. Other indirect controls result from government investment in joint public-private ownership of media and in management of the flow of news through the staging of events or the selectivity with which officials release information to the public.

To gain a perspective of the government-media relations for the entire region of Latin America, this volume also compares and contrasts the relatively small number of republics having true freedom of the press and broadcasting and those nations suffering official censorship.

This volume has been written for more than one interest group; it provides information on government-media relationships and the status of the mass media in reporting on politics and other aspects of public life. Students of political science, other social sciences, journalism, and broadcasting can each find the key elements they seek in analyzing Latin America's public life and national cultures.

Over the years, first as a news correspondent then as a political scientist in almost every one of the Latin American republics, I have watched governments try to account for their stewardship of office. Whether the government in question was authoritarian, dictatorial, benevolently autocratic, democratic, or a mixture of political postures, each seemed to court public opinion to bolster its own feeling of legitimacy. The democratic administrations worked to gain a positive image through public relations and publicity techniques far removed from unconstitutional restraints. The undemocratic regimes tended to rely on direct application of their power, forcing the media to develop mass support for their administrations. At the time of this writing, Latin America prepares to enter the 1980s with most government attempts at guidance of the media still being practiced, though happily press freedom continues to reappear in some Latin American nations after periodic absences.

For those seeking a history of the inter-American group of journalists fighting press censorship since 1926, Mary A. Gardner's *The Inter-American Press Association* (Austin: University of Texas Press, 1967) will prove helpful. For those seeking a profound analysis of newspaper editorials as they relate to political crises in a major Latin American republic, Alfred Stepan's *The Military in Politics: Changing Patterns in Brazil* (Princeton, N.J.: Princeton University Press, 1971) will be essential as a model reference. For those seeking continuing updating on the never-ending struggle of Latin American newspapers to overcome governmental pressures, the monthly *IAPA News*, and the annual *IAPA Freedom of the Press Report* (Inter-American Press Association, Miami, Florida) and the *IPI Report* (International Press Institute, Zurich, Switzerland) are invaluable. For verbatim excerpts of significant Latin American radio and television broadcasts, the *Foreign Broadcast Information Service* (National Technical Information Service, U.S. Department of Commerce) is the only daily source available.

To specifically thank all those who helped me gain, from 1947 to 1979, the information used in this book would be impossible. In a meager paragraph of acknowledgement, only a few of those providing major help can be listed.

Richard F. Staar, associate director, Hoover Institution of Stanford University, provided me with the research facilities for a quarter term as a visiting fellow.

Arizona State University provided a faculty research grant to investigate government control of newsprint distribution.

The Fulbright Commission made possible my acquiring academic field experience as a visiting professor in Peru and Nicaragua.

Russell Tornabene, a vice-president of NBC news, made it possible for me to gain invaluable experience as a news correspondent in Latin America.

James B. Canel, executive director of the Inter-American Press Association, provided important data about Latin American newspapers through the years.

Journalism professors John C. Merrill, John T. McNelly, Mary A. Gardner, Michael Sewell, and Jerry Knudson provided invaluable information.

Political scientists Martin C. Needler, Robert E. Scott, Roderic A. Camp, L. Vincent Padgett, Riordan Roett, and Frederick C. Turner provided advice, as did historians Stanley R. Ross and James W. Wilkie.

Luigi Einaudi, now of the Department of State, gave vital orientation when at the RAND Corporation.

My wife Beverly and our sons Sander and Joseph adjusted their schedules and needs to accommodate to my field trips and long periods of uninterrupted research.

MARVIN ALISKY

Arizona State University
Tempe, Arizona
September 1980

An Overview

EACH government in Latin America, whether democratic or dictatorial or somewhere in between, seeks to present as positive an image of itself as possible, publicly stressing every semblance of success and ignoring or rationalizing those failures that have not yet risen to nationwide disputes or been incorporated into the slogans of advocates of violence.

Censorship evokes a negative connotation: the silencing of critics before their accusations can be printed or aired, the suppression of stories challenging the legitimacy of governments in power, and the elimination of reports questioning the soundness of official policies or implying that such policies benefit the entrenched few at the expense of the majority of citizens. Governmental guidance of media, however, suggests official exploitation of the media to mobilize popular support for those in power and mass cooperation for their programs and ideologies. From the 1820s to the 1940s, traditional Latin American *caudillos,* or strong-man presidents, often silenced the press so as to minimize political opposition. But Juan Perón in the 1940s and Fidel Castro in the 1960s utilized the mass media to "reeducate" Argentines and Cubans into embracing ideologies and life-styles breaking radically from the past. Rafael Trujillo, in power in the Dominican Republic from 1931 to 1961, required newspapers and broadcasting stations to praise his rule—with adulation for him personally.

Since 1968 in Peru, the generals waging a revolution from the top have not been content to minimize media criticism. Juan Velasco and Francisco Morales Bermúdez

1

sought, instead, to utilize the press and broadcasting of Peru to engender mass support for their social reform programs.

One widely used method of influencing Latin American mass media has been bribery, but inasmuch as no government ever makes public its records of monetary payments or the awarding of jobs or favors in return for sympathetic press coverage, a scholarly survey can provide only a few glaring examples.

A kindred control, which is legal and therefore does appear in government budgets, is the device of government subsidies. A government may gain sympathetic coverage of officialdom in return for subsidizing the price of importing or manufacturing newsprint, printing presses, or broadcasting station equipment. Such subsidies may be appropriations, tax rebates, or both.

Latin America consists of a continent and a half in territory; is the home of more than 330 million people; and is grouped into twenty-one republics plus Caribbean dominion islands. Unlike most of the developing nations of Asia and Africa—only recently converted into independent countries—the Latin American republics have more than a century and a half of experience as nation-states. During the recent decades when Asian and African countries were acquiring national independence, the concept of government-owned media already had become widespread in Europe. But the Latin American press evolved in the 1820s, an age in which newspapers universally tended to be privately owned and independently operated.

Although this book groups Latin American nations into three categories—nations with censorship, nations with press freedom, and nations with various direct and indirect controls for guidance and influence—the classifications are not mutually exclusive. For example, during the apex of Juan Perón's power in Argentina, he employed direct censorship. But for the outstanding holdout newspaper, *La Prensa,* which did not publish under censors, he utilized less direct methods of harassment. The rolls of newsprint were impounded at warehouse docks for "improper" payment of import taxes or other trumped-up technicalities. Similarly, a radio station cannot transmit without power tubes. And like newsprint, such vital parts of a transmitter often are imported into a Latin American nation and can be delayed in customs indefinitely by a government determined to pressure a broadcaster.

News perhaps ranges from what people want to know to what they ought to know, from sports scores and gossip about popular entertainers to financial reports and biographical sketches. But the heart of the news of any nation centers in government and politics, the entities formulating the legal framework within which daily life itself must be conducted. A government determined to constrict the flow of news most certainly will attempt to manage and shape the quantity and quality of information the various entities of the state furnish newspaper and broadcasting reporters.

Any Latin American government reacts favorably when the news carries stories about its national development. In recent years the Argentine government actually tried to specify that 50 percent of the news published on any given day be about Argentina, but the availability of such stories could not be made to respond to that arbitrary law, which simply could not be carried out in practice. (For more information see "Second Perón Era" in Chapter 9.) In Cuba, Communist party ideology shapes the selection of news stories, but even in a controlled society, whether Marxist or right-wing, no government can guarantee that reporters in the field will encounter sufficient newsworthy data in prescribed proportional categories.

Major newspapers in Latin America publish far more news about their own country and more world news than they do news of other Latin American nations. Latin Americans sometimes know as little about some of their hemisphere neighbors as many North American newspaper readers and television and radio listeners do. Spot checks by the author over the past two decades have indicated that Mexican newspapers regularly carry some stories of significance about Central America but often neglect all but one or two South American nations on any given day. Writing in *Times of the Americas* (Jan. 4, 1978) about the surprising mutual ignorance between neighboring Venezuela and Brazil, William Giandoni, Latin American editor of the Copley News Service, put the problem this way:

> Venezuela's President Carlos Andrés Pérez, after a quick trip to Brazil . . . sounded surprised by his encounter with

Brazilians. . . . There are no highway or railroad links between Venezuela and Brazil. The 900 miles of border they share is mostly undeveloped jungle.

There is also a language barrier. Latin America's largest nation, Brazil, is Portuguese speaking, whereas each of its neighbors speaks Spanish. But even across the many borders in Latin America where Spanish is the common language, the number and length of stories about neighboring nations remain disappointingly meager. Within each Latin American nation, however, the feeling of nationalism coupled with growing systems of mass media insures continuing sensitivity between government and press, with the resulting types of governmental guidance being the locus of emphasis of this volume.

For many decades, political philosophers have warned that if a government requires that the newspapers of a nation must be filled with good news, then that nation's jails may be filled with good people. If a government prevents critical or negative news from being published, it may also be restricting the political liberties of those trying to correct mistakes of administrators in power or those who publicly call attention to national problems not being solved. Press freedom in Latin America does not guarantee that problems will be solved but the converse holds that when press freedom is lacking both leaders and citizens do not face problems openly or solve them in ways that are equitable for all citizens.

1

Latin America:
Mass Media and Class Media

A majority of the nations of Latin America display varying degrees of authoritarian government in their political systems and a minority display varying degrees of democratic government. Each nation's press and broadcasting naturally reflect the political system in which the mass media must operate. The quantity and quality of the information about the public life of each nation the mass media transmit to the citizens contribute to the change or continuity of all the other public institutions of that nation. Thus the governments exert an impact on the media but the media also exert an impact on the government.[1]

If the press and broadcasting stations can maintain some autonomy in their operations and are allowed to gather and report the news without government direction or supervision, then that government may learn about problems and errors confronting the nation as quickly as it learns about achievements. When censorship or varying degrees of guidance hamper the press, the government may learn of malfunctions in its own agencies or in the economy by hapchance, rumor, or word-of-mouth clues. Naturally, government administrators at every level wish to present the most favorable portrayal possible of their own stewardship of office. Reporters and editors free of government restraint are more likely to make known the negative factors in the news than are the officials involved in such stories.

Where authoritarian government prevails, it demands that the mass media help mobilize citizens for national development. If the government attempts undemocratic controls to suppress its opposition, full censorship ensues. The libertarian theory contends that a free press allows the public to check on government.[2] Libertarian press situations have been fully enjoyed by only a few Latin American republics: Venezuela, Colombia, Costa Rica, and before the 1970s Uruguay and Chile.

Latin American newspaper and magazine readers tend to be from the middle and upper classes. They are more likely than the working class to be literate, to be able to afford the price of a paper or periodical, and to be sufficiently politically active to require detailed news about government. Economic and literacy factors in more than half of the Latin American republics tend to make newspapers a "class" medium. By contrast, thanks to inexpensive transistor receivers, radio news remains a mass medium throughout Latin America, serving the illiterate and semiliterate low-income majority.

The Physical Setting

Latin America stretches from the United States border southward to Tierra del Fuego, where Argentina and Chile pinch together into a continental tip called Cape Horn which juts into the frozen waters approaching the Antarctic. It encompasses islands of the Caribbean ranging from Cuba, ninety miles south of Florida, to tiny isles with English-speaking blacks crowded onto enclaves in a demographic region where hybrid Spanish-Indian (*mestizo*) ethnic norms prevail.

These nations range from one-third of an island called Haiti (French speaking) to the half-continent called Brazil (Portuguese speaking). Haiti, 90 percent illiterate with complete press and broadcasting censorship by the Duvalier dictatorship, does not yield enough significant activity for an instructive case study. Brazil in 1978 shifted from censorship to cautious press freedom under mild dictatorial political guidelines.

Argentina, Uruguay, and Costa Rica have populations with European-origin majorities. Brazil, Cuba, and Panama have large black minorities. The typical Latin American is a *mestizo.* When the English came to Virginia in 1607, archaeologists estimate that in all of what is today the United States, ½ million Indians roamed a relatively empty North America. When Hernán Cortés and his conquistadores came to Mexico in 1519, an estimated 25 million Indians populated what today makes up Mexico and Central America and another 15 million made up the Inca Empire of South America. During three centuries of Spanish colonialism, from the 1520s to the 1820s, only 300,000 Spaniards came to the New World to find their fortunes. They came as soldiers or explorers, leaving their families in Europe and beginning new hybrid families among the Indians.[3]

By contrast, the English, Dutch, and French journeying to North

America brought their wives and children and cleared the wooded terrain as they planted cotton and tobacco. Spaniards sought the gold and silver of the Aztec and Inca empires. North America had the "colonization" and Latin America had the "conquest."

The Andes and other mountain ranges of Latin America tended to limit populations to the coastal plains, whereas in North America rolling plains made possible the spread of people throughout the interior of the continent.

Language and Communication

The Spanish language predominates in eighteen of the Latin American republics. Yet more than 121 million Brazilians speak Portuguese and millions of Indians in southern Mexico, Guatemala, Ecuador, Peru, Bolivia, and Paraguay speak Nahuatl, Maya, Quechua, Aymará, and Guaraní. In 1978, of the estimated 330 million Latin Americans, more than 15 million spoke primarily Indian tongues.[4] In the Caribbean nations of Jamaica, Trinidad-Tobago, and Guyana, English is the national language.

In addition to minority languages the factors limiting newspaper reading are the high degree of adult illiteracy, plus the high prices of newspapers and magazines that inhibit buying by the majority of Latin Americans struggling with low incomes. Their meager purchasing power further limits television ownership, but radios can be found everywhere. The inexpensive transistor receiver has made radio the number one mass medium.

Uruguay is 92 percent literate, Argentina 91 percent, Chile and Costa Rica each 90 percent, and Venezuela 88 percent. And, appropriately, these nations traditionally lead the other Latin American republics in sales of daily newspapers per 1,000 population.[5]

In the highly literate nations, the official literacy rate and the functional adult literacy rate match. In Colombia, with 60 percent adult literacy, the figures also match. However, in several other republics, Ministry of Education or Census Bureau percentages for adult literacy are based on minimum ability to read a limited number of basic words including the names of the respondents. Functional literacy at the level permitting understanding of a newspaper or magazine story would yield far lower percentages. Brazil claims 81 percent literacy, but perhaps only half its adults can read the news. Mexico and Peru each claim better than 70 percent literacy, but in each case better than one-third of the population should be considered functionally illiterate.[6]

For a majority of Latin Americans—the millions of poor, working-class men and women—inflation, unemployment, and underemployment have kept their purchasing power not much above the level of barter trade. With transistor radios, however, music gives them daily entertainment, thanks to a battery that lasts six months to one year and costs the equivalent of twenty United States cents or less. Daily serialized dramas, known in English as "soap operas" and in Spanish as "novelas," reduce their boredom. News may be limited and in bulletin form without the details they could find only in a newspaper, but radio diminishes their isolation and links them to the world.[7]

In Guatemala, Ecuador, Bolivia, and Paraguay, governments have been slow to incorporate fully their large Indian minorities into the urban national way of life. But in Peru, by contrast, since October 1968 military reformers running the government have tried to institutionalize a social revolution, including launching for the first time provincial schools in which the language of instruction is Quechua, not Spanish, and in which the viewpoint of the courses is Indian rather than Hispanic.[8] Peru has some radio programs in Quechua and in the late 1980s the Ministry of Education plans to publish a simplified newspaper in that language.

As in the other developing areas of the world (Asia and Africa) so too in Latin America the absence of adult literacy in the dominant language of a nation inhibits not only newspaper readership but also direct, meaningful, political participation.

Yet the converse of that hypothesis is not true. That is, the presence of literacy does not by itself guarantee either avid daily attunement to the flow of news or widespread democratic political activism with the implied yield of representative government. Remember that in Nazi Germany under Hitler, 95 percent literacy did not prevent fascist totalitarianism. During 1933–1945, every German was expected to read newspapers daily. Those papers brainwashed, inflamed, and instructed what the government line was and demanded conformity. In the Soviet Union at the time the Bolsheviki took power in 1917, Russia suffered high adult illiteracy. Under the tutelage of a Communist dictatorship, the Soviet Union became a highly literate nation, but that literacy alone has not brought freedom from news censorship nor democracy with competing political parties and the public tolerance of divergent viewpoints. The situation depends upon the presence or absence of various other factors combining to yield freedom of information or conspiring to yield government-imposed indoctrination.[9]

As we focus on Latin America, we must distinguish between "press freedom," which is the right to publish freely, and "freedom of information," which is the right to gather news from official and unofficial sources without government interference.[10]

In Latin America's Communist state, Cuba, the government controls the mass media completely, but all publications are not owned by the government. The principal mass medium of Cuba is the daily newspaper *Granma,* which is owned not by the government but by the Communist Party of Cuba (Partido Comunista de Cuba or PCC). Even a cursory study of the Cuban power structure shows that the apex of policy formulation is the PCC, not the executive branch of government,[11] even allowing for changes promulgated in the 1975 Constitution. Similarly, in the Soviet Union the apex of power resides in the Central Committee of the Communist Party, as political scientists point out when referring to the top leader of the USSR as the party chairman rather than the prime minister of the government.

A new model of governmental guidance of the mass media arose in Peru in 1974 when the military rulers created a system of custodial publishers. Each vocational interest group of workers had an expropriated daily newspaper assigned to it. In 1978, however, the government drastically curtailed that model, to allow workers at the newspapers or former owners to puchase stock, as policy formulators sought new mechanisms for a transition from military to elected civilian government.[12]

Newspaper Ownership

In Chile, the government for decades owned and published *La Nación,* one of the major Santiago newspapers competing with privately owned rival dailies. It supported the administration of whoever was president: the Conservative party's Jorge Alessandri in 1958–1964; the Christian Democrats' Eduardo Frei in 1964–1970; and Marxist Salvador Allende in 1970–1973. With the advent of the military regime of General Pinochet in 1973, the paper was suspended.

In Mexico City, the daily *El Nacional* originally was incorporated by the Central Executive Committee of the government's dominant political party, the Institutional Revolutionary Party (Partido Revolucionario Institucional or PRI), but later the federal government itself bought majority stock control even though it already set editorial policies through its entwinement with the PRI.

Under the rule of General Omar Torrijos in Panama from 1968 to 1978, the government increased its investment in the nominally privately owned newspapers to insure editorial control.

Of the approximately 960 daily newspapers published in twenty-three Latin American nations in 1978, fewer than twenty-four were owned outright by governments, but several dailies had private publishers in partnership with governments that had bought significant minority stock holdings.[13] Sometimes over-the-counter stock purchases make accurate tabulations on the extent of such holdings impossible to document. Sales records at stock exchanges simply do not show these investments. The clues come from the budgets of Latin American government development banks or from the annual reports of the public corporations in which these banks have invested.[14]

A majority of the most influential daily newspapers in Latin America have been owned by publishers who were also leaders of the most powerful or major political parties in their nations.

In every Latin American republic except Brazil, the major dailies of the nation cluster in the national capital. Provincial dailies often remain relatively weak organs of political commentary in terms of shaping a nation's public opinion. In Brazil, Mexico, Colombia, and Ecuador, leading provincial dailies do affect national public opinion, but in almost every Latin American republic, the most prestigious dailies in the capital are the principal forums for defining national issues. In Brazil, the leading dailies are in Rio de Janeiro and São Paulo, whereas the capital is Brasília.

Broadcasting Ownership

When radio pioneers set up the first stations in Latin America during 1920–1925, governments and private broadcasters both established stations. However, the pattern was soon set with a large majority of the stations being privately owned and a minority being government owned until recently.[15]

In Cuba, since the advent of the Communist government in 1961, all radio and television facilities have been owned by the government. In Peru, since 1971, the government has owned 51 percent of all private television stations and 25 percent of all private radio stations, but the dominant radio service, *Radio Nacional,* has been a government entity for decades.

In Colombia the government owns the television networks and stations, and operates its own radio network in competition with private networks. In Mexico, in the 1970s, the government invested in two Mexico City television stations and their provincial networks and in a holding corporation which competes with the commercial networks and stations. Latin American television began in Mexico City in 1950, when privately owned Channel 4, XHTV, went on the air. In 1951 Latin America's second television station went on the air in Buenos

Aires; it was controlled by the government of President Juan Perón through a private-public mixed corporation, with shares held by private investors and by the government. In the 1970s the Argentine government expropriated the private television stations but remained content to control the private radio stations through censorship.

In all the Latin American republics the basic control mechanism has been the licensing of stations to assigned frequencies and power, with licenses being renewed periodically. In the 1970s, broadcasting censorship was practiced in Chile, Uruguay, Paraguay, Bolivia, Ecuador, Panama, Nicaragua, Honduras, El Salvador, Guatemala, Haiti, and Cuba. In Brazil, broadcasting censorship began in 1964, eased in 1974, and ended in 1978, just as it was being intensified in neighboring Argentina.

In the Caribbean the independent dominion in the British Commonwealth, Jamaica, has 2 million English-speaking citizens in its island nation of 11,000 square miles. After the socialist government of Prime Minister Michael Manley took office in 1972, the government expropriated the radio and television stations and networks of the nation: *Radio Jamaica* and the Jamaica Broadcasting Corporation, and the *Daily News.* As Clifton Neita, managing editor of the *Daily Gleaner,* reported, in 1979 the government formulated a five-year communication plan which could lead to the takeover of the only remaining mass medium independent of the government, the *Gleaner*.[16] This plan called for a Third World perspective from all the nation's media and full support for the government. The *Gleaner* has been politically independent, neither supporting the government's party nor the opposition party.

News Flow: Into and out of Latin America

As journalism professor John T. McNelly of the University of Wisconsin has observed, the information about world news coming into a nation directly affects the concepts about the world that nation's editors, readers, listeners, and televiewers possess. His research in Latin America suggests the special significance of the mass media as sources of informational mobility among the less privileged citizens of a nation.[17] Whether meager or extensive, news of the world helps to form the concepts citizens hold about the world and about their own nation.

In 1893 the three largest news agencies in the world were the Associated Press, a private company in the United States; Reuters, the

British news agency, privately owned but with financial ties to the government; and the then French news agency Havas, succeeded after World War II by Agence France Presse.

These three agencies agreed to divide the world among themselves for purposes of gathering and distributing news to client newspapers. The AP would gather and supply news in Latin America, Reuters in Asia and Africa, and Havas in Europe. However, other news agencies were beginning to grow in Germany, Italy, Spain, Russia, and Japan and they had no intention of limiting their own quest for clients. Not since Pope Alexander VI in 1493 had apportioned the world between the two Catholic empires, Spain and Portugal, for the seeking of converts, had any leaders made such global assumptions for providing basic services.[18]

In the aftermath of 1893, newspaper publishers of the developing nations simply did not recognize this division of the world into three spheres of news coverage. As small news services expanded, the big three agencies faced real competition. By 1917 the upstart United Press had beaten AP to the biggest newspapers in Latin America as clients.[19] By the 1920s, UP had more newspaper subscribers than AP in every Latin American nation. In recent decades some non-Marxist newspapers and broadcasting stations in Latin America have added the wire service of the Italian news agency ANSA, the West German agency DPA, the Cuban government's news service Prensa Latina, or the Soviet Union's news service TASS.

In San José, Costa Rica, at a conference sponsored by UNESCO on July 21, 1976, various Latin American governments endorsed a plan whereby in the future they would finance a news service and thereby control the content of stories this projected Latin American service would gather and disseminate. This proposed official news agency would "stress the achievements of the nations of Latin America instead of the negative emphasis on reporting crises" carried by the independent news services.[20]

The privately owned newspapers and broadcasting stations of the Western Hemisphere, represented by the Inter-American Press Association and the Inter-American Broadcasters Association, rejected the UNESCO encouragement of government "guidance" of the flow of news, calling it an attempt to substitute political propaganda for objective reporting. Nevertheless, at the final session of this Intergovernmental Conference on Communication Policies in Latin America of UNESCO, a resolution passed favoring the plan.[21]

At the UNESCO conference in Paris in November 1978, the general asembly voted down a similar plan for a worldwide news service funded and controlled by Third World nations. The *Washington Post,* in covering the conference, pointed out how different the Reuters version of the general assembly was from that of Tanjug, the Yugoslav news agency serving as the Third World's pooled news service. Reuters told of behind-the-scenes pressures by the Soviet Union and its allies for the government news service, whereas the Tanjug report did not.[22] Further, the Tanjug editors rejected statements from Colonel Quaddafi, the Libyan head of state, that conflicted with views from the leaders of other Moslem nations. The incident illustrated the problem, or perhaps impossibility, of a pooled agency of governments conducting world news coverage on a daily basis if each story had to have the political sensitivities of each nation considered ahead of the basic professional concerns of news gathering: Who did what, how, where, when, and why? For editors independent of governments, these questions must be answered no matter which leaders might like or dislike the answer. Latin American government leaders not committed to press freedom always charge that their nation's image has been damaged when stories about their public life include failures as well as successes of government programs or even errors in judgment.

In a majority of the Latin American republics, domestic reporters usually are inhibited by their governments from probing deeply or consistently into the malfunctions of officialdom. It remains for foreign correspondents to uncover such matters when permitted to do so. Bureaucrats bent on guiding the flow of news into and out of their nation can then blame the outside news services for contributing to national problems by having reported that they exist or by having revealed in detail their extent.

In the larger Latin American republics, some privately owned national news services have continued to function. In Argentina, the Saporiti News Service, founded in 1900, has managed to survive that republic's periods of dictatorship and censorship. In May 1968 the Argentine government bought the previously private Telenoticiosa Americana news agency (better known as Telam) and added the administration of government advertising to its function as a news service for Argentine mass media.[23]

In Mexico, from 1950 on, the privately owned newspaper chain of thirty-seven dailies, the Cadena García Valseca, had operated its own news service nationwide. In 1972 the Mexican government's SOMEX corporation bought the CGV and has continued to operate its news service.[24] Mexico's privately owned news agencies, cooperatively operated by member newspapers, include the Asociación de Periódicos Independientes or API (Independent Newspapers Association), the

Asociación de Editores de los Estados or AEE (Association of Editors of the States), the Agencia Mexicana de Información or AMI (Mexican News Agency), and the Mexican Press Service. Several private feature syndicates and public relations agencies provide background stories on sports on a fee basis. The Mexican government operates the Notimex service to distribute news about major government policies and programs.

Similarly, in Brazil numerous private agencies provide national or regional news or features to client newspapers, magazines, or broadcasting stations. The media corporation, Diários Associados, founded by the late Francisco de Assis Chateaubriand, began its DA news service primarily for the thirty-two newspapers, twenty-four radio stations, eighteen television stations, and four magazines it owned and then took on any other media subscribers who wished to purchase the DA service. DA reached its peak in 1964; after 1968 it began accepting government subsidies, which restricted its independent operations.[25] Even the ending of government press censorship in 1978 did not end the subsidies.

News from Latin America in the United States

News about Latin America usually receives scant space or air time in the mass media of the United States. It took a missile crisis in 1962 and Castro's troops fighting in Africa in the late 1970s to insure the publishing of much news about Cuba. Not until the 1977 Senate debate over transfer of sovereignty of the Panama Canal to Panama did that republic rate headlines except for a few times when tensions or coups spelled out violence. News of Mexico centered in tourism until the late 1970s, when Mexico's large numbers of migrants coming into the United States became continuing news and its recently discovered large petroleum reserves became significant to a fuel conscious North American public.

Back in 1949 Harry B. Murkland, editor of hemispheric news for *Newsweek,* analyzed the news blind spot U.S. editors had about Latin America. He observed that a majority of the news personnel and their readerships and audiences were of European origin and had been brought up on European history. If a news story came from Moscow or Paris or London, the reader or listener had some general knowledge about the country involved. But if a story came from Bogotá, that person might not even know the nation involved was Colombia, let alone much about its public life.[26]

In the three decades since that observation, the situation has changed somewhat in terms of news personnel because more editors and reporters of Latin American origin are now working for newspapers, broadcasting stations, and networks. Yet Latin American history or other studies of the area still have not become mainstream curricular offerings in either high schools or universities.

Also, because of the several hundred thousand refugees from Castro's Cuba who settled in Florida, the Puerto Ricans in New York, and the millions of Chicanos in the Southwest and West, significant numbers of Spanish-speaking Americans have made Spanish a popular foreign language in the schools. Travel writers everywhere plus editors and reporters in the Southwest and Florida have increased news coverage of the Mexican borderlands and the Caribbean. But consider one of the largest nations in the world in terms of land area or population, Brazil. Its language, Portuguese, remains basically unknown and untaught in the United States. This republic of 121 million Brazilians increased its industrial output by 7.5 percent during 1978, with a 16.3 percent boost in its automobile industry, which turns out more vehicles than does either the Soviet Union or Britain.[27] Yet Brazil rarely rates coverage even on the financial pages of newspapers, with the exception of the *Wall Street Journal,* which monitors it regularly.

After the Pearl Harbor attack bringing the United States into World War II, after the Korean War, and after the longtime struggle in Vietnam, news of Asia did increase on occasion in U.S. newspapers and broadcasts. The dramatic East-West struggles for power in the nations of Africa helped improve that continent's coverage. The flow of news from Latin America, however, has remained more sporadic. Compared with a battalion of U.S. news correspondents in key capitals of Europe and Asia, a mere corporal's squad of reporters file back to North America from the largest Latin American cities.

Not that the AP and UPI do not carry over their wires daily several thousand words of news about Latin America. Also, the handful of broadcast network correspondents telephone New York or Los Angeles daily to record stories or relay by satellite communication or airline flights reels of film and video tape. A tiny portion of what correspondents send to New York or Los Angeles actually ever captures space in print or air time. The frustration of uncovering significant events south of the border and filing them to an editor back home, only to have most of such stories discarded without capturing an audience, discourages correspondents from increasing their daily coverage. The gatekeeper editors and producers, presuming their readers, listeners, and viewers are not interested in many stories about Latin America, make their assumption self-fulfilling by not offering the stories. In my own experience, after serving as a news correspondent in Latin America for NBC, I felt that teaching in a university, where the findings of one's investigations can be shared with a small but appreciative audience each day, instead of being unshared most of the time, would bring greater satisfaction.

A specific illustration will show the hapchance of propelling some news stories from Latin America into prominence and the smothering of others before they can be circulated. Reference is not to censorship but to the casual combining of circumstances. In 1960 I served in Nicaragua as a Fulbright professor to establish a School of Journalism and Social Sciences at the National University. Anti-Somoza rebels attacked across the border from Honduras at Jícaro but soon were defeated by the Nicaraguan National Guard. Jícaro, an isolated town, has no roads or highway connections. General Anastasio Somoza, Jr., commander of the armed forces, stated that there had been no fighting at the border. His statement was carried in Managua by the AP and UPI and circulated in the United States.

One of the university students, a news photographer, was at the military hospital in Managua when the soldiers wounded at Jícaro had been flown in and took photographs of them, though he could not get them published in Nicaragua without ending his own career.

At the military hospital I talked with the wounded back from Jícaro and wrote down their names. A telephone call to New York got my story about the abortive invasion of Nicaragua taped; it was aired on NBC radio and repeated on the hourly news several times. The AP then sent my story across the United States and back into Latin America on its main circuits.

Thus the story of an unsuccessful revolutionary thrust was circulated in the United States because an American correspondent with academic status had been free to communicate it. The AP and UPI news bureau chiefs in Managua were Nicaraguans and would have had to live there with possible negative results had they tried to defy quickly imposed censorship. The question arises: How many other Jícaro-type outbreaks erupt regularly in Latin America but go unreported because local correspondents cannot defy their own government? Probably many, unless an outside observer who is qualified as a correspondent happens to learn of such events and can verify them.[28]

Nicaraguan correspondents could not directly challenge General Somoza's denial of a battle any more than local correspondents could have challenged Chile's Pinochet, Paraguay's Stroessner, Panama's

Torrijos, Guyana's Forbes Burnham, or Cuba's Fidel Castro. In only a handful of the Latin American republics can national leaders be challenged directly by news reports flatly contradicting them.

Even during the most prosperous economic periods of the 1950s and 1960s, U.S. television and radio networks hired very few full-time news correspondents to cover Latin America. Part-time correspondents (universally known as stringers) had to file most of the reports away from the major cities of the largest republics. By the end of the 1970s the increased rate of inflation in the United States had prompted budgetary economies in all of the network news departments, with even some of the part-time correspondents in Latin America being dropped. A network reporter might be flown out of Los Angeles or New York to as far away as Buenos Aires if a specific news event seemed big enough. That might happen very few times during the course of a year.[29]

Associated Press in Latin America

Let us consider the Latin American coverage of the Associated Press, the largest news agency in the world in terms of the volume of stories filed to it each day and the volume of stories the AP in turn makes available on its wires to all its subscribers. The Latin American division of the AP World Service, transmitting news to and from more than 110 nations, is the Prensa Asociada Division, with headquarters in New York. In 1971 the AP computed that 1 billion persons outside the United States saw or heard AP news each day.[30] No specific total has been calculated since then, but in 1978 the AP estimated that the total had reached 2 billion. By 1978 the AP Latin American bureaus had 100 editors and writers.[31]

Professor Albert L. Hester's landmark study of the AP Latin American news flow covered the period June 28 through July 18, 1971. He found that stories about violence and crime dominated the news from Latin America that the AP in New York selected to send to its newspaper and broadcasting subscribers throughout the United States.[32]

Nearly 72 percent of the stories sent from Latin America to the AP headquarters in New York fell into just four subject categories: sports, domestic politics and government, international relations, and crime and violence. Hester categorized all the news into eighteen subjects, with the descending order of percentages: sports, international relations, domestic politics, violence and crime, accidents, economics-business, human interest features, labor relations, prominent personalities, military activities, entertainment-culture, education, science and medicine, agriculture, and religion.

Hester found the high attrition of news transmitted from Latin American bureaus yielding a distorted emphasis on violence after that news had been received in New York. Of the reports received from Latin America, editors selected only a small number for wire circuits to newspapers and broadcasting stations throughout the United States. Of 1,636 news reports sent from Latin America to headquarters, only 128 were retransmitted out of New York on domestic news wires to media throughout the United States. Thus only 7.8 percent of the stories sent from Latin America actually reached the mass media within the United States.

Hester found that of all the foreign news stories the AP circulated to newspapers and broadcasting stations in the United States, news about western Europe predominated, making up 38.5 percent of the total. News of Asia accounted for 25.8 percent, of the Middle East 9.9 percent, and of Latin America only 9.9 percent of all foreign stories circulated.

At the time Hester made his study, the Vietnam conflict accounted for many world headlines and a high percentage of foreign news whereas the Middle East was enjoying a period of relative quiet, accounting for the low percentage of Middle East news. One could choose other time periods, even when the Panama Canal treaty discussions were top news in 1977 and 1978, and still find Latin American news with a lower percentage of any day's total budget of foreign news than that from Europe.

Hester found news from Africa made up 7 percent and news from eastern Europe 6.4 percent of the total foreign news circulated during that 1971 time period. Certainly the crises in Angola in 1975 and in Uganda and Rhodesia in 1978 would increase Africa's percentage. President Carter's 1979 visit to Mexico and negotiations with that republic for purchase of oil would increase the Latin American percentage of the foreign news total.

Professor Hester also completed a systematic sample of evening news broadcasts on the three major U.S. television networks for a three-year period, 1972–1974, and found a tendency on the part of television news editors to associate the public life of Latin America with violence.[33] His cross-regional comparison of eighteen coded subject categories shows that the category for "crime, violence, terrorism" stories sometimes accounted for two-thirds of the stories the networks decided to film or videotape.

Such quantitative probing does not touch on the vital content analysis of major stories from Latin America for qualitative factors, even in the small number of U.S. daily newspapers with continuing emphasis on news coverage of Latin America. Such dailies include the *Miami Herald,* the *Los Angeles Times,* the *New York Times,* the *Arizona Republic,* and the *Christian Science Monitor.*

As journalism professor Jerry Knudson has observed, news coverage of Latin America in the United States seldom includes any emphasis in depth of social trends or reforms.[34] Knudson in 1973 completed a monograph study of the social revolution that had gone on in Bolivia from 1952 to 1964 and its relationship to the Bolivian press. This study did not include U.S. coverage. But even the most cursory inspection of U.S. newspapers shows the absence of any stories from Bolivia except during violent eruptions or when elections or expropriations have been held. Knudson pointed out that during a twelve-year period Bolivia redistributed one-third of its agricultural lands to formerly landless peasants.[35] That basic social reform went almost unchronicled as far as U.S. mass media were concerned. Yet once the 1952 social revolution became institutionalized, the National Revolutionary Movement (Movimiento Nacional Revolucionario or MNR) leaders who governed Bolivia ended press censorship. Not until the armed forces overthrew the MNR on November 4, 1964, did repression of the media return. The MNR government's newspaper, *La Nación,* attempted to outshout, rather than silence, opposition newspapers.[36]

During the 1952–1964 period in Bolivia, foreign news correspondents could have constructed an ongoing profile of changing public life by contrasting the claims and counterclaims of *La Nación* and the opposition dailies *El Diario, Ultima Hora,* and *Presencia.* During the 1970s, such an opportunity vanished.[37]

Freedom to Obtain News

In recent decades both social scientists and journalists have concerned themselves with the presence or absence of press freedom in the Latin American countries. "Press freedom" can be defined as the independence of newspapers, magazines, and radio and television stations from direct control of government.[38] This journalistic autonomy involves the writing, editing, printing or broadcasting, and circulating of news.

Press freedom became one of the basic criteria for measuring degrees of democracy and dictatorship in the various Latin American nations in the continuing surveys pioneered by the late political scientist R. H. Fitzgibbon and continued by Kenneth F. Johnson, based on composite ratings by several scholars every five years, 1960 to 1965 to 1970 to 1975. Those of us who helped compile the ratings of the Latin American republics for degrees of political democracy considered press freedom as one of the most important measuring factors.[39]

A related concept has not been measured, however. That is the more illusive factor of "freedom of information," which has been defined as the freedom of reporters to gather facts from official and unofficial sources upon which news stories are based and the freedom of the mass media to protect confidential news sources.[40]

In the United States, various states passed "shield laws" in the 1950s and 1960s so that reporters could protect confidential news sources, thereby insuring some access to information about improper or illegal government activities.[41] Throughout the 1970s, however, from time to time reporters in the United States were fined or jailed anyway in trials involving murders. In Latin America the concept of protecting news sources, even in the small number of republics with genuine press freedom and no formal governmental pressure on the media, has not been widely accepted.

A token step in protecting news sources was attempted in Costa Rica in 1954 when a reporter for the *Diario de Costa Rica* refused to reveal the name of the employee in the Ministry of Finance who furnished the names of plantation owners who had failed to pay export taxes as required by law. The reporter was threatened with a jail term but remained silent and remained free and was never indicted. President of Costa Rica José Figueres publicly ordered the judge in the case not to infringe upon Costa Rican constitutional freedoms and the judge agreed.[42] A few times since then, through the 1970s, reporters in Costa Rica refused to reveal confidential news sources and did not incur any penalty.

A few similar cases of journalists protecting news sources occurred in Chile and Uruguay, but in both republics since 1973, strong press censorship has removed even basic press freedom as well as any hope of shielding news sources. A pioneer case in Uruguay took place in July 1967 when reporters for *Radio El Espectador* refused to tell the attorney general of the republic their source for a story on smugglers bringing untaxed automobiles across the Brazilian border into Uruguay at Rivera. The story proved to be true, the smugglers were convicted, and the attorney general withdrew his threat to prosecute the radio reporters.[43]

The 1979 president of the Inter-American Press Association and publisher of the daily *El Caribe* of Santo Domingo, Germán Ornés, felt modest press freedom gains had been made in Latin America in 1978, including freedom of information, but he warned that many Latin American government administrators continued to use superficially attractive phrases that were misleading. He singled out the phrases "a new order of information" and the government's "right to communicate" as euphemisms for restrictions on the freedom of the mass media to report objectively about government.[44]

Media and National Development

As John C. Merrill has observed: "A nation's communication media develop as the nation develops. Significant changes in the scope, sophistication, and purpose of the mass media are evidences of political modification in a society."[45]

Obviously, a nation's political system reflects the country's total development. The mass media play a key role in any nation's development process through various complex relationships. Considering all the Third World nations, the Latin American republics register higher on a variety of economic, political, and social indicators, including the mass media, than do a majority of the nations of Asia and Africa.[46] Latin American nations tend to have higher per capita incomes and per capita distribution and use of mass media than most Asian and African nations. In addition, most Latin American nations have been independent nation-states for more than a century and a half as contrasted with most African and many Asian nations which have achieved political independence only in recent decades.

For citizens of any Latin American republic to participate actively in the economic, political, and social systems of their country, they must receive basic information about the activities of their government. With 200 radio receivers in daily use for each 1,000 Latin Americans, multiplied by several listeners per receiver, that minimal information does get received.[47]

A typical study of media habits of both urban and rural citizens in Panama, Honduras, and El Salvador showed that almost every adult heard some radio program daily.[48]

In 1977 in the west central region of Venezuela, urban and rural inhabitants were found to use their radios an equal amount, with nine out of ten listening to radio daily. As for television, 79 percent of the urban Venezuelans and 61 percent of the rural dwellers watched some television more than once a week as contrasted with 75 percent of the urban and 50 percent of the rural respondents reading a newspaper at least once a week.[49]

In 1969 in various neighborhoods in metropolitan Lima, Professor John T. McNelly and Peruvian sociologist Julio Molina surveyed male heads of households, testing them on knowledge of international affairs, including identification of such world leaders as President Richard Nixon (correctly identified in a news photo by 58 percent) and Mao Tse-tung (50 percent identification). In an analysis of the lower socioeconomic stratum of respondents, regular exposure to radio vied with newspaper and magazine use measurements as a significant correlate of knowledge of world affairs. The frequency and amount of time spent with media made a greater difference for the lower-status men than for those of higher status (with more than a primary school education), suggesting that the media may offer a route to informational mobility for the economically less privileged. To the extent that they use the media, they may be able to compensate in part for their lack of education in learning about the outside world.[50]

Researchers should not try to design a priori guidelines or theories about the effects of mass communication within any nation without first seeking empirical evidence. Each case study in each nation may reveal different media impact upon national development. In this volume we will examine the various degrees of guidance or censorship or press freedom governments in the different Latin American nations extend to the mass media. No universal formula covers all Latin American nations, except for the assumption that most of them have governments that exert some pressure on the media in the hope of aiding national development.[51] A study was made encouraging students of developing nations to reexamine the nature of the mass media and the conditions under which they function as part of larger studies of national development.

It becomes easier for a government to accept press freedom when the reporters and editors of the mass media perform at a professional level, exhibiting regard for verification of facts and a nonpartisan or objective approach in presenting stories. Beginning in the 1950s, journalism schools began to multiply in Latin America, their programs ranging from the type originating at the National Autonomous University of Mexico to the trade school programs in Central America. Most of the university programs encountered the problem faced by the University of Chile's School of Journalism in Santiago, which furnished a degree at a professional level equal to law or economics only to find that available jobs for graduates did not justify such advanced training in most cases.[52]

During the administration of President Camilo Ponce Enríquez in Ecuador during 1956–1960, press freedom flourished, and brothers Carlos and Jorge Mantilla Ortega developed the Quito daily *El Comercio* into a responsible, newsworthy newspaper. Encouraged by this, UNESCO convened a conference on education for the mass media in Quito from March 28 to April 1, 1960, for the establishment of the International Center for Higher Journalism Studies for Latin America (Centro Internacional de Estudios Superiores de Periodismo para la América Latina or CIESPAL).[53] I was the U.S. delegate to that founding conference.

CIESPAL since 1960 has provided professional training in journalism for a limited number of outstanding reporters and editors sent to the Quito center by their publishers to be groomed for top-level posts. In courses lasting two months or more, students have come from most of the Latin American nations.

The late Ricardo Castro Beeche, publisher of the San José daily *La Nación,* along with the founding dean, Jorge Fernández, who had been *Comercio's* managing editor in Quito, helped design the original curriculum.[54] Through the years, lecturers from U.S., European, and leading Latin American newspapers and networks have taught at CIESPAL. Danton Jobim, journalism dean at the University of Brazil, in the 1960s gave CIESPAL graduates credit for bolstering the struggle of Brazilian newspaper editors to maintain press freedom. Similar endorsements have come from Colombia, Venezuela, Costa Rica, Mexico, and the Dominican Republic.

CIESPAL is funded by UNESCO and various nonprofit foundations and its students are maintained by publishers or broadcasters from other Latin American nations. In the 1970s, when the military government pressured or censored Ecuadorian media, the Center, in its own isolated plant, was undisturbed. It has diplomatic status.

Helping to upgrade journalism standards in some leading Latin American newspapers, in addition to CIESPAL and some of the journalism schools, are the Fulbright exchange programs and the newer journalism exchange programs among the United States and various Latin American republics sponsored by the Partners of the Americas, a surviving entity from the Alliance for Progress. These programs continued in 1980.[55]

Jack McLeod, Ramona Rush, and Karl Friederich, in a study of Quito, Ecuador, concluded that there are two types of political knowledge, and only the more superficial type seems to increase with mass media exposure in a city with professionally produced newspapers and broadcasting.[56] This civics type knowledge involved merely being able to identify government and civic leaders, agencies, and programs. However, they found that a deeper political knowledge, which involved a respondent's ability to recognize political problems and their solutions, did not seem to be related to media exposure. Therefore, citizen understanding of public life as a factor in national development depends only in part on further upgrading of Latin America's mass media operations. Factors ranging from experience to the formal education of individual citizens may be involved.

References

Ackerman, Henry S. "Correspondents South of the Border," *Inter-American Press Association Fund*, Mar. 4, 1971, pp. 1–6.

Alisky, Marvin. "Argentina" in John C. Merrill, Carter R. Bryan, Marvin Alisky, *The Foreign Press*, 2nd ed. (Baton Rouge: Louisiana State University Press, 1970), p. 201.

_____. "Central America's Radio," *Quarterly of Film, Radio, and Television* 10 (Fall 1955): 51–63.

_____. "Early Mexican Broadcasting," *Hispanic American Historical Review* 34 (November 1954):515–26.

_____. "U.S. News Coverage of Latin America," *Proceedings of the Arizona Latin American Conference of 1975* (Tempe: ASU Center for Latin American Studies, Paper 2, 1976), pp. 2–7.

Asante, M. K., Eileen Newmark, and C. A. Blake, eds., *Handbook of Intercultural Communication* (Beverly Hills, Calif.: Sage Publications, 1979), 496 pp.

Barron, Louis, ed. *The Americas: Worldmark Encyclopedia of the Nations*, vol. 3 (New York: Harper & Row, 1971).

Brazilian Government. "Economics: Industry," *Brazil Today* (Brazilian Embassy, Washington, D.C.) 4 (Mar. 8, 1979): 1–2.

Brucker, Herbert. *Freedom of Information* (New York: Macmillan, 1949), 307 pp.

Cappon, R. J. "Personnel," *Report of the General News Editor of the AP*, Summer 1971, p. 12.

Chaffee, Steven, ed. *Political Communication* (Beverly Hills, Calif.: Sage Publications, 1975), pp. 218–19.

Cross, Harold L. *The People's Right to Know* (New York: Columbia University Press, 1953), pp. 3–11.

DePalma, Samuel. "Freedom of the Press, an International Issue," *U.S. Department of State Bulletin*, Nov. 14, 1949, pp. 724–40.

Desmond, Robert W. *The Press and World Affairs* (New York: D. Appleton-Century, 1937), pp. 65–68.

Drysdale, Robert S. and Robert G. Myers, "Continuity and Change: Peruvian Education," in Abraham F. Lowenthal, ed., *The Peruvian Experiment* (Princeton, N.J.: Princeton University Press, 1975), pp. 254–301.

Fagg, John E. *Latin America: A General History* (New York: Macmillan, 1963), pp. 129, 153, 207.

Fisher, Hans-Dietrich and John C. Merrill, eds. *International Communication* (Hastings House, 1970).

Gerbner, George, ed. *Mass Media Policies in Changing Cultures* (Somerset, N.J.: Wiley-Interscience, 1977).

Giandoni, William. "Latins Don't Know Each Other Well," *Times of the Americas*, Jan. 4, 1978, p. 2.

González, Edward. *Cuba under Castro: The Limits of Charisma* (Boston: Houghton Mifflin, 1974).

Graham, Fred P. *Press Freedoms under Pressure* (New York: Twentieth Century Fund, 1972), pp. 65–81.

Hester, Albert L. "Foreign News on U.S. Television," (Paper at International Association for Mass Communication Research conference, Leicester, England, September 1976).

_____. "The News from Latin America, Via a World News Agency," *Gazette* (International Press Quarterly, Amsterdam), 20, no. 2 (1974): 85–92.

Hill, K. Q. and P. A. Hurley. "Freedom of the Press in Latin America," *Latin American Research Review* 15, no. 2 (1980): 212–18.

Hocking, William E. *Freedom of the Press* (Chicago: University of Chicago Press, 1947), pp. 200–27.

Huth, Don. "World Services: By Satellite, Landline," *AP World* 29 (Summer 1971): p. 12.

Inter-American Press Association. "The UNESCO Fight," *IAPA News,* October-November 1976, pp. 1–2.

_____. "Ornés Warns of Dangers," *IAPA Updater,* March 1, 1979, p. 2.

Inter-American Statistical Institute. *América en Cifras* (Washington, D.C.: Organization of American States, 1975).

Johnson, Kenneth F. "Scholarly Images of Latin American Political Democracy in 1975," *Latin American Research Review* 11 (Summer 1976): 127–37.

Knudson, Jerry. *The Press and the Bolivian National Revolution* (Minneapolis, Minn.: Association for Education in Journalism Monographs, No. 31, 1973).

_____. "Whatever Became of the Pursuit of Happiness: The U.S. Press and Social Revolution in Latin America," (Paper at International Communications Division, Association for Education in Journalism, San Diego, California, August 1974).

Lent, John A. "Commonwealth Caribbean Mass Media: Historical, Cultural, Economic, and Political Aspects" (Ph.D. diss., University of Iowa, Iowa City, Iowa, 1972).

Lowenthal, Abraham F., ed. *The Peruvian Experiment* (Princeton, N.J.: Princeton University Press, 1975).

Martin, Richard R., John T. McNelly, and Fausto Izcaray. "Is Media Exposure Unidimensional?" *Journalism Quarterly* 53 (Winter 1976): 619–25.

Matthews, T. S. *The Sugar Pill: An Essay on Newspapers* (London: Victor Gollancz, 1958).

McDougall, Curtis D. *The Press and Its Problems* (Dubuque, Iowa: William C. Brown, 1964).

McLeod, Jack M., Ramona Rush, and Karl H. Friederich. "Mass Media Exposure and Political Knowledge in Quito, Ecuador" (Paper at International Communications Division, Association for Education in Journalism, Boulder, Colorado, August 1967).

McNelly, John T. "International News for the Third World Masses?" *Journal of Communication* 26 (Spring 1979).

_____. "Mass Communication and Family Planning," *Organization of Family Planning Programs* (Washington, D.C.: Smithsonian Institution Interdisciplinary Communications Program, Monograph 8, 1976), pp. 149–82.

McNelly, John T. and Julio Molina. "Communication, Stratification and International Affairs Information in a Developing Urban Society," *Journalism Quarterly* 49 (Summer 1972): 316–26, 339.

Merrill, John C. *Gringo: The American as Seen by Mexican Journalists* (Gainesville: University of Florida Press, 1963).

_____. *The Imperative of Freedom: A Philosophy of Journalistic Autonomy* (New York: Hastings House, 1974).

Merrill, John C., Carter R. Bryan, and Marvin Alisky. *The Foreign Press,* 2nd ed. (Baton Rouge: Louisiana State University Press, 1970).

Morello, Ted. "Journalism School Beside the Andes," *Quill* 43 (July 1955): 10, 14–15.

Morris, Joe Alex. *Hōra de Cierre a Cada Minuto* (Buenos Aires: Ediciones Gure, 1959), pp. 110–18.

Murkland, Harry B. "Editors' Blind Spot," *Américas* 1 (May 1949): 12–14.

Nixon, Raymond B. "UNESCO's Program in Journalism," *Editor & Publisher,* May 7, 1960, p. 27.

Pierce, Robert N. *Keeping the Flame* (New York: Hastings House, 1979).

Ramos, Samuel. *Profile of Man and Culture in Mexico* (New York: McGraw-Hill, 1963).

Reis, Edgardo. Correspondent for *O Globo,* interviewed in Washington, D.C., by Marvin Alisky, November 16, 1978.

St. John, Jeffrey. "The Third World and the Free Enterprise Press," *Policy Review* 2, no. 2 (1978): 59–70.

Schramm, Wilbur. *Mass Media and National Development* (Stanford, Calif.: Stanford University Press, 1964).

SOMEX. *Memoria de la Sociedad Mexicana de Crédito Industrial* (México, D.F.: SOMEX, 1973).

United Nations. *United Nations Statistical Yearbook 1978* (New York: United Nations, 1978).

United States Information Agency. *A Study of Media Habits in El Salvador, Honduras, and Panama* (Washington, D.C.: USIA, 1970).

Wilkie, James W., ed. *Statistical Abstract of Latin America 1978* (Los Angeles: UCLA Latin American Center, 1978).

Newspapers: *Diario de Costa Rica,* San José; *Excelsior,* Mexico City; *New York Times; Wall Street Journal; Washington Post.*

SECTION **2**

Nations with Media Guidance

MEXICO, Peru, and Brazil are three Latin American republics with elaborate government guidelines for their mass media. Each of these republics has different degrees of active political opposition that affect the functioning of those guidelines.

Mexico represents the nation in Latin America with institutionalized control mechanisms from a political and economic establishment that can permit relative press freedom but still guarantee support for the Revolutionary coalition which has dominated Mexican public life for more than sixty years.

After the military reformers came into power in 1968, Peru's governmental guidance lapsed from time to time into censorship and then improved into relative press freedom. As that republic moves from military to elected civilian government in the 1980s, the pluralistic nature of the left-center political spectrum might work in favor of less governmental guidance and less frequent lapses into censorship.

Brazil's military administrations, from 1964 to 1978, relied on censorship to maintain political support, and then decided on February 2, 1978, to rely instead on governmental guidance and pressures, after testing limited broadcast time for the opposition candidates of the Brazilian Democratic Movement in the 1974 congressional elections. At the time of this writing, the administration of the new president, inaugurated in 1979, had not yet projected its long-range media guidelines, but during 1980 considerable editorial latitude was allowed.

2

Mexico's Bandwagon Journalism

A headline across the front page of Mexico's leading daily newspaper, *Excelsior,* in December 1978, proclaimed: "Registration of the Opposition Exterminates Adventurism."[1] For half the front page and half an inside page, the story emphasized the claim that qualification of additional minority parties in the 1979 congressional elections constituted a functioning democratic process, though in actuality this event was more cosmetic than substantive.

For decades, the Institutional Revolutionary Party (Partido Revolucionario Institucional or PRI) has dominated public life, monopolizing the presidency, the governorships of all the states, and most of the seats in the federal Congress and municipal councils.[2] Mexico's leaders carry out policies in the name of a presumed consensus, and persuade or pressure the mass media into supporting the goals of the institutionalized reforms. Opposition newspapers and magazines, with relatively small national readerships, range from Marxist to far right, but these periodicals, with a genuine impact upon the national political and social systems, practice a self-induced, loosely defined, supportive communication that might be termed "bandwagon journalism." That is, mainstream mass media tend to rally around the established leadership, a power elite that replenishes governmental and political vacancies from within its own ranks.[3] Public policies are carried out in the name of the "Revolution," always capitalized in Mexico to denote an ongoing or institutionalized program of social and economic reforms.

The Revolution

For a century after Mexico's independence from Spain in 1821,

28

Mexican political culture, fragmented by violence, underscored the absence of consensus on fundamental government goals.[4] Since the 1920s, however, a power elite organized as a Revolutionary coalition has carried out policies in the name of an institutionalized reform program. The Revolutionary coalition brings together top-level bureaucrats, industrialists, labor leaders, agrarian spokesmen, and entrepreneurs. Those who hold effective decision-making power include major publishers and broadcasters. Executives in the mass media fields who are outside the ranks of political leadership share a mutual self-interest in the continuation of the domination of public life by the Revolutionary coalition. They perceive that their own continued well-being depends on political power not being transferred to far right or far left politicians.[5]

Mexico began this century with an inherited dictatorship under Porfirio Díaz going back to 1876. Beginning in November 1910, a struggle against the past began with military battles and evolved into elaborate social reforms embodied in the federal constitution of 1917. The civil war between rebels seeking social justice and the entrenched forces of age-old landed gentry raged for a decade, until 1920, in which 1 million Mexicans—out of a population then of only 15 million—lost their lives. Out of so much bloodshed came the ongoing institutionalized social reform called the Revolution, spelled in Mexico with a patriotic capital "R" to distinguish it from the many revolts and coups d'etat which preceded it.

Political freedoms for individuals seemed central to the slogan "Effective suffrage, no reelection" espoused by the articulator of the Revolution's theory, ill-fated President Francisco Madero, who was murdered in 1913. However, the principal goal of those peasants who actually won the battles was the slogan "Bread, land, and justice," the credo of peasant general Emiliano Zapata.

With the exception of a few years under Benito Juárez in the mid-nineteenth century, Mexico suffered a political history of government censorship of the press from the days of the first periodicals of the Spanish colonial era to the promulgation of the 1917 Mexican Constitution. Press freedom and other political freedoms did not become top priorities of the Revolution. Government-directed integration of economic and social life took precedence as the principal priority of Mexican public life.[6] The goals of truly representative government— including a completely independent system of mass media and effective opposition parties—have been periodically postponed until the Revolution can create a middle-class majority and an expanding economy, yielding an improved internal distribution of national income. Thus, for sixty years, leaders of the Revolution have continued to insist on projecting a good image and involving the press and broadcasting in encouraging massive support for the dominant party, the PRI, and for the government establishment.

Mexico's leaders have not had to resort to overt censorship to insure that their views predominate in the press and broadcast coverage. For built within Mexican political and government structures are the mechanisms of control, ranging from the informal techniques of "management of the content and emphasis of news" through official sources to the official regulatory agencies.

The Physical Setting

Demographic disequilibrium strains the communication and distribution facilities of Mexico, insuring the dominance over national life by Mexico City and the two largest provincial metropolitan centers of Guadalajara and Monterrey. Although Mexico's national territory of 750,000 square miles ranks it the third largest Latin American republic, after Brazil and Argentina, its 1979 estimated population of 69 million ranks it second only to Brazil.[7] Half of all Mexicans live in 14 percent of the national territory, the central region or Valley of Mexico, with industrial payrolls overwhelmingly bunched in the three largest metropolitan areas.

A tortuous terrain—more than half of mountainous Mexico rises 3,200 feet or more above sea level—conspires with a climate ranging from deserts to swamps to reduce natural rainfall cultivation to 7 percent of the total land. Hydroelectric projects, however, have added irrigated farming so that 14 percent of Mexico's surface is now being cultivated or grazed. Some 66 percent of Mexico's population is now urban yet a majority of the potential work force remain peasant farmers ("campesinos"), intensifying a high rate of unemployment and a high rate of migration into the United States for seasonal work.[8]

After decades of education reform and adult literacy campaigns, the Revolution had reduced adult illiteracy from its 1910 level of 70 percent down to 20 percent by 1960. But the annual net increase in population of 3.6 percent has eroded part of that victory, with Mexico entering the 1980s with one-third of its adult citizens unable to read a newspaper story. Better than 95 percent of all Mexicans obtain their daily news from radio whereas less than one-fifth of the adults buy or read daily newspapers.[9]

Although the republic of Mexico has 240 daily newspapers, provincial papers have grown slowly, due in part to the Mexico City dailies that circulate nationally among government and civic leaders. In 1978 the three largest metropolitan centers—greater Mexico City, greater Guadalajara, and greater Monterrey—had 60 percent of the total daily newspaper circulation of the republic. The remainder of Mexico, with 80 percent of the total population, bought only 40 percent of the newspapers.[10]

Government Control Mechanisms

Political scientist Evelyn P. Stevens has analyzed the vigorous support Mexican newspapers give the government and the Revolutionary coalition:

> To read a Mexican newspaper is to venture onto a factual desert in the midst of an ideological hailstorm. Headlines scream, news stories bellow, and columnists and cartoonists belabor "enemies of the Revolution" with sledgehammer sarcasm.[11]

During a fourteen-month period, from January 1965 to March 1966, she surveyed major daily newspapers in the Federal District and found enthusiastic descriptions of the republic's material progress. I have been reading these same dailies off and on since 1947 and have likewise found that vaguely described government projects have been consistently presented as if they were accomplished facts.

But some Mexican publications on occasion do offer strong warnings against the uncritical reporting of government programs in the daily press. The pro-Marxist voice of the Popular Socialist Party (Partido Popular Socialista or PPS), the weekly magazine *Siempre,* never attacks the president of Mexico directly, but does challenge the establishment in this manner:

> The man in the street in Mexico lives in an atmosphere of fiction which is dangerous because it gives him the impression that what has been constructed and inaugurated is just a sample of the general progress achieved at all levels all over the nation . . .[12]

Siempre went on to warn that the proestablishment press has misled Mexicans into believing that much more has been accomplished than might be the case decades in the future.

Proestablishment periodicals also from time to time emphasize topics that top government officials would rather not have mentioned or at least portrayed differently. Luis Echeverría was president from December 1970 to December 1976. Until April 1972 he consistently opposed any government program for birth control. Then he reluctantly permitted announcements of the first Family Planning Centers being established.[13] Not until 1974 did most papers and magazines begin to describe in vivid detail the extent of the danger to Mexico's economy and stability from the population explosion. Yet a leading proestablishment weekly news magazine, *Tiempo,* from 1972 on had been running reports on the misery of the poorest Mexican families, without hope of finding employment. Echeverría was irritated but no government retribution befell *Tiempo,* even when it featured on its cover a photograph of nine ragged children hovering around their impoverished peasant mother.[14]

Mexican bureaucrats read the Mexico City daily newspapers attentively, not only to learn the current line from the apex of power, but also to know how to comport themselves as vital sources of the news and as part of an extensive, informal control system.

Not all major news stories stem from official sources, but an overwhelming majority of the events and announcements shaping Mexican public life certainly do. After all, Mexico's mixed public-private economy finds the government a senior partner in significant enterprises that range over the entire spectrum of economic activities. Thus the various entities of the government itself serve as control mechanisms for the content flowing into the mass media because these government entities function as the primary sources of news.

The Mexican presidency, the cabinet ministries, the semi-autonomous agencies, the public corporations, and the state and municipal governments—all dominated by federal policies[15]—in their daily operations help the power elite manage the flow of news, shaping its emphasis and regulating its quantity. These primary news sources can voluntarily offer information or attempt to withhold it in ways which contribute to the headline priorities and the descending order of importance of a day's newsworthy events.[16]

Government controls of the distribution of newsprint (paper), the importing or manufacturing of printing presses and parts, the placing of official advertising, and loans and subsidies all constitute government guidance of the Mexican press. But the person-to-person interaction of officials and news personnel offers a primary guidance at the juncture where the news itself originates.

Camarillas and Padrinos

Based on the economic and social standards prevailing within the republic, economist Ifigenia Martínez de Navarrete, combining official and unofficial sources, has divided Mexican society thusly: lower class,

65 percent; middle class, 30 percent; and upper class, 5 percent.[17] Among the upwardly mobile and upper groups, one can examine the political cliques or *camarillas*.[18] Each camarilla consists of a political leader and his entourage, a group of friends and former classmates from school or university days. These collaborators work for their chief's advancement and he in turn tries to reward them with promotions, patronage, or government contracts, or he may act as their ombudsman in cutting official red tape to finalize projects or solve problems.[19]

Camarillas are quasi-permanent, hierarchical, cooperative structures that are crucial to the proper functioning of Mexican government and politics. These groups are formed horizontally by peers and vertically across age levels, as the human linkage within Mexico's officialdom and its mass media system. Continuing communication at the personal and mass levels remains one of the most important ongoing functions within a camarilla and among camarillas, as wheels within wheels keep everything in public life moving.

Political scientist Roderic Ai Camp has performed an invaluable service by compiling the biographies of Mexican leaders from 1935 through 1975.[20] His summaries show that these "old boy" or "old school tie" networks function at every level of Mexican government and politics and in most other entities of public life, especially the mass media. Every six years a presidential term ends, and the presidency is at the apex of power in a system in which the executive branch dominates the legislative and judicial branches of federal government and all three branches of state and local government. Therefore, as each new chief executive takes office, a fascinating game of political musical chairs takes place. Former governors become cabinet ministers, former deputies become senators, former senators become governors, former cabinet ministers become senators, and various directors of agencies move vertically or horizontally into new appointments.[21]

Most of these appointees or nominally elected officials belong to camarillas, with retirements, deaths, or new alliances assuring space for recruitment of young, upwardly mobile administrators.

At every level up the administrative ladder of government, or the executive ladder of industry or commerce, Mexican leaders find some of their camarilla duties entailing work with the press. Over a period of a few years, networks of friendship among public administrators and newspaper editors and reporters develop. Those whose status gives them some of the benefits of the establishment relate as news sources or communicators within Mexico's bandwagon journalism.

A front-page story in the December 12, 1978, *Excelsior* illustrates the interpersonal relationships between men who have served in various federal posts or elsewhere in public life and functioned as news sources as they rose in national prominence. Such public figures automatically rate headlines, for reporters and editors think of them as the wellspring of nationally significant information.

The story in question carried the headline "AMD, the Major Decision: Fidel." The initials stood for Alfonso Martínez Domínguez, who was being nominated by the Mexican Federation of Labor (CTM) as a favorite for the PRI candidacy for governor of the state of Nuevo León. The first name identification of the person asserting that this was a major political decision was Fidel Velázquez, head of the CTM for thirty-two years. With that tenure, he could be recognized in a headline by his first name.

Martínez Domínguez typified the upwardly mobile member of the camarilla of Adolfo López Mateos when the latter became minister of labor in 1952. During López Mateos' presidency (1958–1964), Martínez Domínguez served as secretary general of the National Federation of Popular Organizations of the PRI. Then Martínez Domínguez became president of the PRI during 1968–1970, then director general of the government's development bank, Nacional Financiera.

In an open society, such as that found in the United States, the privately owned news media themselves conversely influence government by stressing or ignoring fledgling official attitudes through the emphasis or de-emphasis in their coverage of government programs and performances.[22]

In the less open society of Mexico, privately owned newspapers, magazines, radio stations, television stations, and networks exert some similar influence, but not anywhere near the amount achieved by their U.S. counterparts. For in Mexico, the media feel numerous direct and indirect government pressures absent in the United States. At the personal level, reporters and editors do feed ideas and views back to the government if they happen to be a *padrino* or godfather of the offspring of the official they regularly contact. Padrinos not only serve as godfather for each other's children, but also symbolize the ties of lifelong friendship which simulate an extended family and relate to the more political camarillas. In Mexico, personal friendships allow journalists leeway with government administrators and in turn enhance a built-in sympathy on the part of journalists covering government, whether or not the news personnel ever receive favors for themselves or for their relatives.

The Revolutionary coalition, however, never trusts these interpersonal relationships alone to maintain the sympathetic treatment government enjoys in the press. Effective use of administrators as news sources at all levels is a more reliable control. And as added insurance, the system of the *mordida* (bribe) flourishes.

Every government entity has a special fund to pay the reporters assigned to cover the agency in question. If unmentioned, such payments are called *igualas* and usually neither the public administrator nor the reporter will mention the payments. If absolutely necessary to make some budgetary accounting for the funds, the payments are listed as consultant fees for public relations, despite the fact that the government itself is overstaffed with personnel whose duties are involved with informational services.[23] Payments to editors or reporters to run specified stories in the news columns are called *gacetillas.* Though common in provincial newspapers, in recent years they have not generally been accepted in the major Mexico City dailies.[24] At the presidential and cabinet-minister levels, neither igualas nor gacetillas are ever necessary, since the other Revolutionary coalition pressures of bandwagon journalism are already in control of the news.

Control of Newsprint

A newspaper must have newsprint (paper) in order to publish, so the most basic noncensorship control a government can possess is the authority to distribute newsprint. Newspapers and magazines must continuously acquire newsprint suitable in texture for direct-type or offset printing, at prices feasible for the financial solvency of the publications. In Mexico, under federal law, all production of newsprint, its importation, and its distribution come under the authority of the joint private-public corporation PIPSA (Productora e Importadora de Papel, S. A., or Producer and Importer of Paper, Inc.).[25]

PIPSA was established in 1935 as a government-financed corporation to administer, and to subsidize when necessary, the importation and domestic production of newsprint. If a publisher tries to purchase paper directly from a foreign producer, he will have to pay an 80 percent ad valorem tax on that newsprint, whereas publishers pay a 5 percent tax on all newsprint, whether imported or domestic, received from PIPSA, no matter how few or how many metric tons in each purchase.[26]

Publications receive newsprint quotas based on their paid circulations and the number of pages customarily printed for each issue, and may contract for both imported and domestically produced paper, as

PIPSA's authority extends to every publicly owned or privately owned newsprint plant.

Modern large-scale production of paper geared to domestic needs began in Mexico in 1936 with the founding of the Titan Corporation by the Garza Sada financial investors group in Monterrey.[27] In the fifties, the government's development bank, Nacional Financiera, launched the joint public-private Celulosa Corporation with Kimberly-Clark as a partner, in the state of Chihuahua, and in 1958, the newsprint plant, Papel Túxtepec, in the state of Oaxaca.

On June 1, 1976, the Villa de Reyes newsprint mill opened in the state of San Luis Potosí, giving Mexico its first paper plant able to recycle old newspapers in the production of newsprint. The older newsprint plants in the state of Mexico require fresh pulp.

Mexico has continued to import more newsprint than it produces domestically in order to meet its national publishing needs. The imported paper comes mainly from Canada, Sweden, Finland, and the United States. In 1978 Mexican newsprint plants achieved an annual production of 120,000 metric tons, or 40 percent of the newsprint needs of Mexican newspapers and magazines.[28] In 1960 Mexico had imported 82 percent of its newsprint. Thus during an eighteen-year period, the annual percentage of newsprint that had to be imported was reduced from 82 to 60 percent.

Aside from prices on the world paper market and any Mexican government subsidies or tax relief for imports, a technical factor enters into the matter of allocation between imported and domestically produced newsprint. The weight of a square meter of newsprint is 45, 49, or 52 grams depending on the quality of the paper, with the finer textured paper being required for magazines or newspapers printing photographs in color. The best quality textured paper must be imported because domestic production of less expensive newsprint absorbs the capacity of Mexican plants.[29]

In 1978 imported newsprint was selling for 11,215 pesos per metric ton, whereas domestically produced newsprint cost 9,750 pesos per metric ton. Depending on technical needs, PIPSA made both types of newsprint available to all periodical publishers, regardless of the quantity of annual purchases of each type.[30]

Twice since the end of World War II, PIPSA announced across-the-board reductions in the amount of imported newsprint available to all publishers, with corresponding increases in allocations of domestic newsprint to meet each periodical's annual needs. In 1973 Canadian and Scandinavian producers were short by one-fourth of the newsprint expected from them during a six-month period. Extra purchases in the

United States and increased domestic production made up most of that difference.[31] In 1976 a warehouse fire destroyed 50,000 metric tons of imported paper, again causing a temporary reduction in newsprint sales to all publishers.[32]

PIPSA furnishes warehouse facilities for the smaller and medium-sized publications. The largest newspapers stockpile paper at their own plants.

PIPSA will supply newsprint on credit and has wide latitude in deciding the terms of payment for individual publications, a powerful weapon with which to reward proestablishment periodicals and to punish noncooperative ones. With assets estimated in 1978 at 200 million pesos, PIPSA had leverage with numerous government and private banks in arranging loans for purchase of paper.

If a publication has stockpiled more paper than it can use for its own regular publishing, it can sell the excess to small and specialized trade journals that are unable to obtain quota assignments from PIPSA for reserve stockpiles.

PIPSA's ability to extend credit to periodicals with cash flow problems or periods of advertising revenue slumps assures considerable self-restraint among most newspapers when criticizing government actions and programs.[33]

PIPSA's board of directors consists of publishers from Mexico City's major dailies and magazines, plus the current head of the Association of Newspapers of the States. Substitute board members are designated to serve during the absence of regular board members or when a vacancy occurs during a regular six-year term. In addition, the government designates three commissioners to coordinate the administration of policies enacted by the board. These *comisarios* sit with the voting board members and the nonvoting substitutes at annual meetings.[34] The board names an executive director of PIPSA every six years upon receiving a recommendation from the newly inaugurated president of Mexico.

Working with PIPSA's administrators is the government's Publications Classification Commission (Comisión Calificadora de Publicaciones or CCP), which enforces sporadically and rarely a code of ethics.[35] Inciting a breakdown of law and order would be a violation of the code, prompting PIPSA to stop distributing newsprint to an accused publication, pending a hearing by the federal judiciary.

Mexican publications range the political spectrum from left to right, with a vast majority of them classified as either progovernment, neutral, or benignly antiestablishment. Analysts of Mexican public life, in classifying newspapers and magazines, should not use as calipers for political orientation solely the government benchmark but rather should use the Revolutionary coalition, which entwines key governmental, industrial, labor union, and business leaders.

The Magazine *Política*

In June 1962, the semimonthly news magazine *Política,* Marxist in philosophy and editorially pro-Castro, for two weeks did not receive PIPSA newsprint deliveries. This prevented the full nationwide circulation of the issue, though limited numbers were circulated. (*Política,* scheduled for national circulation on June 14, 1962, was distributed in small quantities before its distribution warehouse was locked up by federal police, armed with a writ from the federal Attorney General, who had been petitioned by the Ministry of Gobernación to investigate newsprint irregularities.) That issue was aimed at the visit of President John F. Kennedy in Mexico City. It featured personal, abusive attacks on President Kennedy, charging him with the exploitation of Mexican farmhands in the United States because the U.S.–Mexican Bracero Treaty was slated to end in December 1964. (I was serving in June 1962 as a freelance news correspondent, covering the meeting of President Kennedy with President Adolfo López Mateos in Mexico City for the NBC Radio Network.)

Política reported only 5,000 paid subscribers to tax authorities but claimed 257,000 street sales at three pesos (then 24 cents) each. In 1968, after the magazine had ceased operations, a government audit charged that 75 percent of its operating costs had come not from its meager advertising sales nor subscribers nor street sales, but rather from subsidies from foreign and domestic Communist sources, including the Communist Party of Mexico, and from various committees in Cuba. More than 200,000 copies of each issue, twice a month, had been given away to aid political propaganda, PIPSA noted in ending newsprint sales to the magazine in late 1967.

Política's publisher, Edmundo Jardón, had been chief of the Mexico City bureau of Prensa Latina, the news service the Cuban government had created to compete with the Associated Press and United Press International in Latin America. Shortly after it stopped receiving newsprint, the magazine itself closed down permanently, making the announcement of its going out of business on January 3, 1968. Its final edition bore the date December 1–31; the issue to have been dated December 1–15 never appeared.

PIPSA board members had halted newsprint shipments to *Política* based on a CCP ruling that the magazine had violated the ethics code of the nation. Although the magazine in late 1967 had gradually increased its hints that it would encourage protestors against the government's hosting of the 1968 Olympics in Mexico City—a protest that did materialize in July–October 1968, culminating in bloody riots—no issue of the magazine during the last quarter of 1967 triggered the adverse CCP ruling. Rather, the issue dated June 1–14, 1967, had been the edition serving as the basis of the CCP indictment.[36] The cover story for that issue was headlined "Press Freedom in Mexico?" It charged an absence of any real freedom of the press, which the CCP considered a defamation of the government.

Since 1950, when the Mexican government finally gained total control over newsprint distribution, only a very few suspensions of newsprint sales have taken place. In most of these cases the suspension has been for a Marxist publication rather than for one on the far right, although the fascist threats in one 1969 issue of the weekly *Orden* almost caused a suspension. This far right Sinarquista movement periodical attacked the memory of revered nineteenth century reformer Benito Juárez.

The movement began in 1939 as a Mexican far right group, proclaiming sympathy with the Axis and the fascist forces then in power in Europe. *Orden* further attacked the government's distribution of free textbooks to primary schools because a historical reference to the Catholic Church in the textbooks was severely critical. *Orden* demanded that public education be phased out in favor of parochial schools. Newsprint delivery to *Orden* was delayed five days before the CCP decided that the ethics code had not been violated. PIPSA then supplied the paper, allowing *Orden* to publish late.

Control through Stock Purchases

A major example of stock-purchase governmental "guidance" occurred in 1972 when the government-owned Mexican Industrial Credit Society (Sociedad Mexicana de Crédito Industrial or SOMEX) took over the García Valseca chain of thirty-seven daily newspapers.[37]

Over a twenty-year period, Colonel José García Valseca, an advertising salesman and investor, built himself into the largest publisher of provincial dailies in Mexico, with newspapers in thirty-six provincial cities plus Mexico City. However, by 1970, he had spent far beyond his income or earning potential, and could not make payments on loans from the government's development bank, Nacional Financiera, nor to his private creditors, nor even to the government for social security taxes for his employees. President Luis Echeverría in 1972 had the government's SOMEX purchase the controlling interest in the GV chain, its pending insolvency proving convenient.[38]

Another major move by the government to change a leading newspaper's management involved President Echeverría with Mexico City's *Excelsior.* The leading daily of Mexico, *Excelsior,* has been rated by scholars and specialists alike as Mexico's most influential newspaper.[39] Ostensibly it had become a cooperative in 1932, though fewer than ninety of its key employees shaped policies, and its board of directors chose, retained, or changed editors.

At the riotous general assembly of *Excelsior* stockholders on July 8, 1976, the presiding chairman and every orator he allowed to hold the floor were identified as members of the camarilla of Echeverría. Armando Vargas, then *Excelsior's* chief correspondent in Washington, described the meeting as a "scenario of intimidation."[40]

Each speaker had been groomed for the assembly coup by public relations experts in a group associated with José Pagés and Luís Suárez, publisher and editor of the weekly news magazine *Siempre.* That magazine supports the Popular Socialist Party but in practice gave support and advice to PRI leaders behind the leftward thrust of Echeverría from 1970 to 1976.

Julio Scherer García, executive publisher of *Excelsior,* and five top editors were fired at the July 8 assembly. Not one word was raised about their competence or professional standards and no charges were specified against them. In fact the Scherer staff had won numerous honors ranging from the María Moors Cabot awards of the Columbia University Graduate School of Journalism to those of the Inter-American Press Association.

One week prior to the July 8 assembly, those slated to attend had been contacted by the federal attorney general's office, or the Ministry of the Presidency, or the PRI. At the entrance to the assembly hall, private guards, sporting business suits and shoulder-holster pistols, checked and challenged those entering. Adolfo Aguilar y Quevado, *Excelsior's* legal counsel, commented that unparliamentary procedures, ineligible voters, and arbitrary rulings by presiding officers made the assembly vote to fire the newspaper's management illegal.[41] However, no government authority has challenged the action in Mexico's politicized courts.

Scherer had served as a political reporter for *Excelsior* since 1947, being promoted to assistant publisher in 1963 and executive publisher in 1968. Until then, a prominent politician could purchase a front-page story praising himself for 100,000 pesos (then $8,000), a practice belatedly revealed in the prosecution for corruption among Echeverría administration leaders during 1976–1977 by President José López Portillo's attorney general.[42] Scherer ended that practice abruptly, and added topflight writers to his staff, ranging from historian Daniel Cosío Villegas to novelist Octavio Paz to essayist Ricardo Garibay.

When the Scherer editoral staff was fired, some 200 other *Excelsior* reporters, editors, and photographers walked off the job to protest. Some never returned, whereas others stayed away only for a few weeks. Prominent newspapers of the world—the *New York Times, Le Monde* of Paris, the *Washington Post, O Estado de São Paulo* of Brazil—editorially condemned the firing.

Echeverristas, meantime, had acquired stock in rival newspapers, in partnership with a government corporation, and seemingly wished to depose *Excelsior* from its pinnacle as the leading paper in Mexico. In February 1976 Echeverría and his close associates became major shareholders in the Mexican Editorial Organization (Organización Editorial Mexicana or OEM). Immediately OEM purchased the Mexico City daily *El Universal,* which for decades had been owned by the relatives and heirs of the Lanz Duret and Palavicini families of journalists who epitomized the conservative nonactivists who were neutral in the rivalries among Revolutionary coalition leaders.[43]

Echeverristas soon took over the key posts at OEM, with Echeverría's former Minister of Foreign Relations, Emilio O. Rabasa, joining *Universal's* board and the OEM board.[44] OEM then purchased a block of stock in the SOMEX subsidiary owning the García Valseca newspapers and installed Fausto Zapata as publisher of these papers. Zapata had been undersecretary of the presidency in the Echeverría cabinet and prior to that, public relations director for the Mexico City daily *La Prensa,* a prolabor paper.[45]

OEM newspapers reported that on June 10, 1976, dozens of slum dwellers invaded a 218-acre property owned by the *Excelsior* cooperative on the outskirts of Mexico City. The land was slated to become the site of a housing development. The poor (land squatters) were led by an unlikely affluent organizer, Congressman-elect Humberto Serrano, an Echeverrista spokesman in the PRI. Serrano promised that the squatters would not leave the site until Scherer was expelled from *Excelsior.*

Police made no effort to evict the squatters who had been transported to the site in buses belonging to the governor of the state of Guerrero, another member of the Echeverrista camarilla.

When the newspaper appealed to the federal attorney general, he stated that he would enforce the law against the squatters only after the *Excelsior* general assembly had been completed on July 8. The newspaper denounced this government stand in an editorial in its July 7 edition.[46] That evening, network television news commentators thereupon attacked the newspaper's editorial and its protests.

For some months after getting a new, inexperienced staff of editors, *Excelsior* evidenced less vigorous investigatory reporting. The paper had customarily emphasized stories about civil rights violations in both rightist and leftist regimes, abroad and within Mexican states. *Excelsior* had reported on human rights problems in Brazil, the Soviet Union, and Uganda, and had sent its own reporters to investigate abuses in Uruguay, Chile, and Bolivia. Now the paper began to recapitulate summaries of earlier dispatches, but without articles on any abuses in provincial Mexican cities and towns.

Universal, other OEM papers, and García Valseca papers gained slightly in circulation in 1977, perhaps not because of the shake-up at *Excelsior* as some manipulators had hoped but rather because of vigorous promotion by the circulation salesmen of these rival papers.[47] *Excelsior* remained the leading daily in the republic and regained some of its previous investigatory reportorial energy. From June to August 1979 the paper ran stories critical of the government's handling of an oil spill in the Gulf of Mexico, a subject the president himself preferred not to discuss.

Criticism of Corruption

Corruption has been a part of public life in Mexico since the colonial era, when viceregal administrators traded knighthoods from the Spanish crown for vast plantations. During the Porfirio Díaz dictatorship from 1876 to 1911, special favors for high fees reached rotten depths. The Revolution blew a few cobwebs of bribery temporarily from officialdom under President Lázaro Cárdenas from 1934 to 1940 and under President Adolfo Ruíz Cortines from 1952 to 1958. However, in recent decades, the accepted practice of paying up to 8 percent of the value of a government contract to get finalization became an extralegal fact in Mexico.

Postauditing of government spending has been rare in Mexico, and through the years various highly placed administrators have been able to siphon official funds into their own hands. When José López Portillo became president on December 1, 1976, he quietly took inventory of Mexico's national resources and its bank reserves, and went over the books of every key government budget.

What he found shocked him into the most sweeping investigation and indictment of bribe-takers and politicians pocketing the taxpayers' money ever witnessed in modern Mexican political history.[48]

Not that a few Mexican newspapers from time to time had not exposed some officeholders who misappropriated funds, but these newspapers only did so after the official in question had fallen from favor with the president of the republic. For example, in the state of Sonora in 1975 and 1976, the Hermosillo daily newspapers *El Imparcial* and *El Regional* chronicled the troubles of the former governor of the state. These papers are published by José Healy, whose independence from state-level influence has contrasted with the other Hermosillo daily, *El Sonorense,* published by a group associated with former Sonora governor Luis Encinas, who went on to become head of the government's National Bank of Agricultural Credit.

As one of Mexico's most properous states, Sonora indicated some tendency to challenge the guidance of Mexico City when the conservative opposition, PAN (National Action Party), won the municipal elections in eight of the sixty-nine municipalities of Sonora in July 1967. Even though the Federal Electoral Commission had often tampered with tabulations to insure a victory by the dominant PRI in many municipalities, newspapers throughout Mexico had customarily reported only the cries of "fraud" from the losing candidates rather than editorialize themselves against the establishment. By contrast, *El Imparcial* for months before the July 2 balloting had warned the PRI not to tamper with vote counting because of a widespread ground swell for the PAN in Hermosillo.[49] The state capital, Hermosillo, did indeed elect a PAN mayor and council.

In October 1975, Sonora's Governor Carlos Biebrich was ordered to resign by President Echeverría after state police killed seven farmers and wounded fourteen others for squatting on disputed land. Biebrich had been a protegé of Echeverría until the month before, when the governor had challenged the PRI leadership by favoring Interior Minister Mario Moya for the PRI presidential nomination just as the party endorsed López Portillo.

During 1976, *El Regional* and *El Imparcial* published dozens of stories about a federal warrant against Biebrich, citing 36 million pesos in state funds missing. Biebrich remained in hiding until a 1978 amnesty. The Hermosillo papers furnished details about the missing funds and improperly filed contracts.[50]

The state of Yucatán for years has also displayed a tendency toward political independence from the Mexico City establishment, echoed and encouraged by the state's leading newspaper, *El Diario de Yucatán* in Mérida. In November 1967 the PAN candidate defeated the

PRI candidate for mayor as the daily kept a vigil against vote-count fraud.[51]

A decade later, the *Diario* eagerly chronicled each investigation in Yucatán that President López Portillo ordered.[52] These probes found that the government-owned and government-operated credit institutions had dozens of employees and consultants who were no longer working for the government but drawing pay. In several cases, an administrator had honored the memory of several departed friends, keeping their ghosts on his payroll and pocketing their paychecks. He plea-bargained a suspended sentence on condition that by 1981 he repay 80 percent of what he had stolen. Even though this administrator had been a prominent member of the PRI and the Revolutionary coalition, once the president of Mexico had ordered the housecleaning, candid reporting of the investigation appeared not only in Mérida, but also in Mexico City in *Excelsior.*

President López Portillo launched his 1977 campaign against corruption in government by having tax and treasury experts audit the botched $22 million government real estate project, the Bahía de Banderas Development. Alfredo Ríos Camarena, project director, fled to the United States. Mexico City newspapers reported:

> A federal judge in Miami, Florida, has refused a defense plea to release Alfredo Ríos Camarena, who faces extradition to Mexico for alleged fraud . . . of defrauding more than 100 million pesos in public funds.[53]

Mexico federal Attorney General Oscar Flores Sánchez requested U.S. Secretary of State Cyrus Vance to extradite Ríos Camarena to Mexico. Minister of Foreign Relations Santiago Roel stressed to Mexican reporters that ample evidence would bring about that extradition.[54] Mexican newspapers were thereby assured that the anticorruption campaign would continue with the full backing of the president, and the coverage of the investigations grew in detail and intensity.

In March 1978 the Mexico City daily *Novedades* and its English-language affiliate, *The News,* stressed the fact that the returned project director had served in the previous administration:

> Alfredo Ríos Camarena was extradited from the United States and faced a Mexican judge Friday on charges of defrauding the government . . . as head of the Banderas Trust in the administration of former President Luis Echeverría.[55]

As Ríos Camarena began to testify and involved dozens of other high-level bureaucrats, his associates were jailed and convicted. The case received continuous front-page coverage.

Féliz Barra García, minister of agrarian reform in the Echeverría cabinet, had directed the expropriation of large numbers of middle-class farms in the states of Sonora and Sinaloa while disputed titles were being appealed by a writ of injunction to the Supreme Court during the waning days of the Echeverría presidency.

The government charged Barra García with extorting 1.2 million pesos from landowners, and wrapped up the case with witnesses, photographs, and a tape-recorded conversation. Newspaper reporters were present when he publicly admitted that he had taken the money. After telephoning his wife, she brought a suitcase containing the funds directly to the federal district attorney's office.[56]

Novedades political columnist Joaquín López Doriga broke the news that President López Portillo in April 1978 had ordered a full continuation of investigations of corruption among public officials.[57] "No exceptions" the newspaper columnist quoted the chief executive as saying. Then came the arrest of the most prominent administrator in the Echeverría presidency. Eugenio Méndez Docurro, who had been minister of communications and transportation, had been retained in the López Portillo administration as subsecretary of public education. The spectacle of an ex-cabinet minister hanging on to public life by taking a demotion to a subcabinet post was rare in Mexico. Even rarer were the newspaper headlines and broadcasts that Méndez Docurro would be tried on charges of taking 80 million pesos from government communications and transportation operations. The federal attorney general showed reporters stacks of faked invoices and canceled checks.

In addition to having been a cabinet minister, Méndez Docurro had been president of the National Polytechnic Institute, head of the National Science and Technology Council, and one of the republic's foremost educators and a leader in the PRI. Not since that dominant party had been organized in 1929 had such a high-ranking government official, still in power at the time of his arrest, been so publicly confronted with misdeeds. Normally, in the past, if corruption had been serious enough, an offender would resign for reasons of health or be given a diplomatic post on the other side of the world, with the newspapers in the know remaining silent. Not so in 1978, for the president and the top leaders of the Revolutionary coalition had made it clear that full reporting of such investigations would not bring official repercussions.

Also in April 1978 federal police arrested Fausto Cantú Peña, director general of the government's Mexican Coffee Institute, after the Ministry of Finance filed complaints against him alleging coffee contraband and tax evasion. Auditors found that the Institute had connived with 125 private exporters to evade 230 million pesos in taxes. *Novedades,* and later the other Mexico City dailies, quoted on the front page the offer of the federal attorney general:

> If Cantú Peña and his companions pay back the 230 million pesos, the charge of fiscal fraud will be dropped. The accused will then be released on bail bond to face penalties for lesser charges.[58]

Cantú Peña and his associates did repay the 230 million pesos to the government and then had to worry about the lesser charges, just as the newspapers had predicted.[59]

Excelsior, Novedades, El Sol, El Heraldo, and *La Prensa* correctly editorialized that President López Portillo had done more to restore respect for the Mexican presidency than any other leader since the crusading days of reformer President Lázaro Cárdenas, 1934–1940. The daily newspaper *El Nacional* commented in more subdued praise since through the years it has always had to portray whomever had been in office as excellent. *El Nacional* is owned by the government itself, with some of the publishing corporation's stock owned by the dominant party, the PRI.

Other Press Criticism

The anticorruption investigations were not the only news events of recent years which permitted Mexican newspapers to publish extensive criticism of establishment leaders. During university student riots from July 26 to October 2, 1968, various newspaper and magazine columnists severely criticized the Ministry of Gobernación (Internal Affairs) and the federal police for the way they handled the explosive situation, and for not realizing that Marxists among student strike groups had escalated the controversy with exchanges of rifle fire with police. Some 200 students were killed. When students paraded past the presidential palace with placards insulting the President of Mexico, Gustavo Díaz Ordaz, the photographs and stories did appear in print, for the event so shocked Mexico that the outbursts could not be ignored or played down.[60]

In February 1977 *Excelsior* began its editorial campaign against landlords who had amassed enormous holdings in rental properties. A top-of-the-page headline read "90% of the Housing of the Federal District Controlled by a Few Millionaires." The story asserted:

> The National Federation of Renters has charged that a few millionaires through holding companies . . . control 90 percent of the Mexico City rental units.[61]

The Mexico City daily newspaper *Uno Más Uno,* staffed by many reporters and editors who had been purged from *Excelsior* in 1976, in June 1978 began to criticize directly the president of the PRI, Carlos Sansores Pérez, who later resigned over party disharmony. The paper summed up its criticism in a cartoon showing a wall plastered with posters declaring support for the head of the PRI. One man in the cartoon says to another: "I don't understand why they don't nominate Roca. He's the only one who's more unpopular."[62] Roca was the coach of the hapless Mexican World Cup soccer team which suffered a big defeat in the 1978 regional playoffs.

Papers Peek inside the PRI

Unlike the political parties in the United States, which reflect genuine opposition to each other and among party factions, in Mexico no open conventions or primaries struggle to select nominees. Mexican newspapers are unaccustomed to presenting on their front pages very much about which PRI leader will receive the nomination from the Revolutionary leadership's inner circle, which includes the incumbent chief executive of the nation.

Breaking with precedence, the National Executive Committee in April 1975 announced the names of six men who met the formal and informal criteria for the PRI nomination for president of the republic and who were deemed more qualified than any other hopefuls. They were: Minister of Finance José López Portillo, Minister of Gobernación Mario Moya Palencia, Minister of Labor Porfirio Muñoz Ledó, Director of Social Security Carlos Gálvez Betancourt, Minister of Agrarian Reform Augusto Gómez Villanueva, and Minister of the Presidency Hugo Cervantes del Río.[63]

Normally, not until September 1975, when the PRI made its nomination public, would so much have been known about the possible successor for the July 1976 election. By this unprecedented move, the Revolutionary coalition leadership unleashed five months of speculative reporting about each of the six favorites for the party nomination. From April into September, the Mexico City dailies reported every major action or statement of all six potential presidents. Most of the newspapers tended to lead their readers into believing that the favorite for the PRI nomination was Interior Minister Moya Palencia or Cervantes del Río. None of the newspapers, in detailed coverage and in many analyses, accurately predicted that the party nomination would go to López Portillo.

Proceso's Alternate Views

Most major Mexican magazines—*Tiempo, Impacto, Hoy, Revista de Revistas*—consistently reflect a proestablishment editorial stance, giving mild and restrained criticism of government on occasion. Hard-hitting magazine criticism by the news weekly *Por Qué* ended when that periodical filed for bankruptcy in 1974, having lost its largest advertisers. However, in September 1976, Julio Scherer García, who had been ousted as head of *Excelsior,* established the weekly magazine *Proceso* and brought to its pages some of the columnists he had published at the newspaper.

For example, in one issue in October 1978, *Proceso* featured an article by novelist and philosopher Octavio Paz entitled "We Must Reconcile with Our Past." He challenged Mexico's policymakers as to the republic's foreign and domestic positions:

> A majority of Mexicans, between 1930 and 1960, were sure of our path . . . now they question . . . economic problems are grave and have not been resolved. On the contrary, inflation and unemployment grow.[64]

In the same issue of *Proceso,* another article charged that in the campaign against narcotics venders in the state of Sinaloa, the army and state police used torture in the course of interrogation. Three other articles in that same issue dealt with criticism of the way the government had ended the student riots of 1968 just before the Olympics opened in Mexico City.

Two weeks later, *Proceso* featured an article about Mexico's problems with the International Monetary Fund, in which the government was accused of mismanaging price and wage controls, compromising national interests in order to refinance huge foreign debts.[65] Another article in that same issue of *Proceso* accused the Ministry of Communications and Transportation of utilizing unconstitutional means in settling a strike by airport control tower operators.

Large display advertisements in major daily newspapers from time to time raise similar criticisms but almost always take the form of an open letter to the president of the republic, or some high placed administrator, and appeal to that official as a wise and understanding leader to rectify whatever problem has been raised. For instance, in July 1978 the farmers of Las Delicias Cooperative in Cuautla published an open letter advertisement to the president of Mexico asking for his help in reversing their being evicted, claiming that illegal procedures had been employed.[66] Mexico City dailies each have averaged one such protest advertisement per week since the custom became established in the early thirties.

Some of the former staffers of *Excelsior* who quit or were fired in 1976 work for the Mexico City daily *Uno Más Uno*, started by Scherer García to reflect the same independent outlook found in his magazine *Proceso.* James Nelson Goodsell, Latin American editor of the *Christian Science Monitor,* said the new newspaper provides diversity of viewpoints:

> *Uno Más Uno* says it will contribute to the national debate on issues, and it appears that Mr. López Portillo's government is eager to have such a debate since numerous government officials welcomed the new daily even, as one said, "if it goes against what we are doing."[67]

Establishment Reporting

When the government indicates that an event directly affects the nation's economy or development, most newspapers quickly respond. In October 1978 the U.S. government announced that it wanted to build a substantial fence along the Mexican border because millions of Mexican migrants illegally enter the United States each year seeking work. That migration constitutes an escape valve for Mexico, burdened with high unemployment and annual population increments.

The daily *El Sol de México* in a front-page headline referred to the proposal as a "Berlin Wall."[68] *Excelsior* quoted President López Portillo as calling a new fence "a grave, discourteous decision."[69] Other dailies featured interviews with the head of the Mexican Federation of Labor repudiating a wire fence, the PRI calling the idea repressive, the farm workers' leaders labeling it a "tortilla curtain," and the bishop of Mexicali demanding that the Catholic Church intervene to prevent the building of a new fence.[70] The United States decided to postpone indefinitely constructing the fence.

The Monterrey conservative daily *El Norte* through the years has been a consistent antiestablishment newspaper. Unlike the far left criticism, which has charged the Revolutionary coalition with not maintaining social reforms, *Norte* has challenged most major government programs and policies as being too extensive. In early 1979 the newsprint authority, PIPSA, for some weeks arbitrarily limited the supply of paper to *El Norte* without any public explanation. Within a generalized atmosphere of press freedom, government pressures on an effective voice of criticism were still a possibility. However, the newspaper's editorial positions remained unchanged during the restriction period and afterwards.

In general, most Mexican newspapers voluntarily support the Revolutionary coalition's policies. The republic's bandwagon journalism appropriately has reflected not only the thinking of the nation's leaders but also the hopes of a majority of its citizens. Their laical faith in their nation has for decades been based on the Revolution's long-range goals.

References

See references at the end of Chapter 3.

3

Mexico's Broadcasting: Private and Public Stations with Assistance from Gobernación

NOT only in Mexico, but in the other Latin American republics as well, the number one medium of mass communications is radio. Newspaper sales (per 1,000 population) remain highest in the republics with the highest rates of adult literacy, but in no Latin American republic do total daily newspaper sales begin to approach the total of radios in use. Given the rates of inflation in the 1970s, a newspaper costs more than a loaf of bread or its cornmeal equivalent, whereas the battery for a pocket-size transistor radio gives six months of daily listening for the price of a Sunday newspaper. Millions of impoverished dwellings without electric current have transistors. The Organization of American States, the United Nations, and other data sources greatly underestimate the number of radios in use, for they tabulate receivers that plug into electric circuits, not the tiny portables that have invaded even remote villages.[1]

Of Mexico's estimated 69 million persons in 1979, family clusters averaging seven individuals to a dwelling unit divided the population into approximately 10 million family households, 95 percent of which had a radio in daily use.[2] Some 6 million television sets are in daily use; approximately the same total as the number of daily newspapers sold.[3] With one adult in three not functionally literate, a majority of Mexicans hear the news rather than read it.

As of 1978 the Ministry of Communications and Transportation (Secretaría de Comunicaciones y Transportes or SCT) had licensed 585 commercial and 17 cultural AM radio stations, 118 commercial and 5 cultural FM stations, 7 commercial and 11 cultural shortwave radio stations, and 83 commercial and 3 cultural television stations.[4] These broadcasting stations reached every municipality in Mexico with one or more radio services. Television transmissions could be received in nine out of ten cities and towns.

In 1923 radio broadcasting began daily service in Mexico and in 1950 television began with privately owned commercial stations.[5] Through the years most stations have remained privately owned since the government has been able to guide the content of programs and set the limits for news coverage. The government also requres airing of publicity for its own projects, without buying the stations. However, in the 1970s the government did begin to purchase television stations and invest in both radio and television networks.

Licensing of Stations

By its very nature, broadcasting requires government regulation. Two competing stations cannot occupy the same frequency nor even transmit on frequencies that overlap within the same geographical listening area. The alternative of unassigned frequencies would result in cacophony.

The fundamental legal basis for licensing and regulating stations springs from the Federal Law of Radio and Television (FLRT) of 1960 as amended in 1969, 1975, and 1978.[6] Article 4 proclaims:

> Radio and television constitute an activity of public interest; therefore, the State must protect that activity and will be obligated to be vigilant towards the required social function compliance.[7]

Article 5 then gives four specific guidelines:

> Radio and television have the social function of contributing to the strengthening of national integration and the betterment of human existence. To effect this their transmissions shall:
> I. Affirm respect for moral principles, human dignity, and family relationships;
> II. Prevent negative disturbances for the harmonious development of children and youth;
> III. Contribute to the raising of the cultural level of the people and conserving national characteristics, customs of the nation, traditions, exalting the values of Mexican nationality, and,
> IV. Fortify democratic convictions, national unity, and international friendship and cooperation.[8]

In recent years various officials of the Inter-American Broadcasters Association, familiar with Latin American broadcasting laws, have told me they consider the fundamental goals of the Mexican law to be the most idealistic of any preamble in the hemisphere.

Only Mexican citizens who can prove financial solvency and who have applied for a frequency that is vacant may receive full-license hearings for a commercial station. And only legally recognized educational entities or units of government may apply for a cultural station.

Licenses for radio and television stations in Mexico are issued for periods of five years, with renewals invariably automatic.[9] Since 1934 not one broadcasting license has been permanently revoked in Mexico, though several stations have been suspended from broadcasting for brief periods for violating either the FLRT or the operating regulations, which reflect the requirements of the Federal Electoral Commission. Some corporate owners have been pressured unofficially into selling to new owners.[10]

In 1966 in Morelia, capital of the state of Michoacán, five radio stations continued to air detailed reports of student riots, despite a warning from the Ministry of Gobernación (Interior or Internal Affairs) that such broadcasts violated Section II of Article 5 of the FLRT regarding negative disturbances "for the harmonious development of children and youth." These stations were each required to suspend operations for several days and to pay fines.[11]

In February 1942 radio station XEG in Monterrey continued to sell time for daily news commentaries by a spokesman for Nazi Germany after the Mexican government had declared war on the Axis. The Ministry of Gobernación jailed the commentator on charges of subversion and forced the corporation owning the station to sell controlling stock to new owners and to change the staff managing the station.[12]

In 1964 a candidate for municipal office in Mérida, capital of Yucatán, scheduled a campaign speech over a radio station, then a violation of federal laws and regulations. A Gobernación official telephoned the station manager from Mexico City to cancel the broadcast.[13] Beginning in 1973 political campaign broadcasts were authorized by the amended Federal Electoral law, but in 1964 no such authorization existed.

Surprisingly enough, during the various student riots from July 26 to October 2, 1968, considerable coverage of the riots was aired on radio and television. That hundreds of students were parading in the Zócalo (principal plaza) of downtown Mexico City in front of the presidential palace and at the National University of Mexico campus obviated any government thoughts about treating the uproar as a minor news event.

On March 14, 1974, when radical student groups interrupted President Luis Echeverría while he gave an address on the campus of the National University of Mexico, television and radio coverage was live. Even when students began hurling objects, the broadcasts remained on the air.[14] Mexico's laws give the government standby power to order live coverage of rioting off the air, yet in both 1968 and 1974, the government did not silence the coverage. In 1974 I watched evening newscasts in which videotapes of the daytime violence had been condensed, perhaps thereby increasing sympathy for the government.

Chapter Two of the FLRT contains the specifics for revoking the license of a station. A radio or television owner could lose the license by not keeping to the assigned frequency or power, or by changing any of the technical elements assigned to daily operations. For allowing unauthorized personnel to broadcast, a sixty-day suspension of operations can be imposed.[15] If a station broadcasts in a manner that incites a breakdown of law and order or endangers the security of the nation, then the "Federal Executive . . . will have the right to acquire the properties of the concessionaire . . . through expropriation. . . ."[16]

Political Broadcasts

Even though the SCT issues the licenses and administers license renewal procedures, it does not help influence the content of programs. The guidelines for programs, especially news and political broadcasts, come from the Ministry of Gobernación.[17]

Under a 1969 amendment to the federal broadcasting law, the Ministry of Gobernación could convene a special commission consisting of the Ministers of Gobernación, Finance and Public Credit, the SCT, Public Education, and Health and Welfare to determine the best utilization of public service messages from the government that all radio and television stations in the republic must transmit.[18] The regulations for Radio and Television in 1973 created a National Council of Radio and Television, expanding the 1969 commission to further emphasize the authority of Gobernación to impose sanctions for any violations of the broadcasting law or its regulations.[19]

Until 1977 Gobernación had as subministries a bureau dealing with cinema and another bureau dealing with broadcasting. With the 1977 reorganization, Gobernación formed a Bureau (Dirección General) of Radio, Television, and Motion Pictures, headed by the sister of the president of Mexico, Margarita López Portillo, a writer.[20] Certainly having this bureau of the Ministry of Internal Affairs directed by the president's sister added considerable extralegal pressure on broadcasters to remain proestablishment by the very implications of the nepotism. The chief executive's own family was absorbed with the nature of programs.

Until 1973 political campaigning had been prohibited from broadcasting stations and networks in Mexico under the 1942 Law of Broadcasting.[21] In January 1973, however, a new federal electoral law was promulgated, and existing broadcasting regulations were amended in April to conform to the new right to discuss politics on the air. Each of the parties qualified to be on the ballot in the federal elections—in the July 1973 congressional elections. That meant the PRI, PAN, PPS, and PARM during each two-week period, for three months preceding the July election day, were given ten minutes of radio and television time, in which to present their campaigns in each congressional district and state.[22]

For the 1979 federal congressional elections, the Federal Electoral Commission on October 24, 1978, again promulgated new broadcasting regulations, this time giving four hours of free radio and television time per month to all political parties.[23] In addition to the four parties on the ballot in 1973 and in recent past elections, in 1979 the Communist Party of Mexico (Partido Comunista de México or PCM) and two new minor parties received free air time. Production and time costs are underwritten by the federal government for the fifteen-minute segments, but the privately owned stations and networks actually had to accept the requirement that the air time itself be donated by the broadcasters.

Government Programs

Under the federal broadcasting law and regulations, the government has always been able to obtain air time for announcements and news about federal and regional programs and projects. In June 1969 the federal tax law was amended to require every radio and television station to provide 12.5 percent of its daily hours of transmission for public service announcements from the government. This providing of free air time to the government was defined as a tax on broadcasting paid in service instead of money:

The Ministry of Finance and Public Credit is authorized to receive from broadcast concessionaires . . . payment of the said tax . . . with twelve and a half per cent of the daily time of transmission of each station. . . . The State will use the time . . . to realize campaigns of collective interest. . . .

Times of transmission will be distributed proportionally throughout the total schedule of transmissions. . . .[24]

Stations are obligated to air announcements of educational, cultural, social, political, athletic, and civic events. Other items entitled to receive broadcast time are government reports about national industry, agriculture, and mining; imports and exports; commercial development; social security; and transportation and communication; federal, state, and municipal election results; meteorological bulletins; and public health.

The regulations for broadcasting specify:

Programming shall include reports about new laws, activities of the Executive and the Congress, the political parties, campaigns and elections throughout the Republic, discussions of national issues, and round-table discourse (by a group of discussants).[25]

Before the 1969 requirement of 12.5 percent of daily air time for the government, the public service requirement for stations was thirty minutes per day.

The oldest continuing program produced by the government is the "National Hour," established in 1937, and still aired each Sunday from 10:00 to 11:00 P.M. over a special network of every licensed radio station in Mexico.[26] Before the growth of television, low-cost tapes, and recordings in working-class households, the audience for the "National Hour" was presumed to be vast, since it possessed a monopoly on all radio receivers that happen to be tuned in at that hour.

The Ministry of Gobernación has a special entity, *Radio Gobernación*, to produce this hour of entertainment and news. That agency hires the republic's leading writers, directors, announcers, and artists from all phases of the entertainment and information fields to intersperse announcements about government programs and projects with songs, comedy routines, and dramatic sketches.

Throughout the 1950s the Belden audience surveys in major Mexican cities showed from two-thirds to three-fourths of the radio receivers tuned in during the "National Hour."[27] With the growth of the Sunday night television audience in the 1960s, however, the impact of the "National Hour" on radio began to lessen. The government decided to rely more on daily reports from and about key government entities scattered throughout the broadcast day. Sometimes as newscasts, spot announcements, or special programs, the public service broadcasts deal with everything from adult literacy campaigns to public health lessons about inoculations against disease.

Inasmuch as radio and television announcers in Mexico must be certified the same as technicians and engineers, the government finds it easy to recruit the best on-the-air personalities to present its own reports. In the United States, transmitter engineers must have licenses from the Federal Communications Commission but studio technicians, such as cameramen, need only membership in unions at the network level or at stations that are unionized. Writers and performers likewise need no government certification. In Mexico, by contrast, not only are all broadcast employees members of various unions at the local stations or networks, but announcers must obtain SCT licenses. Chapter V, Article 86 of the *Ley Federal de Radio y Televisión* specifies that announcers with bachelor's degrees from preparatory schools qualify for Class A announcing licenses for any type of air work, whereas announcers with a secondary school education (ninth grade) receive Class B licenses, which may restrict some on-the-air activities.

Upon being licensed, announcers are given an excerpt from the *Reglamento* that reminds them the law forbids news reports threatening the security of the nation, endangering public order, violating decent language, obstructing justice or promoting crime, discussing religious matters, or advertising prostitution or vice.[28]

Publicizing Family Planning

In 1978 small town housewives in Guanajuato paused during their late morning cleaning and other household chores to tune in stations carrying the government's Radiofonía Rural service, featuring the daily serialized drama or soap opera "María the Forgotten One." This half hour radio drama, Monday through Friday, ran for sixty episodes. Originally the programs were produced in Mexico City by the Ministry of Gobernación's *Red Nacional*, a taped programming service, and broadcast over the leading commercial radio station of the republic, XEW, from 12:30 to 1:00 P.M., July to October 1976. XEW's repeater transmitters also carried the original series to listening areas representing 30 percent of the national daytime audience.[29]

This dramatic series in late 1977 and early 1978 was aired over a radio station in the port city of Lázaro Cárdenas in the state of Michoacán, where it again drew large female audiences.[30] In 1979 and 1980 the taped series was aired in thirty states, with provincial stations also enjoying good public response.

For the first time since daily radio broadcasting had come to Mexico, a dramatic series, "María la Olvidada," directly attacked "machismo," the cult of male virility that is proved by the impregnation of females, either one's wife or lover or any other consenting female.[31] This widely held philosophy, coupled with a lowering death rate, has given Mexico an annual net increase in population of 3.6 percent.[32]

In this popular radio series, the heroine, María, worked in a factory with her lover, Juan Carlos, who made her pregnant. She quit her job to have the child and Juan married her. María then finds out that Juan has other children and unburdens her sorrow to a doctor at a free clinic:

MARÍA: Why does Juan flaunt the children of that other woman? Why does he play with my feelings?

DOCTOR: María, that's how we show we are "macho" . . . virile males. . . . For a Mexican male, the more women he has sexually, the more macho he feels when these women have children.

MARÍA: But why? Is Juan Carlos emotionally sick?

DOCTOR: Not just as an individual. It's society which is sick, with values which corrode men's souls . . .

MARÍA: How do Mexican men get that spiritual sickness?

DOCTOR: By treating a woman as an object and by fathering many children, because deep inside themselves, men feel insecure . . .[33]

María Elena Becerril, a young broadcast dramatist, won a government contest to become the writer of this series, sponsored by the National Population Council (Consejo Nacional de Población). The series represents the strongest dramatic statement the government has encouraged to promote birth control, after ignoring the problem of the rapidly increasing population and its ensuing pressures until 1972.

On television, on Channel 13—a government-owned station in Mexico City—on Wednesday evenings, the question-and-answer program "Thanks, Doctor," in recent years has drawn a large audience. Physicians from social security and the Ministry of Public Health and Welfare answer questions on family planning mailed or telephoned in.[34]

Similar questions about birth control pills, abortion, intrauterine devices, and the free sterilization program of the government are aired on other television question-and-answer broadcasts, marking a basic departure in Mexico from previous inhibitions about public mention of such topics. On radio the daily morning program "Dialogue Without Fear," over the XEW network, has fielded the same questions about birth control.

Even the escape valve of the United States, where several million illegal migrants from Mexico annually seek work, has not solved Mexico's over-population dilemma. More than one adult in four has been unemployed in recent years and the economy cannot expand fast enough to absorb the annual increment in the potential work force. In response the government opened its first Family Planning Centers in January 1973, under the Ministry of Health and Welfare and under Social Security clinics. By 1979 more than 4,000 Family Planning Centers were operating seven days a week throughout the republic. To get Mexicans to avail themselves of the centers' free services, the government hopes that radio will reach the poor semiliterate and illiterate families who need the centers the most. The National Population Council found in 1978 that only 26 percent of childbearing aged women were utilizing the centers. Yet without the centers and without the government's mass media campaign for "Responsible Parenthood," the annual net increment in population might have risen to 3.8 percent.

The government's publicity campaign to make Mexicans aware of the need to practice family planning at the leadership level concerns distribution of paperback books and magazine articles and holding seminars for community officials by the Mexican Population Association (Asociación Mexicana de Población or AMEP). At the popular level, aimed at working-class adults without much education and at middle-class adults without higher education, the National Population Council circulates leaflets, booklets, and a comic book entitled "Better Life for Mexico's Population." Slogans about "Responsible Parenthood" become radio and television spot announcements and advertisements in magazines and on billboards. One radio public service announcement throughout 1978 urged married couples to stop by a center to get a free sixteen-page pamphlet of cartoons about family planning so that in the future children could be fed and when they become adults have a chance to find jobs.

The earlier radio announcements of 1974 stressed a negative phraseology: "Millions of our children will not find jobs, schools, or health care without responsible paternity."[35] By 1978 the radio announcements had become more positive in tone, promising an upward mobility for those who planned ahead to have fewer children.

Government Investments in Television

In addition to financing educational outlets from its budgets, the government achieves control by ownership of regular commercial video stations and their affiliated networks.

For the first two decades of television service in Mexico, all video stations were privately owned and operated, but by the 1970s, the government also operated two Mexico City channels and their network services.[36] These government-owned commercial video outlets are Channel 8, with five network affiliates in three states, and Channel 13, with a network of twenty-six affiliates in twenty-three states.[37]

Television began in Mexico as a privately owned commercial system in 1950, when Rómulo O'Farrill, Sr., opened XHTV, Channel 4, as the first full-time television station in Latin America. O'Farrill, publisher of the Mexico City daily newspapers *Novedades* and *The News,* also operated radio station XEX.[38] In 1951 the late Emilio Azcárraga, Sr., owner of radio station XEW and its networks, launched XEW-TV, Channel 2. Also in 1951 Guillermo González Camarena established the third commercial television station, Channel 5. Later these three rival Mexico City stations merged into the Telesistema Corporation, and still offer separate programming schedules today, from studios located adjacently at the Televicentro.

Each of these three pioneer commercial stations has become the anchor outlet feeding a network of provincial affiliates. Channel 2 heads a network of thirty-seven affiliates in twenty-one states. Channel 4 heads a network of eight stations in four states. Channel 5 heads a network of eighteen stations in eighteen states.

On January 8, 1973, the government devised a holding corporation, Televisa, with an umbrella ownership of commercial Channels 2, 4, and 5, and the government's 8. Channel 8 went on the air originally September 1, 1968, as a commercial station owned by Monterrey industrialists who later sold controlling stock to government subsidiaries. Each station competes for advertisers and audiences although all of the stations are tied to the same corporation. The news director of the system is Miguel Alemán, Jr., son of the former president of Mexico (1946–1952), Miguel Alemán, Sr.[39]

The Mexican government can have official views televised directly or indirectly through the basic laws regulating the operations of all licensed stations. It can also do this through government investments in television stations and networks and the consortium linking private and public video operations. Government reports can claim the 12.5 percent of all air time reserved for public service programs and announcements. The government can simply send its messages to Channels 8 and 13 and their networks. Or the government can work indirectly through Televisa to help formulate news selection and emphasis on the privately owned commercial channels and their networks.[40]

In 1970 the news departments of Channels 2 and 4 spent eight months planning the best-financed and most elaborate ninety-minute news program on television anywhere in Latin America. As a result, in September 1970 Telesistema began the nightly news program "24 Hours," aired from 11:00 P.M. to 12:30 A.M., under the management of Miguel Alemán, Jr., and edited and anchored by Jacobo Zabludovsky.[41] More than 120 persons—reporters, editors, correspondents, cameramen—work on the weeknight roundup under the technical direction of Arturo Vega Almada. News correspondents, via satellite live or on tape, add top news stories from the United States, Western and Eastern Europe, and Central and South America. Some of the editors and writers have worked with the Telesistema news team for twenty years, and skillfully combine news that the government considers top priority with the free flow of news stories streaming in from all over Mexico and the world.[42]

The highlights of all tapes and films used on "24 Hours" Monday through Friday nights are edited and late-breaking weekend stories added for the Sunday night edition "Today Sunday." Substantial portions of the program aired on Channel 2 at night are repeated on Channel 4 the following morning.

Broadcast Budget Emphasis

Budget analysis often yields the relative importance and scope of various entities in the public life of a nation. Utilizing that premise of political scientists and public administrators, a glance at the National Polytechnic Institute's Channel 11 and the government's commercial-style Channel 13 in Mexico City, may give some clues as to the relative emphasis the government gives to each type of operation.

For 1978 Channel 13's budget totaled 480 million pesos ($21.6 million) for operations, whereas Channel 11's budget totaled 42 million pesos ($1.9 million).[43] That is, the station the government operates as a commercial-type outlet with emphasis on entertainment had a budget approximately eleven times that of the educational station the government finances through the National Polytechnic Institute.

Unlike the situation in the United States, where the Public Broadcasting System obtains not only government funding but also generous grants from philanthropical foundations and large corporations, in Mexico educational stations subsist on whatever funds the government appropriates. Thus Channel 11 cannot hope for outside funds to purchase British dramas, Italian operas, or any other cultural series. With strong pressure from the labor unions to pay its personnel on a par with commercial station employees, Channel 11 finds a relatively large portion of its budget going for payrolls. It must get along with few staffers and a limited selection of programs, in contrast to its commercial rivals. Channel 11 often eagerly accepts free films and taped programs offered by the Ministry of Gobernación.

The government, therefore, could arrange to air as elaborate a production on the educational outlet as it can on its commercial-type station. That it seldom chooses to do so can be explained in terms of audience ratings. Channel 13 draws much larger audiences for its light comedies, popular musical reviews, and dramas than does Channel 11 with its discussion panels, programs on science, adult education courses, and old movies.

Government Series

Since 1976 Gobernación has supplied to both television and radio stations various series ranging from dramas to commentaries, each running from twenty-six to thirty weeks.

For television these series have included "Artists, Museums, and Galleries," "History of Mexico," "Invitation to Read," "Concert in Your Home," "Our Common Destiny," "Twenty-First Century Science," "The Physician," "Our Civilization," "Technology Education," "Traveling with Children," "News for Children," "National Jobs and Goals," "Famous Mexican Films," "Talking About Books," "Sports Today," "Point of View," "Your Home," "Evolution," "Morning Report," "Recreation," "Weekly Dramas," and "World Images."[44]

For radio these series have included "Today and Tomorrow" (sports, business, recreational activities), "Weekend Report on Mexico," "Music of Mexico," "National Reports," "Classical Music," "Foreign Trade," "News from the President's Office," "Biographies of Painters," "Public Health," "Parallel Zero: Interviews with Public Leaders," plus various dramas and soap operas about vocational training, family planning, household budgeting, and family problems.[45]

During the past decade over every radio and television station in Mexico, at least thirty minutes each day is devoted to the government's adult literacy campaign programs, a series called by various names but unofficially lumped together as "Alfabetización."[46] Some series offer formal lesson plans and last six months. Other programs center in informal lectures of shorter time periods.

The quantity and quality of broadcast news and reports in Mexico have continued to increase, but under governmental guidance rather than through the independence of broadcasters.

References

Alba, Victor. *The Mexicans* (New York: Praeger, 1967).

Alisky, Marvin. "Early Mexican Broadcasting," *Hispanic American Historical Review* 34 (November 1954): 514–26.

_____. *The Governors of Mexico* (El Paso: Texas Western Press Monographs of UTEP, 1965).

_____. "Growth of Newspapers in Mexico's Provinces," *Journalism Quarterly* 37 (Winter 1960): 75–82.

_____. "Mexico" in John C. Merrill, Carter R. Bryan, and Marvin Alisky, *The Foreign Press,* 2nd ed. (Baton Rouge: Louisiana State University Press, 1970).

_____. "Mexico's National Hour on Radio," *Nieman Reports* 7 (October 1953): 17–18.

_____. "Mexico's Population Pressures," *Current History* 72 (March 1977): 106–10, 131–34.

_____. "Mexico's Rural Radio," *Quarterly of Film, Radio, and Television* 9 (Summer 1954): 405–17.

_____. "Mexico's 'Watergate' Investigations Oust Hundreds of High-Level Bureaucrats," *USA Today* 107 (January 1979): 11–12.

_____. "Mexico Versus Malthus," *Current History* 66 (May 1974): 200–203, 227–30.

_____. "Radio's Role in Mexico," *Journalism Quarterly* 31 (Winter 1954): 66–72.

_____. "Radio and Television" in Helen Delpar, ed., *Encyclopedia of Latin America* (New York: McGraw-Hill, 1974), pp. 514–16.

_____. *Who's Who in Mexican Government* (Tempe: Arizona State University Center for Latin American Studies, 1969).

Ampudia, Ricardo. Editor of Mexico City magazine *Hoy* interviewed at Stanford University by Marvin Alisky, October 10, 1978.

Azcárraga, Emilio, and Angel Cabrera and Rodolfo Coronado. XEW-TV officials interviewed over XEW-TV on September 7, 1970.

Bagdikian, Ben H. *The Effete Conspiracy, and Other Crimes of the Press* (New York: Harper and Row, 1972).

Balam, Gilberto. *Tlatelolco, Reflexiones de un Testigo* (México, D. F: Editorial GB, 1969).

Belden and Associates. *Radiómetro: el Auditorio de México* (México, D.F.: Editorial Acosta, 1952).

Blair, Calvin P. "Nacional Financiera" in Raymond Vernon, ed., *Public Policy and Private Enterprise in Mexico* (Cambridge, Mass.: Harvard University Press, 1964).

Brandenburg, Frank R. *The Making of Modern Mexico* (Englewood Cliffs, N.J.: Prentice-Hall, 1964).

Cámara Nacional de la Industria de Radio y Televisión. *Anuario 1978* (México, D.F.: CIRT, 1978).

_____. *Directorio de la CIRT* (México, D.F.: CIRT, 1978).

_____. *Disposiciones legales en Materia de Radio y Televisión* (México, D.F.: CIRT, 1976).

Camp, Roderic A. *Mexican Political Biographies, 1935–1975* (Tucson: University of Arizona Press, 1976).

Castaño, Luis. "El Desarrollo de los Medios de Información en la América Latina," *Ciencias Políticas y Sociales* 8 (April-June 1962): 291–306.

Cárdenas, Leonard. "Contemporary Problems of Local Government in Mexico," *Western Political Quarterly* 18 (December 1965): 858–65.

Chaffee, Steven, ed. *Political Communication* (Beverly Hills, Calif.: Sage Publications, 1975).

Chilcote, Ronald. *The Press in Latin America, Spain, and Portugal* (Stanford: Institute of Hispanic American and Luso-Brazilian Studies, 1963).

Cohen, Bernard. *The Press and Foreign Policy* (Princeton, N.J.: Princeton University Press, 1963).

Cole, Richard R. "Mexico and the Foreign Press," *Quill* 58 (January 1970): 18–19.

Coleman, Kenneth M. *Diffuse Support in Mexico: Potential for Crisis* (Beverly Hills, Calif.: Sage Publications, Comparative Politics Series, Vol. 5, 1976).

Consejo Nacional de Población. *México Demográfico Breviario 1975* (México, D.F.: CONAPO, 1975).

Davis, James. "The Press and the President in Mexico," *Inter-American Press Association Special Report,* June 1971, pp. 2–4.

Editor and Publisher. *Editor & Publisher International Yearbook 1978* (New York: Editor & Publisher, 1978).

Erlandson, E. H. "The Press in Mexico: Past, Present, and Future," *Journalism Quarterly* 41 (Spring 1964): 232–36.

Farías, Luis M. Publisher of *El Nacional* interviewed in Mexico City by Marvin Alisky February 2 and July 15, 1962.

Fernández, José Luis. *Derecho de la Radiodifusión* (México, D.F.: Academia de Derecho Radiofónico, 1960).

Gardner, Mary A. *Inter-American Press Association* (Austin: University of Texas Press, 1967).

González Casanova, Pablo. *Democracy in Mexico* (New York: Oxford University Press, 1970).

Grayson, George W. "The Making of a Mexican President, 1976," *Current History* 71 (February 1976): 49–52, 83–84.

Inter-American Development Bank. *Economic and Social Progress in Latin America 1977 Report* (Washington, D.C.: IADB, 1977).

Jagos, Marión de. "Homenaje de Cineastas a Margarita López Portillo," *Mujeres* 10 (May 31, 1977): 8–10.

Johnson, Kenneth F. *Mexican Democracy: A Critical View* (Boston: Allyn and Bacon, 1971).

Krasnow, E. G. and L. L. Longley. *The Politics of Broadcast Regulation* (New York: St. Martin's Press, 1973).

Lowry, Dennis T. "Radio, TV and Literacy in Mexico," *Journal of Broadcasting* 14 (Spring 1970): 239–44.

Macías, Pablo G. *Octubre Sangriento en Morelia* (México, D.F.: Editorial Acasim, 1968), p. 92.

Medal, Conseulo. *El Periodista Como Orientador Social* (México, D.F.: Escuela Nacional de Ciencias Políticas y Sociales, UNAM, 1965).

Medios Publicitarios Mexicanos. "Periódicos," *Medios Publicitarios Mexicanos,* August–October 1976 and February–April 1977.

Merrill, John C. *The Elite Press: Great Newspapers of the World* (New York: Pitman, 1968).

Mexico's International Research Associates. *El Videómetro de México* (México, D.F.: International Research Associates, 1978).

Montaño, Guillermo. "La Otra Cara de la Luna," *Siempre* 64 (November 25, 1964): 77, 86.

Navarrete, Ifigenia Martínez de. *La Distribución del Ingreso y El Desarrollo Económico de México* (México, D.F.: Instituto de Investigaciones Económicas, Universidad Nacional Autónoma de México, 1960).

Needler, Martin C. *Politics and Society in Mexico* (Albuquerque: University of New Mexico Press, 1971).

Nogales, Laura. Sales director for PIPSA interviewed in Mexico City by Marvin Alisky on October 26, 1978.

Norris, R. C. "A History of La Hora Nacional: Government Broadcasting via Privately Owned Radio Stations in Mexico" (Ph.D. diss., University of Michigan, Ann Arbor, Michigan, 1963).

Padgett, L. Vincent. *The Mexican Political System*, 2nd ed. (Boston: Houghton Mifflin, 1976).

Paz, Octavio. "Reconciliémonos con Nuestro Pasado," *Proceso*, 2 (October 9, 1978): 10-11.

Productora e Importadora de Papel. *Papel para Imprimir Periódico* (Mexico, D.F.: PIPSA, 1978).

Purcell, Susan Kaufman. *Public Policy and Private Profits: A Mexican Case Study* (Berkeley: University of California Press, 1975).

Rabasa, Emilio O. Minister of Foreign Relations interviewed in Tubac, Arizona, by Marvin Alisky, on October 24, 1974.

Ramírez, Carlos. "Nuestro Problema Es Político y Social, No Técnico," *Proceso*, 2 (October 23, 1978): 18-19.

Rivers, William L., Susan Miller, and Oscar Gandy, "Government and the Media," in Steven Chaffee, ed., *Political Communication* (Beverly Hills, Calif.: Sage Publications, 1975), pp. 217-36.

Rodríguez González, Bernice. Administrator at the National Population Council interviewed in Mexico City by Marvin Alisky on November 8, 1976.

Ross, Stanley R. *Is the Mexican Revolution Dead?* 2nd ed. (Philadelpha, Pa.: Temple University Press, 1975).

Rubin, Bernard. "Secrecy, Security, and Traditions of Freedom of Information," in Otto Lerbinger and A. L. Sullivan, eds., *Information, Influence and Communication* (New York: Basic Books, 1965), pp. 136-75.

Scott, Robert E. *Mexican Government in Transition*, 2nd ed. (Urbana, Ill.: University of Illinois Press, 1959).

Secretaría de Gobernación. *Ley Federal de Radio y Televisión* (México, D.F.: Gobernación, 1960).

_____. "Acuerdo: 12.5 de Tiempo al Estado," *Diario Oficial*, June 27, 1969, Section I.

_____. *Ley Orgánica de la Administración Pública Federal* (México, D.F.: Gobernación, Dec. 29, 1976).

_____. *Reglamento de la Ley Federal de Radio y Televisión* (México, D.F.: Gobernación, Apr. 4, 1973).

_____. "Reglamento de las Estaciones Radiodifusoras Comerciales, Culturales, y de Experimentación Científica y Aficionados," *Diario Oficial*, May 20, 1942, Art. 114-15.

Secretaría de Programación y Presupuesto, Dirección General de Estadística. *Compendio Estadístico* (México, D.F.: Departamento de Censos, 1978).

Stevens, Evelyn P. "Mexican Machismo," *Western Political Quarterly* 18 (December 1965): 848-57.

Taladrid, José, Director General of PIPSA interviewed in Mexico City by Marvin Alisky on October 24 and 25, 1978.

Turner, Frederick C. *The Dynamic of Mexican Nationalism* (Chapel Hill: University of North Carolina Press, 1968).

Underwood, Robert Bruce. "A Survey of Contemporary Newspapers of Mexico," (Ph.D. diss., University of Missouri, Columbia, Missouri, 1965).

Untel, Carlos. "The University as Sanctuary," *National Review* (Aug. 18, 1978): 1024-25.

United States–Mexico Association. "Mexican Government Takes Over Newspaper Chain," *U.S.–Mexico Border Cities Association*, May 1972, p. 10.

Vargas, Armando. "The Coup at Excelsior," *Columbia Journalism Review* 15 (September-October 1976): 45–48.

Wilkie, James W. *The Mexican Revolution: Federal Expenditure and Social Change Since 1910,* 2nd ed. (Berkeley: University of California Press, 1970).

Newspapers and Periodicals: *Christian Science Monitor; El Día,* Mexico City; *El Diario de Yucatán,* Mérida, Yucatán; *El Heraldo,* Mexico City; *El Imparcial,* Hermosillo, Sonora; *El Nacional,* Mexico City; *El Sol,* Mexico City; *Excelsior,* Mexico City; *La Prensa,* Mexico City; *New York Times; Novedades,* Mexico City; *Política,* Mexico City; *Tele-Guía,* Mexico City; *Tiempo,* Mexico City; *Times of the Americas,* Washington, D.C.; *Uno Más Uno,* Mexico City.

4

Peru: Bolstering Reform through the Media

IN 1968 when military leaders came to power in a coup and launched Peru's social revolution, a new era began in which government has guided the mass media into bolstering social, economic, and political reforms. The military government's "revolution from the top" needed to arouse mass support for programs of basic change in a nation that had been overwhelmingly traditional during most of its history.[1]

From the inception of its independence from Spain in the 1820s until recent years, a majority of the presidents of the republic came from the army, but neither they nor the civilian chief executives did much to mold public opinion. Rather they censored the press to mimimize political criticism. For example, during the eleven-year dictatorship of Augusto B. Leguía, from 1919 to 1930, no public ground swell materialized for the airing of complaints against Leguía. Only when the U.S. economic depression hit Peru full force did the jobless revolt and the newspapers chronicle the crisis.[2]

Press censorship remained in force when a civilian banker and engineer, Manuel Prado, succeeded the generals of the 1930s as president in 1939 for a six-year term. Prado began to allow limited editorial criticism and found in 1940 that the most influential Peruvian daily newspaper, *El Comercio,* was criticizing him for advocating the extension of the social security system.[3]

In the spring of 1945, when a new presidential campaign began, President Prado lifted all censorship. Newspapers were at last free to publish criticism of the candidates. This period of press freedom continued until October 1948 when General Manuel Ordría took over the government in a coup and reinstituted press censorship. In July 1956 press freedom returned to Peru but was later abridged by the newspaper expropriations of 1970 and the sweeping law of 1974 assigning newspapers to various workers groups. In 1978 came another modification that allowed stock in the newspapers to be purchased on the open market. However, Peru entered the 1980s with governmental guidance of press and broadcasting still discernible.

The Setting

Peru's national territory of almost ½ million square miles equals the size of Alaska and is divided into three parts. The eastern forest and jungle, some 60 percent of the republic's land area, contains less than 10 percent of the population. Nine out of ten Peruvians live either in the coastal plain or the highland regions. In 1976 the population totaled 16 million and has been increasing at the rate of 2.9 percent a year.[4] Public health measures have sharply reduced the death rate among infants and half of all Peruvians are younger than seventeen years of age. Thus only 9 million of the 1980 estimated population of 18 million are adults, the primary group of the mass media and politics.

Language further limits potential newspaper readership. The 1972 census showed that one-third of all Peruvians spoke Quechua, Aymará, or another Indian language, with 11.7 percent of the total population being strictly monolingual Indians. Language also reduces the primary group reached by broadcasting, since radio programs are broadcast mostly in Spanish.

The 1972 Education Reform Law created provincial primary schools with instruction in Quechua, but so far this plan has not yet had time to lead many Indians from literacy in transliterated Quechua to literacy in Spanish or even to increased fluency in spoken Spanish.

Literacy has risen in the past two decades, with the government now claiming that 70 percent of the adults can read. However, they are literate only in a rudimentary way, being able to recognize their name, street signs, and basic words. Probably only half the adults can read a newspaper or magazine story with any true comprehension.[5]

Of the 1978 total daily newspaper circulation of 1,186,000, some 88 percent—or 1,045,000 copies—represented sales by the Lima dailies, which are also national papers, circulating among the civic leaders of the provincial cities and towns.[6] Those most active politically throughout the republic tend to read the Lima dailies. *La Prensa* publishes a separate limited edition for each major region of the republic, dropping some international news or national news in order to run regional stories. These regional editions result in a form of news management in which each provincial region reads stories emphasizing its own interests.

As anthropologist Paul L. Doughty has observed, true nationwide communication comes from radio, with one-fifth of all radio stations in the nation being in the Lima area, hooked to the provincial stations via networks and repeater transmitters.[7] The greater Lima metropolitan area, including Callao, with a 1980 estimated population of 4.5 million, accounts for one-fourth of the republic's inhabitants. Therefore, better than one Peruvian in four resides within the primary audience areas of Lima radio and television stations. In 1977 Peru had 3.8 million family dwelling units and more than 3.6 million radios, including transistors, in daily use, putting most Peruvian adults in continuing radio contact. In 1969 political scientist Howard Handelman interviewed provincial community leaders in Cuzco, Junín, and Pasco. He found only a minority who felt they could influence government policies.[8] Yet these leaders remained in daily contact with Lima or provincial cities through radio news.

From Press Freedom to Censorship and Back

Early in 1945, for the final six months of his first term, President Manuel Prado ended Peru's longtime censorship of the press, thereby insuring an open presidential campaign eventually won by José Bustamante, diplomat and judge.

The American Revolutionary Popular Alliance (Alianza Popular Revolucionaria Americana or APRA), which had been outlawed in the 1930s, was active in the new Congress. APRA began as a leftist reform movement in 1924 and through the years grew more conservative and anti-Marxist in its own kind of nationalism and reforms.[9] In recent decades it has remained Peru's largest party. In September 1945 Apristas in Congress, smarting over. editorial criticism in the Lima dailies *El Comercio* and *La Prensa,* forced a bill into law returning press censorship but President Bustamante refused to sign it and a second law was enacted canceling the first measure.[10]

Learning to live with press freedom, reformers and the conservative editors of the Lima daily *La Prensa* fought politically and traded insults in editorials and letters to the editor. On January 7, 1947, the *Prensa* board chairman was shot and killed in his office.[11] An Aprista member of Congress was formally charged but years passed without any court decision.

In a coup in October 1948 General Manual Odría took over the government, reinstituted press censorship, and outlawed the Aprista party. Not only the liberal publications, but the conservative dailies also began a nine-year period of trying to report national affairs over the arbitrary objections of the government. Under the constitution the presidential term was six years, and with the constitutional powers returned to civilians in 1956, aging Manuel Prado won his second term. As soon as he was inaugurated on July 28, he ended censorship of the press.

Within two years the mass media freedom of Peru would be tested twice. First in May 1958, with the visit of the then vice-president of the United States, Richard M. Nixon, angry mobs in demonstration against the policies of the United States subjected him to jeers, stones thrown at the automobiles in his entourage, and other street violence. I was a consultant for the Fulbright Commission at Catholic University in Lima from June through August that year, and after analyzing the Peruvian press I found only the leftist radical weeklies had advocated the violent demonstrations.[12] Most of the dailies had reflected some frustration over inflation and the U.S. lead and zinc tariffs, but had not directly aided the outburst. The Peruvian government felt embarrassment over the rude treatment received by the vice-president but did not use the occasion to censor even the most violent criticism of the weeklies.

El Comercio, oldest extant newspaper in Peru, having been founded in 1839, had always supported public order and the governing establishment. As a post-Nixon trip series, during ten consecutive issues that July, *Comercio* ran editorial-page analyses on foreign policy mistakes of the United States and Western European nations, entitled "The Errors in the Fight Against Communism."[13] The United States was criticized for neglecting its best customers, the Latin American republics, in its preoccupation with the affairs of major European and Asian nations.

President Prado, nearing the age of seventy, decided in mid-1958 to end his marriage of forty-three years in order to marry a thirty-nine year old companion. To do this he found a cooperating committee of three bishops to declare his church marriage "annulled." The Roman Catholic church would not recognize this action, which had not been processed through the Sacred Roman Rota, the tribunal of appeal at the Vatican. Hundreds of protesting women swinging rosaries picketed the presidential palace for two weeks as the Peruvian mass media reflected the indignation of many citizens in overwhelmingly Catholic Peru. Even the popular tabloids as well as the Aprista daily *La*

Tribuna joined in the chorus of criticism. To his credit as a chief executive pledged to press freedom, Manual Prado took the criticism for weeks and weeks, and never once attempted to restore press censorship.

One Lima daily, *La Nación,* founded in 1953, did cease publication in 1956, early in the Prado administration. This paper had been a supporter of the Odría dictatorship and became a target of its many creditors, who never collected $320,000 in debts.

President Prado himself owned the corporation publishing the daily *La Crónica,* which had both a morning and an evening edition, and which operated the popular station *Radio La Crónica.* During 1958–1963 his station vied with *Radio Central* and *Radio Panamericana* for the largest audiences for soap operas and musical programs. All three stations trailed the government's own network, *Radio Nacional,* for audiences for the news programs.

In the 1962 presidential election, Víctor Haya de la Torre was the Aprista candidate. Fernando Belaúnde was the candidate of the Popular Action (AP) party, with support of the Christian Democratic Party (PDC). The third candidate turned out to be former President Manuel Odría, who had retired as a general and had renounced past dictatorial postures. The popular vote divided three ways, but the constitution required a winner to receive more than one-third of the votes. Otherwise, the Congress was supposed to sit as an electoral college and choose the president.

Commanders of the armed forces accused the Apristas of fraud in an alleged arrangement in Congress. The generals then staged a coup, nullified the election, and announced that a junta would rule for one year, and that in June 1963 the election would be held again. For two weeks a junta resorted to censorship, then allowed the press to return to full reporting of national news. Another close threat of curtailing information had passed.[14]

The same three major candidates ran again in June 1963, and this time Belaúnde won the presidency with 39 percent of the votes. In Congress the four political parties grouped into two rival coalitions, with the Aprista-Odriísta group holding a majority over Belaúnde's AP-PDC alliance.

Utilizing the Peruvian tradition of executivism, Belaúnde launched some education, agrarian, and housing programs, and encouraged new industrialization including automobile assembly plants.

During 1966 Lima newspapers reported that the agrarian reform had not been very successful. During 1967 in many issues of the new magazine *Oiga,* the divisions within the Belaúnde administration became evident. For two decades the Peruvian currency, the sol, had remained steady at twenty-seven soles to the dollar, then in 1967 it sank to forty to the dollar.

In 1968 one of the crises involved the International Petroleum Company (IPC), a subsidiary of Standard Oil of New Jersey, whose La Brea and Ariñas oil fields represented a major petroleum reserve for the republic. Belaúnde and his cabinet ministers negotiated an agreement whereby IPC would return the oil fields to Peru in exchange for a monopoly in refining and other concessions and payments. The newspapers published a detailed description of the widely unpopular and controversial agreement after the magazine *Oiga* printed it in full, much to the anguish of the government.[15] The continuing uproar in the press contributed greatly to the downfall of the Belaúnde government.

Day after day the conservative daily *El Comercio* reported in detail on the irregularities of the IPC agreement and published severely critical editorials that encouraged the coup d'état the military leaders were contemplating. Political scientist Carlos A. Astiz observed:

> . . . it seems apparent that *El Comercio* was very important in molding public opinion against Belaúnde and in favor of an alternative, which could only come from a coup d'etat.[16]

The public works programs of the Belaúnde administration coupled with its inability to reform the tax system had forced Peru to borrow from abroad. Foreign debt rose as international trade contracted and capital continued to leave the country.

In the Belaúnde cabinet, the minister of finance, Manuel Ulloa, had been an officer of the Deltec Banking Corporation, a major creditor that had extended loans to Peru at high interest. Ulloa negotiated with Deltec on August 9, 1968, for still another large loan.[17] Within a few days Ulloa issued a decree that reversed protective legislation and allowed foreign banks to take control of Peru's private banking system. Press reports of this action inflamed not only the military but civilian nationalists. The Ulloa-Deltec negotiations symbolized in the mass media a shocking conflict of interest.[18]

In addition to the IPC deal and the Ulloa-Deltec arrangements, the leadership of the president's own Popular Action party split deeply over candidates for the 1969 presidential and congressional elections. On October 3, 1968, the top generals and admirals of the armed forces ousted the Belaúnde government and assumed power through a junta.

General Juan Velasco became president, backed by military cabinet ministers and the Advising Council to the Presidency (Comité de Asesoramiento a la Presidencia or COAP), forty-two generals and admirals committed to institutionalizing social and economic reforms in Peru.[19]

These military leaders of 1968 differed from those of the past who had been pledged to maintain order and the status quo. The newer military leaders came more from the middle class and from provincial cities, and had risen from colonel to general or captain to admiral by studying at the Center for Higher Military Studies (Centro de Altos Estudios Militares or CAEM). Founded in 1950, CAEM courses stress economic problem solving, national development, and public administration techniques.[20] CAEM graduates became the catalytic agents for revolutionary chemistry in the body politic. Political scientist Luigi Einaudi, formerly with Rand Corporation and now with the State Department, found these military leaders to have self-images as technical innovators whose skills were needed if Peru was to develop its full potential as a modern nation.[21]

After expropriating IPC and creating a government-owned petroleum industry, Petroperu, on October 9, 1968, the Velasco government promulgated between June 1969 and March 1972 basic reform laws for land and agriculture, mining, industry, fishing, and education. The junta broke with Peru's past through expropriation of large estates, forcing the sale to the government or to Peruvian investors of percentages of stock in industries, and creating workers cooperatives. Press censorship did not return with the military, and in the early years of the revolution, diversity of editorial opinion was tolerated by the government reformers with irritation.

The military reformers suspended activities of the political parties, and would not lift that ban until 1977. The reformers knew they must stimulate mass support for the revolution and sought to influence the mass media through positive public relations. With formerly powerful civilians being subjected to expropriations and controls in the name of a social revolution, obviously a consensus on national goals did not result from discussions and debates.

The Press Statute

President Velasco and the COAP in late 1969 sought standby guarantees that editorial comments by the press, and its reporting of criticism by political opponents of the government, could not present a serious challenge to the power of the military administration. In early 1970 President Velasco promulgated by executive decree the Press Statute.[22] This misnamed Law of Press Freedom provided that a publisher could be fined or jailed for defamation of any citizen, but the libel would be considered aggravated if directed against a government official or public entity.

This law, therefore, discouraged undocumented attacks against the government's reform laws. Velasco indicated that the press law would help mobilize citizen support for the revolution by allowing the government to expropriate any newspaper whose editorial policies opposed the reform laws.[23]

Rather than place censors in all privately owned newspapers to insure support for the revolution, the military leaders decided to expropriate opposition newspapers, and to evolve some type of custodial-publisher system under which each daily paper would be assigned to a specific group of workers representing one of the sectors of the economy. This long-range plan took five years to unfold, and then another three years to be attempted unsuccessfully. In 1978 private stockholders were invited to return to the public publishing corporations.

The Expropriations

The government's first major move against the opposition press came on March 4, 1970, when the minister of the interior expropriated the Lima daily newspapers *Expreso* and its afternoon affiliate *Extra*. These dailies were owned by Manuel Ulloa, the beclouded finance minister under President Belaúnde, who had been sent into exile. Management of these newspapers was turned over to an Employees Board of Directors representing the printers and journalists unions.[24]

Also expropriated in 1970 were the daily newspaper *La Crónica* and its broadcast affiliate *Radio Crónica* when the corporation declared bankruptcy. Assets were recovered by an auction. The *Crónica* media had been owned by former Peruvian President Manuel Prado (1939–1945 and 1956–1962), whose family in 1970 lost control of their banks and vast real estate holdings through expropriations as part of the reform laws. *Crónica's* breezy tabloid style and morning, midday, and afternoon editions had made it the circulation leader among the nation's newspapers at that time. Under government guidance during most of the 1970s, its circulation became smaller than that of five rival dailies.

Also in 1970 the courts expropriated the daily newspaper of the Aprista political party, *La Tribuna,* for nonpayment of taxes, but instead of turning it over to a progovernment union or workers society, the Supreme Court ruling abolished this paper and the government then sold the printing equipment.[25]

After the other newspapers that politically opposed the military government's revolution had been expropriated, the large conservative daily *El Comercio* chose to censor itself rather than risk a government takeover. *El Comercio,* the second oldest continuing daily newspaper in Latin America, was owned by the Miró Quesada family, aristocrats who trace their lineage back to the Spanish conquest of the Inca Empire in 1532. From 1971 until its 1974 expropriation, *El Comercio* voluntarily restrained itself from editorially opposing the government.

Another large daily newspaper independent of the government was *La Prensa,* published by Pedro Beltrán, who had been head of the presidential cabinet during the second Prado administration. Under technicalities of the 1970 Press Statute, a Peruvian publisher must not remain out of the country more than six months in any one year. Beltrán left Peru on July 10, 1971, to be a visiting professor of economics at the University of Virginia and returned to Lima on January 21, 1972. The government ordered his removal as publisher for violating the residency restriction, and on April 6, 1972, he had to sell his 50,504 shares of stock to the 508 employees of *La Prensa.* His nephew, Pedro Beltrán Ballen, carried on as executive publisher under restraints for two more years until expropriation.

La Prensa had continued during 1971 to feature on its front page stories about the suspended Aprista party. For example, in February 1971, on the front page of a Sunday edition, a large headline read "Haya in Aprista Meeting Gives a Call to Create a Civilian Front." The story itself, taking up one-fourth of the front page and part of page two, stated:

> The Chief of the Aprista Party, Víctor Raúl Haya de la Torre, proposed last night the formation of a civilian front . . . to begin the fight for the recuperation of democracy and the full vigor of the Constitution.[26]

The military government of President Velasco tried to answer such challenges to its authority and social revolution by creating an agency to stimulate peasant and working-class support for reform programs. Established in 1971 the agency was the National System of Aid for Social Mobilization (Sistema Nacional de Apoyo a la Movilización Social or SINAMOS).[27] The Decree of June 22, 1971, establishing SINAMOS, declared that this entity would act as a link between the government and the people, helping make bureaucracy more responsive to the public and helping citizens express their desires to the government. Coordinating squatter settlements, peasant organizations, and cooperatives, SINAMOS set up offices in each region of the republic, with dozens of field agents sending news stories and reports to newspapers and to every radio and television station. To reach provincial working-class Peruvians, radio remained the appropriate principal medium. In 1978 SINAMOS suspended its operations.

Broadcasting Controls

From the inception of daily radio broadcasting in Peru in 1925, privately owned commercial radio enjoyed a monopoly of the market until 1935 when the government added its own broadcasting services. Not until 1971 did the government gain control of radio and television.

On June 20, 1925, commercial station OAX in Lima inaugurated daily broadcasting in Peru with music, the poetry of Ricardo Palma, and a speech by the president of the republic.[28] For years the pioneer stations aired only news headlines taken from newspapers and weather reports.

The president of Peru, Oscar R. Benavides, in 1935 contracted with the Marconi Company to create the government's own network of radio stations, *Radio Nacional,* with transmitters in Lima and in provincial capitals, with broadcasts repeated via shortwave. Now the republic had full newscasts mornings, afternoons, and evenings, a service soon copied by the commercial stations.[29]

Although *Radio Nacional,* through its Marconi contract, traces its heritage to Peru's first full-time station, OAX , in 1925, and to the amateur stations of Callao of 1923, not until 1935 did the government itself attempt to produce or air broadcasts.

In 1958 the Locke Audience Surveys for Lima showed that Peruvians were listening to serialized dramas or soap operas and musical programs over commercial stations *Radio La Crónica, Radio Central, Radio Miraflores,* and *Radio Inca.* For news programs, however, the government's *Radio Nacional* network, which also reached audiences throughout the republic, had the highest ratings.[30] This pattern continued into the 1970s.

In November 1971 COAP, the cabinet ministers, and President Velasco decided to insure government control of the broadcasting industry. A presidential decree promulgated Law 19020, a new General Law of Telecommunications.[31] It permitted the government to expropriate 51 percent ownership of privately owned television stations.

In Lima the government had owned Channel 7 since video came to Peru in January 1958, when that station was launched atop the Ministry of Education building. In November 1958 privately owned

Channel 4 inaugurated commercial video, and later was joined by three other commercial outlets in Lima. The university system began Channel 13.

The four commercial channels in Lima and the commercial channels in thirteen provincial cities had not employed their own news directors before expropriation. Television news commentators had been under contract to sponsors, and by 1971 the major sponsors of television news programs were government corporations that had been created to run the petroleum, fishing, and similar industries. So the gaining of majority stock by the government did not substantially change the prevailing sympathetic video coverage of Peruvian political events and the television reports about the programs of the social revolution.

Article 15 of the 1971 Telecommunications Law permitted the government to purchase 25 percent ownership of each privately owned radio station. But inasmuch as a minority of the Peruvian radio stations aired any substantial amounts of news in their music-oriented programming, only eleven of the twenty-seven Lima radio stations were directly affected by the government's 1971 stock purchases.[32]

Even with competition from twenty-seven other radio stations in Lima, *Radio Nacional* had consistently drawn the large audiences for news programs for twenty years, according to surveys by the Catholic University School of Journalism. Similarly, throughout the provinces before the expropriations, *Radio Nacional,* via standard-band and shortwave repeater transmitters, also had more listeners for news than the privately owned stations did. RN aired more extensive newscasts more frequently than did other stations. Thus with substantial numbers of the adult population either functionally illiterate or otherwise nonreaders of daily newspapers, even before the 1971 expropriations, government-furnished radio news already had become the leading source of daily news for a majority of Peruvians.

In January 1976 the government expressed concern over the content of nonnews programs on television that might detract from a national commitment to Peruvian values in carrying out reforms of the revolution. The Ministry of Transportation and Communications reviewed various imported television series, and decided to ban the importation of several "escapist" shows, including the British-produced "The Avengers" and the Hollywood-produced "Streets of San Francisco." These shows allegedly oversimplified the extensive police efforts needed in real life to control dangerous criminals.

The Telecommunications Bureau states that the banned series

constituted a distraction from developing Peruvian culture and a needless dependence on foreign cultural values to escape involvement with the Peruvian national way of life.

Newsprint Control

On November 18, 1971, a presidential decree put all importation of newsprint (paper) under the government's National Industrial Commercialization Enterprise Corporation (Empresa Nacional de Comercialización Industrial or ENCI).[33] The ENCI now allocates and distributes all newsprint used by Peruvian newspapers and magazines. Presumably, if a publication attempted to incite the overthrow of the government, ENCI could cut off its supply of paper, thereby ending a threat to the government by a direct means other than censorship.

Through the ENCI, civilian governments in the 1980s will be able to aid or slow down expansion of various publications in terms of the number of pages per issue or in terms of the circulation of each publication. The new constitution presumably offers some legal safeguards against arbitrary denials of supplies by public corporations.

Custodial Publishers

In May 1974 the government promulgated the Law of Social Property Businesses, climaxing much discussion about a concept considered central to the Peruvian revolution.[34] Social property would henceforth be the Peruvian version of worker-owned and worker-managed enterprises, with profit sharing similar to that in a cooperative. Social property would be a distinct form of ownership, neither "private" nor "state," as a vital part of the military reformers' commitment to a pluralistic economy.

With that concept legally defined, the military reformers were now ready to devise a system of distributing expropriated newspapers to various workers societies. These societies would include labor unions within a vocational calling, but they would be broadly defined groups of workers within an entire trade, occupation, or professional calling. Each would be assigned a daily newspaper as its property in trust. As a custodial publisher, a workers group would be assured an ongoing journalistic forum to acquaint officialdom and citizens in general with the trends and problems within that group.

On July 28, 1974, President Velasco announced that all remaining privately owned newspapers were being expropriated. Newspapers with circulations of 20,000 or more were classified as "social property" and given to organized sectors of society.[35]

The government would allow one year before publishing the decree establishing the organizational structure for the interest groups that would become publishers.

In November 1974 the government closed the English-language weekly *Peruvian Times* after it reported a Peruvian contract with Japan for a loan to finance an oil pipeline. The contract permitted Japanese arbitration of financial disputes in the construction, which the Lima Bar Association condemned as a compromise of the social revolution. The Velasco government contended that the story damaged the economic nationalism needed in public works projects.[36] The *Peruvian Times* was allowed to resume publication as the *Lima Times* in 1975.

For printing the same Japanese financing story, the government also suspended the news magazines *Oiga* and *Opinión Libre* for several months. Their editors, Francisco Igartua Rovira and Guido Chirinos, plus three reporters who severely criticized the government, were deported.

In December 1974 the government continued to pressure press critics by deporting two prominent journalists, César Martín Barreda, former financial news editor of *La Prensa*, and Enrique Chirinos Soto, former editorial writer for *Correo*.[37]

With the major newspapers of the nation expropriated, the Velasco administration decided that suspending publications or exiling journalists would not mobilize mass support for the social revolution. The government would have to put the custodial publisher plan into operation.

On July 1, 1975, Velasco issued a decree giving the regulations for custodial management of expropriated newspapers by the various interest groups or Civil Associations.[38] Decree 04–75–TR proclaimed:

> Daily newspapers will be oriented in the direction of the integral education of the people, pursuing the building and maintaining of a free society in which everyone can be fulfilled. . . .
> Each civil association daily newspaper will be formed by a general board and a council, both with three-year terms . . .
> The General Board will be the supreme entity of the association and will nominate members of the Directive Council. Each Board will consist of 30 members, elected from among basic organizations (of the Association).
> The publisher of the daily newspaper and the managers will be named by the government.[39]

Even though an elaborate system of entwining influence from

various workers entities within a trade or economic sector was created, the government retained strategic control by continuing to select the publisher.

The daily *El Comercio* was assigned to farm workers. Its thirty-member board represented the National Agrarian Federation, agricultural cooperatives, peasant worker communities, Indian communities, and incorporated Agricultural Societies of Social Interest. The Ministry of Agriculture supervised elections of board members by the agricultural groups.[40]

La Prensa was assigned to the industrial workers association, with a thirty-member board representing unions, cooperatives, telecommunication workers societies, and related-services workers. The Ministry of Industry supervised election of board members, with the Ministry of Energy and Mines supervising the election of board members representing the energy industry workers.[41]

Publisher of the daily *Expreso* was the education sector association, whose membership ranged from teachers and librarians and superintendents to the nonteaching employees of schools, universities, and cultural and instructional entities of all types. The Ministry of Education conducted elections for the General Board from teachers unions, administrators and teachers of adult education, primary school workers, secondary school workers, communal education groups, vocational education groups, and other organizations of workers in the field of education.[42]

The daily *Ojo* was assigned to the custodial publisher of the cultural and fine arts services workers association. Theater, music, painting, and other fine arts were represented not only by actors, writers, artists, and similar performers, but by nonperforming workers in these various fields of entertainment and fine arts, including clerks and office personnel.[43]

Workers in the construction, banking, insurance, retail commerce, and transportation industries became a civil association publisher for the daily *Ultima Hora.*[44]

Workers groups and unions in the health care, pharmacy, medical, dental, hospital, and optical fields became part of the civil association publishing the daily *Correo.*[45] A provision was made for adding representation for workers in other professional fields later.

After surveying press systems of major nations of the world, the public relations director of *La Prensa,* Antonio Fernández Arce, launched social communication discussions throughout Peru with the declaration that the new custodial system was unique in the world.[46]

For the various groups within each civil association to communicate their priorities and positions on major policies of each newspaper took from one to two years. In mid-1978 the entire custodial publisher system would be drastically modified by the government with a new decree allowing newspaper stock to be purchased by individuals. But, for the next three years, the principal factor in government-press relations in Peru would be easing and tightening governmental guidance of the news.

General Morales Eases Restrictions

Even after the Velasco administration assigned the daily newspapers to the civil associations, the editors of *El Comercio, Correo,* and *Ojo* kept their positions, but the editors of *Ultima Hora* and *La Prensa* were replaced.[47] Within the COAP, the cabinet ministries, and throughout the Velasco administration, unreported debate raged as to the directions the Revolution (now capitalized in Peru as an institutionalized ongoing reform movement) should take.

On August 17, 1975, the daily *Expreso* published a protest against government deportations of journalists who had been critical of the Velasco administration, and against the closing of the periodical *Marka,* a leftist magazine. Those who signed the protest were questioned by police and released.[48] The Ministry of the Interior released a report questioning the extent of Marxist thinking at *Expreso.*

On August 29, 1975, General Francisco Morales Bermúdez ousted President Velasco, and the COAP named Morales as the president of Peru. The new chief executive assured the nation that the Revolution would continue but that some Velasco policies, including easing controls over the mass media and over political opponents of the Revolution, would be changed for the national good.[49]

On September 2, 1975, President Morales Bermúdez nullified the orders of former President Velasco that had exiled journalists critical of the government.[50] In the same decree, the president permitted publications that had been closed by Velasco to resume publishing, including the conservative journal *Opinión Libre,* the liberal magazine *Oiga,* the English-language *Lima Times,* and the leftist magazine *Marka.*

Then the press in general began to report more candidly than it had under Velasco about the various economic problems as the government sought both national development and better living standards for the working class.[51]

In July 1976 an economic crisis forced Peruvian currency to be devalued 44 percent. Strikers demanded immediate pay raises as workers and students rioted in the streets.[52] This was the most serious challenge faced by the military government since 1968. Again the government responded by closing *Oiga, Opinión Libre, Marka,* and nine other publications that had suddenly questioned the ability of the military reformers to run the government. President Morales Bermúdez promised that suppressed publications would be able to resume publication upon the assurance of their editors that the ongoing social reforms and "public order" not be subverted by inflammatory editorial campaigns. As editorial self-restraint increased, government pressures decreased again.[53]

In 1976 one broadcasting station, *Radio Callao,* was suspended for seven days for failing to clear critical commentary in news programs with the Central Information Office of the executive branch. By mid-November, President Morales Bermúdez publicly reassured the media that they could process most news of national significance and that the news magazine *Caretas* was being compensated for lost revenues incurred when one of its September issues had been suspended.[54]

During 1976 *La Crónica,* which had become the voice of government bureaucrats, reported sympathetically on Cuba's military intervention in Angola, on accomplishments of the Soviet Union, about the dangers of transnational corporations from Western democracies, and about the wisdom of the general amnesty for political dissidents in Peru. By 1977 the political spectrum of Peruvian mass media again ranged from Marxist to conservative, with the stipulation that no publication or station could be permitted to advocate the end of the institutionalized Revolution or the ouster of the government. Already the military reformers were publicly discussing the near future when a constituent assembly would be elected, when political parties would be functioning in a transitional era leading to a return to elected civilian government.

Manuel Ulloa, the exiled former finance minister and former publisher of *Expreso,* and other political exiles received pardons at the end of 1976. By early 1977 they were publicly expressing confidence that the military government could pursue its Revolution without curtailing the liberties of opponents. The Inter-American Press Association in January 1977 noted that controls over newspapers and magazines had been minimized, and that publications ranged from *ABC* of the Apristas to *Unidad* of the Communist Party of Peru (PCP).[55]

Newspapers and magazines began to cover activities of political parties that would not be officially recognized until November 17,

1977, months later. The press eagerly reported on the military government's plans for a 1978 election for the Constituent Assembly to draft a new constitution and preparations for civilians to take over the government. These reports clearly had the approval of the military reformers themselves. Newspapers did not question keeping the long-range reforms of the Revolution, but rather suggested changing some administrative practices to better carry out these reforms.

Jesús Reyes, publisher of the news magazine *Oiga,* in January 1977 stated his periodical had made an agreement with the interior minister to keep criticism of the government and negative news about the Revolution within limits.[56] Enrique Zileri, editor of *Caretas,* who had gone into exile in 1975, returned at this time and made a similar agreement. *Caretas* began publishing protest letters from political opponents who had been jailed by the Velasco administration.

Uncertain Custodial Publisher System Ends

During the three years of the government's attempt to create a corporatist press, relations between the newspapers and the civil associations they were supposed to represent varied. *La Prensa* editors took their civil association leaders seriously for the first year. Then a struggle between leftists and moderates to control the National Congress of Industrial Communities complicated and confused editorial positions.

During August 1977 Dennis Gilbert interviewed the editors and civil association leaders at the Lima dailies. He found at *Correo* that the conservative professional organizations radiated hostility to government reforms, making this input unacceptable to the editors.[57] At *Ultima Hora,* open warfare developed between the civil association and the editors. Only at *El Comercio* did Gilbert find Alex Noriega, a peasant leader and president of the farm workers civil association, having direct influence on the newspaper's editorial policy in agrarian matters.

During June and July 1977, I also had visited these newspapers and found that the civil associations had very little influence on what the newspapers published, and functioned with more form than substance. At the time General César Vinatea, director of the government's National Information Service, had the most direct influence on the newspaper editors.

By mid-1978 the military reformers under President Morales Bermúdez decided to revoke the 1974 and 1975 decrees creating the civil association custodial publisher system. On July 21, Decree Law

22244 created a new system of publishing in which the government would be assured space for its announcements and would control each publishing company's executive board.[58]

The 1978 Press Law formula provided that the employees of the newspapers would have first rights to purchase 25 percent of the stock of each publishing corporation and the former owners would have the right to purchase 25 percent of the shares.[59] The remaining 50 percent of the shares of each newspaper would be sold on the Peruvian Stock Exchange (Bolsa de Valores), and each corporate or individual investor could buy no more than 5 percent of each newspaper's capitalization. A transitional period for changing the structure of the publishing companies had begun.

Alejandro Miró Quesada, former publisher of *El Comercio,* protested that the government was offering to allow former owners of the newspapers to buy back one-fourth of the expropriated shares for which compensation was still pending with valuation undermined because of the devaluation of Peruvian currency during the intervening years.[60]

The transitional period for the press paralleled a transitional period for Peru from a military to an elected civilian government. On July 28, 1978, 100 members of a Constituent Assembly were elected to draft a new constitution, with elections to be held in 1980 for members of a Congress and for president of the Republic, and with political parties fully active again. The Constituent Assembly had thirty-seven Apristas, twenty-five from the Popular Christian party, twelve from the Worker-Farmer-Student Popular Front, six from the Communist party, six from the Revolutionary Socialist party, four from the National Workers and Farmers Front, four from Democratic Unity, two Christian Democrats, two Odría National Unionists, and two from the Peru Democratic Movement. The government continued its direct control over the newspapers during the time when the new constitution was being finalized, reflecting the official views of issues before the Constituent Assembly.

Article 9 of the 1978 Press Law required the newspapers to provide free space up to 200 square centimeters for communiques from the various branches of government. This requirement was to continue even after the ownership formula had changed.

Article 11 required that each March the National Supervisory Commission of Business and Stocks audit the shareholder percentages for each newspaper.

Presumably, in the 1980s with an elected civilian government returned to power, the government would no longer have four representatives on each seven-member executive board of any newspaper.

The government's development bank, Financial Corporation of Development (Corporación Financiera de Desarrollo or COFIDE) was assigned the task of overseeing the financial transition of the newspaper publishing companies.[61]

Changing Government-Press Relations

With the period 1979 and 1980 a transitional era for both government and the press, the curtailment of the custodial publisher system signaled more independence on the part of some Peruvian publications.

In July 1978 the news magazine *Caretas* sued the government for $200,000 for revenue losses incurred during the period it had been suspended. The dailies of the city of Trujillo, *La Industria* and *Satélite,* resumed publishing after twenty-four days of suspension for running "demagogic propaganda." They continued to publish similar severe criticism of government programs after the suspensions.

In November 1978 the news weekly *Kúnan* severely criticized General Oscar Molina, prime minister of the presidential cabinet, for what it termed Molina's ill-advised and unsuccessful official visit to Argentina, a country which disagreed with Peru on various policies toward Chile. The leftist magazine *Marka* also attacked Peru's foreign policies and made accusations against the government-owned airline, Aeroperú, charging its administrators with accepting bribes to lease Lockheed jets. During the same month the probusiness *Opinión Libre* attacked the government's economic policies.[62]

Minister of the Interior Fernando Velit in January 1979 accused several publications of trying to "destabilize" the government with criticism that could hurt the Revolution and the transitional period to civilian government.[63]

When former *La Prensa* publisher Pedro Beltrán died on February 16, 1979, praise of him by government officials indicated a desire on the part of the government to better relations with those who had fought for press independence. However, relations worsened temporarily after February 19 when the government suspended ten news magazines, including the noted *Caretas,* for reporting on Peru's acquiring twelve Soviet fighter bombers from Cuba. In March four of the magazine publishers went on hunger strikes, and the government ended the suspensions.

The civilian constituent assembly during 1979 continued to warn the military government against using censorship. President Morales said that newspapers would be returned to their former owners in 1980. Yet he indicated some newspaper stock would remain with newspaper employees.

Former president Belaúnde won the 1980 presidential election. After he took office in July he vowed to revive press freedom by phasing out government guidance of the media over a period of several months.

In August 1980 the government transferred majority stock control in seven large dailies back to their former owners.

References

Alba, Victor. *Peru* (Boulder, Colo.: Westview Press, 1977).

Alexander, Robert J., ed. *Aprismo* (Kent, Ohio: Kent State University Press, 1973).

Alisky, Marvin. "Broadcasting in Peru," *Journal of Broadcasting* 3 (Spring 1959): 118–27.

_____. "Government-Press Relations in Peru," *Journalism Quarterly* 53 (Winter 1976): 661–65.

_____. *Historical Dictionary of Peru* (Metuchen, N.J.: Scarecrow Press, 1979).

_____. "Peru" in Ben G. Burnett and K. F. Johnson, eds., *Political Forces in Latin America*, 2nd ed. (Belmont, Calif.: Wadsworth Press, 1970), pp. 372–98.

_____. *Peruvian Political Perspective*, 2nd ed. (Tempe: Arizona State University Center for Latin American Studies, 1975).

_____. "Peru's SINAMOS," *Public Affairs Bulletin* 11, no. 1 (1972): 1–4.

_____. "The Peruvian Press and the Nixon Incident," *Journalism Quarterly* 32 (Fall 1958): 411–19.

Astiz, Carlos A. *Pressure Groups and Power Elites in Peruvian Politics* (Ithaca, N.Y.: Cornell University Press, 1969).

Basadre, Jorge. *Historia de la República del Perú*, 5th ed. (Lima, Perú: Editorial Historia, 1961).

Belaúnde, Fernando. *Peru's Own Conquest* (Lima, Perú: American Studies Press, 1965).

Carty, Winthrop P. "Latin American Press Freedom under Attack," *Times of the Americas*, Dec. 10, 1975, p. 3.

Cavero Calixto, Arturo. *El Centro de Altos Estudios Militares* (Chorrillos, Perú: CAEM, 1971).

Chaplin, David, ed. *Peruvian Nationalism: A Corporatist Revolution* (New Brunswick, N.J.: Transaction Books, 1976).

Collier, David. "Squatter Settlements and Policy Innovation in Peru," in Abraham F. Lowenthal, ed., *The Peruvian Experiment* (Princeton, N.J.: Princeton University Press, 1975), pp. 128–78.

Commission of Onis Priests. "Onis Speaks," *Ladoc* (Lima) 4 (November 1974): 36–37.

Dew, Edward. *Politics in the Altiplano* (Austin: University of Texas Press, 1969).

Dickerson, Mark O. "Peru Institutes Social Property as Part of Its 'Revolutionary Transformation,' " *Inter-American Economic Affairs* 29 (Fall 1975): 23–33.

Doughty, Paul L. "Social Policy and Urban Growth in Lima," in David Chaplin, ed., *Peruvian Nationalism* (New Brunswick, N.J.: Transaction Books, 1976), pp. 75–110.

Drysdale, Robert S. and R. G. Myers. "Peruvian Education" in A. F. Lowenthal, ed., *The Peruvian Experiment* (Princeton, N.J.: Princeton University Press, 1975), pp. 254–301.

Einaudi, Luigi R. *Revolution from Within? Military Rule in Peru Since 1968* (Santa Monica, Calif.: Rand Corporation, July 1971).

_____. *The Peruvian Military: A Summary Political Analysis* (Santa Monica, Calif.: Rand Corporation 1969).

Einaudi, Luigi R. and Alfred C. Stepan. *Latin American Institutional Development: Changing Military Perspectives in Peru and Brazil* (Santa Monica, Calif.: Rand Corporation, 1971).

Fishel, John T. "Politics and Progress in the Peruvian Sierra," (Ph.D. diss., Indiana University, Bloomington, Indiana, 1971).

García, José Z. "Military Government in Peru, 1968–1971," (Ph.D. diss., University of New Mexico, Albuquerque, New Mexico, 1973).

Gilbert, Dennis. "Society, Politics and the Press: Interpretation of the Peruvian Press Reform of 1974" (Paper at Latin American Studies Association at Houston, Texas, November 1977).

Graham Hurtado, José. *Filosofía de la Revolución Peruana* (Lima, Perú: Oficina Nacional de Información, 1971).

Grayson, George W. "Peru's Revolutionary Government," *Current History* 65 (February 1973): 61–63, 87.

Handelman, Howard. *Struggle in the Andes: Peasant Political Mobilization in Peru* (Austin: University of Texas Press, 1975).

Haya de la Torre, Víctor Raúl. *Pensamiento Político de Haya de la Torre* (Lima, Perú: APRA, 1961), 5 vols.

Kandell, Jonathan. "Peru's Economic Setbacks Erode Revolution's Image," *New York Times*, May 2, 1976, pp. 1, 22.

Kantor, Harry. *Ideología y Programa del Movimiento Aprista* (México, D.F.: Ediciones Humanismo, 1955), pp. 27–28.

Knudson, Jerry W. "Peruvian Press Law of 1974 (Paper at International Media Conference, Edinburg, Texas, October 1977).

Lowenthal, Abraham F., ed. *The Peruvian Experiment: Continuity and Change under Military Rule* (Princeton, N.J.: Princeton University Press, 1975).

Ministerio de Gobierno y Policía. *Reglamento General de Telecomunicaciones* (Lima, Perú: Gobierno, 1957).

Ministerio de Relaciones Exteriores. "Deltec," *El Peruano*, Aug. 9, 1968, p. 2.

Ministerio de Transportes y Comunicaciones. "Ley General de Telecomunicaciones," *El Peruano*, Nov. 10, 1971, p. 1.

_____. Decreto Supremo No. 04–75–TR, "Reglamento de las Asociaciones Civiles Propietaria de los Diarios de Distribución Nacional," *El Peruano*, July 1, 1975, p. 1–37.

_____. Decreto Supremo 2975, "Periodistas," *El Peruano*, Sept. 3, 1975, p. 2.

_____. "Ley de Prensa," *El Peruano*, July 21, 1978, pp. 2–3.

_____. "Ley de la Libertad de la Prensa," *El Peruano*, Jan. 9, 1970, p. 1.

Niedergang, Marcel. "Revolutionary Nationalism in Peru," *Foreign Affairs* 49 (April 1971): 454–63.

Palmer, David Scott. *Revolution from Above: Military Government and Popular Participation in Peru, 1968–1972* (Ithaca, N.Y.: Cornell University Latin American Studies, 1971).

_____. "Peru: Authoritarianism and Reform" in Howard J. Wiarda and Harvey F. Kline, eds., *Latin American Politics and Development* (Boston: Houghton Mifflin, 1979).

Pike, Frederick B. *The Modern History of Peru* (New York: Praeger, 1967).

Quijano, Aníbal. *Nacionalismo, Neoimperialismo, y Militarismo en el Perú* (Buenos Aires, Argentina: Ediciones Periferia, 1971).

Tullis, F. LaMond. *Lord and Peasant in Peru* (Cambridge, Mass.: Harvard University Press, 1970).

Vargas Escalante, Jorge. *Cuarenta Años de Radio en el Perú* (Lima, Perú: Editorial Vargas, 1944).

Werlich, David P. *Peru: A Short History* (Carbondale, Ill.: Southern Illinois University Press, 1978).

Newspapers and Periodicals: *Arizona Republic; Correo,* Lima; *Diario de las Américas,* Miami, Florida; *Editor & Publisher; El Comercio,* Lima; *Expreso,* Lima; *IAPA News,* Inter-American Press Association; *La Prensa,* Lima; *Latin America,* London; *Latin America Political Report,* London; *Miami Herald; Oiga,* Lima; *Times of the Americas,* Washington, D.C.

5

Brazil: A Subcontinent's Media with Guidelines

AFTER two decades of press freedom and a decade of censorship, Brazil has regained media independence, but within government guidelines.

Brazil, stretching over more than half of South America, a subcontinent of 3.3 million square miles, ranks in land area as the fifth largest nation in the world (after the Soviet Union, Canada, China, and the United States). Its 1980 estimated population of 121 million makes Brazil in terms of citizenry the twelfth largest nation on earth (the 4.2 billion inhabitants of this planet dividing into approximately 200 nation-states).

From other perspectives, Brazilians account for 37 percent of all Latin Americans and constitute the largest Roman Catholic country in Christendom. In terms of resources, the Amazon river and its hundreds of tributaries constitute the world's largest freshwater system. Even with vigorous highway construction since 1964 penetrating into isolated western regions, the Mato Grosso forests of the central western region loom as nature's anteroom for the Amazonian jungles to the north and northwest.

Brazil's five natural geographical regions are the Northwest, with 42 percent of the territory but only 4 percent of the population; the Northeast, with 11 percent of the territory but 21 percent of the people; the Center West, with 22 percent of the land but only 4 percent of the population; the East, with 15 percent of the territory and 34 percent of the population; and the South, with 10 percent of the territory but 37 percent of the population.[1] Both the people and the mass media tend to locate near the Atlantic coastal plain.

Mass Media and Economics:
A Tale of Few Cities

Considering the East and South together, from the port city of Salvador in the state of Bahia along an Atlantic coastline running southwestward to the border of Uruguay, seven out of ten Brazilians reside, on or near that coast. Until the opening of the new federal capital of Brasília in April 1960, some 650 miles inland, the only major cities not on or near the ocean were Manaus on the Amazon River and Belo Horizonte, state capital of Minas Gerais.

Almost 90 percent of Brazil's industry concentrates in four southernmost states, with the heaviest concentration in São Paulo. Until the 1940s, the export crop of coffee alone symbolized the Brazilian economy. After World War II, through import controls on consumer goods and fiscal policies favoring investment in manufacturing, the government made industry the most dynamic sector of the economy. Between 1947 and 1961 the annual economic growth rate reached 9.7 percent, with the volume of industrial production during this period tripling.[2]

From 1961 through 1963, inflation combining with widespread lack of confidence in the blustering administration of President João Goulart slowed drastically the momentum of diversified industrial growth.[3] With the beginning of the era of military government in 1964, foreign investors who had been frightened off by expropriation threats, returned to help underwrite an economic recovery.

By 1969 the annual industrial growth rate had soared to 10 percent, with four sectors—iron and steel, automobiles and trucks, ships, and petroleum products and byproducts—principally responsible. Only sixty miles from Rio at Volta Redonda, the National Steel Company expanded a gigantic integrated iron and steel complex, and then established fifteen provincial branch plants, to become the largest such entity in the Third World of developing nations. By 1979 the states of São Paulo and Minas Gerais shared the distinction of having the largest steel plants.

Production of automobiles and trucks now ranks as the fifth most important industry in Brazil, employing 10 percent of the nation's industrial work force. Brazil stands tenth in the world among all nations producing motor vehicles and its annual automobile production in the late 1970s remained larger than that of the Soviet Union.[4]

Petrochemicals are Brazil's most recently established major industry, significant only since 1958. By 1978 Brazil was ranked tenth among the world's producers of these materials, employing 9 percent of the republic's industrial workers.

By 1977 Brazil's population had become 64 percent urban with a demographic concentration in the southern and eastern coastal cities. The greater metropolitan area of São Paulo City, expanding past dozens of suburban towns, by 1979 totaled 12 million. This thyroidic urbanization made it the fastest growing city in the world. Newspaper circulations and location of television and radio transmitters parallel the demographic disequilibrium, tending to bunch in the metropolitan areas of São Paulo, Rio de Janeiro, Belo Horizonte, Porto Alegre, Salvador, Recife, Fortaleza, Curitiba, and Brasília. Even though Brasília functions as the capital of this federal republic, the former seat of government, Rio de Janeiro, remains Brazil's cultural capital and therefore its daily newspapers, magazines, and radio and television stations vie with those of São Paulo for national dominance.

Although the Ministry of Education in 1978 estimated that the adult literacy rate had reached 81 percent, functional literacy enabling the average citizen to comprehend newspaper stories remains somewhat lower. In some rural communities of Brazil, a citizen's ability to recognize his own name and traffic signs classifies him as literate.[5] Even if adult literacy were universal, newspaper circulation would not surpass national totals of radio audiences because the price of a daily newspaper equals the cost of a glass of milk or of four slices of bread in a nation in which the 1976 per capita gross domestic product income equaled $1,071.[6] Transistor radios require no household electric circuits but merely a tiny battery costing the equivalent of 20 cents for usage running six hours a day for six months.

As political scientist Robert A. Packenham notes, internal distribution of income in Brazil benefits the urban middle and upper classes.[7] In rural areas the ratio between the income of the richest 10 percent of the population and that of the poorest 10 percent is fifteen to one. In São Paulo a top-level manager or government technocrat with a Ph.D. can earn what his U.S. or West German counterpart earns, but a common laborer earns only 7 percent of what his counterpart makes.[8] But rich or poor or in between, greater numbers of Brazilians listen to radio and television news than read the news in dailies and magazines.

Communication for a Nation

As in other Latin American nations, radio remains the number one medium for daily information in Brazil. Nine out of ten Brazilians have either a personal transistor radio or live in a dwelling unit that has a radio in daily use. Some 24 million radios are in daily use whereas daily newspaper sales total 5 million copies.[9] Until 1978, national totals of radio receivers were annually underestimated because the government concentrated on urban sales and tended to ignore rural resale of old radios and illegal importation of transistor models on which import tax had not been paid.

Unlike several other Latin American nations—Peru, Bolivia, Paraguay, Ecuador, Guatemala—Brazil does not have substantial numbers of Indians speaking dialects other than the national language, Portuguese. In the total population a mere 98,000 monolingual Indians, plus a few thousand resident foreigners, have no understanding of Portuguese. Thus broadcasts in Portuguese are understood almost universally within Brazil. In this vital aspect of communication, Brazil possesses a factor of internal unity lacking in such large developing nations as multilingual India or the majority of African republics. This unity is even lacking in the economically developed bilingual Canada or Belgium where linguistic rivalries spill over into cultural frictions and political tensions echoing separatism.

Census officials determined that the estimated 1980 population of 121 million citizens would be living in 25 million households. That dwelling unit total provides a major caliper for measuring radio and television receivers in daily use.[10] Researchers of the recent past who merely totaled radio and television sets from sales and manufacturing records distorted the true role of broadcasting in Brazilian life because they ignored group listening. One receiver inside a home may draw six or more televiewers or radio listeners for a news program.

Inasmuch as broadcasting data for some Latin American nations remain mired in inaccurate UNESCO estimates or optimistic claims of governments, accurate comparisons remain difficult. But probably Brazil leads every other Latin American republic in the percentage of households with radios in daily use. In Brazil, repair service of radio and television receivers has grown into a major skilled occupation, whereas in Bolivia, Cuba, and the Central American republics, repair technicians at the retail level remain scarce. Brazil's huge repair service, available even in villages and city slums, indicates heavy daily use of receivers. Corroborating this assumption are the findings of the nationwide audience surveys in every metropolitan area of Brazil. These include monthly measurements in all cities of at least 20,000 population.[11]

With 25 million households and 24 million radios in daily use, Brazilians are tuned in. The ever-present transistor obviates difficulties in poor dwelling units without electricity.

In 1978 more than 14 million Brazilian households—more than half the dwelling units—had television sets in daily use.[12] The Rio de

Janeiro Parks Department on weekends sets up television receivers in public parks for evening viewing. In some other cities, municipal governments have placed television sets at bandstands and other outdoor sites for broadcasts of soccer matches or other events of wide interest. Given a significant distribution of television sets in such public gathering places as schools, fire stations, and taverns, we may assume that more than half of Brazil's population makes daily contact with one or more television programs.

From Chaos to Regulation

By mid-1920, KDKA in Pittsburgh and WWJ in Detroit had ushered in the age of daily radio broadcasting in the United States. On August 2, 1920, the government in Rio issued the first license for a commercial radio station in Brazil, and on August 27 a similar licensing took place in Buenos Aires. These dates were close enough together to become the basis for decades of claims and counterclaims by Argentina and Brazil as to which nation pioneered in South American radio.[13] Several other republics had transmitters soon thereafter.[14]

With only a few transmitters on the air in the early 1920s, the Brazilian government delayed promulgating genuine broadcasting regulations. Instead, under a federal law covering amateur radiotelegraphy, the government handed out licenses for commercial stations after brief inquiries into the corporate nature of the operations, without any questions about planned programs.

After Westinghouse, Western Electric, and Marconi companies in 1922 established Brazilian commercial radio stations, several unlicensed imitators took to the air at night as the mood hit them, yielding cacophony as unskilled transmitter engineers invaded each other's broadcast frequencies. Finally in 1936 President Getúlio Vargas established the Brazilian Radio Commission, which examined all licensed station operators in detail. New regulations not only required public service announcements from the government on all stations, but also required every privately owned radio station to hook into a special weekly "National Hour" network. These Sunday broadcasts explained government policies, interspersed with music and news of the entertainment world via interviews with Brazilian film, theater, radio, and recording artists. In the 1970s, this "Hora do Brasil" was revived as a nightly, instead of a weekly, feature. The second republic to have a weekly "National Hour" on all radio stations of the nation was Mexico, from the 1950s to the present.[15]

In Cuba, since the coming into power of a Communist regime, all radio stations have become the property of the government and frequently link together for reports. In 1937 Vargas tightened his controls over political opponents, especially through censorship of newspapers and radio stations, as part of his *Estado Novo* or New State. The Vargas state projected the fascist overtones then in vogue in Germany and Italy, but without the Nazi persecution of minorities and with milder restrictions on political criticism than those imposed by Mussolini's dictatorship.[16]

In 1942 Brazil joined the Allies in the war against the Axis. In 1943 the government decided to put 5,000 Brazilian soldiers into battle against Field Marshal Albert Kesselring's soldiers in northern Italy. Their commander, General Eurico Gaspar Dutra, acquired officers with a United States level of professional military technology, by sending to Fort Leavenworth, Kansas, for training a group of colonels that included Humberto Castello Branco and Henrique Teixeira Lott, both destined to be national leaders in post-Vargas Brazil.[17] Dutra himself succeeded Vargas as president after the war.

By March 1945, censors in Rio had so sufficiently eased their guidelines that news correspondent Barreto Leite, interviewing Brazilian officers after their victory in Italy, could publish an article demanding an end to Vargas's arbitrariness in *Diário de Notícias*.[18] Democratization of the political system was forecast along with criticism that Vargas was not practicing at home what he advocated abroad.

October 1945 marked fifteen years since Vargas had come to power. With the end of World War II, Brazil felt the same popular ground swell for representative government that echoed from Europe to Asia to Latin America. Vargas realized that an officer corps would be returning to Rio, exhilarated by defeating fascism abroad and committed to advancing political democracy at home. Cosmetic gestures, such as drafting constitutions in 1934 and 1937 or allowing mild political debate by the PTB and the PSD in 1943, would no longer suffice. Already General Dutra had helped the fledgling Social Democratic Party (Partido Social Democrático or PSD) articulate goals rivaling those of the Vargas group, the Brazilian Labor Party (Partido Trabalhista Brasileiro or PTB).

Vargas tried to calm growing opposition to his administration by asserting publicly that presidential and congressional elections would be nationwide late in 1945, with respect for a secret ballot and monitoring of vote counting by all parties on the ballot. Furthermore, Vargas promised he would not be a presidential candidate himself. Obviously the changing political atmosphere would not permit his continuing at the apex of power.

Eduardo Gomes, presidential candidate of the Democratic National Union (União Democrática Nacional or UDN), added conservative criticism of the government to the mildly progressive criticism of the PTB and the PSD. Election day had been set for December 2, but in late October popular opposition to Vargas among both military and civilian groups reached a crescendo. The president refused to withdraw his nomination of his brother, Benjamin Vargas, as chief of police of the Federal District, arousing suspicion that extralegal force might intrude into the promised honest election after all. A military coup on October 29 removed Vargas from the presidency and sent him home to the state of Rio Grande do Sul.[19]

Neither newspapers nor radio networks and stations achieved freedom from censorship until after Dutra became president in 1945. Then suddenly the strictures on the media were gone, and Brazilian editors and commentators soon displayed skill in investigative reporting and analysis.

Then occurred one of the most bizarre media events in Latin American political history. Vargas, just ousted from a presidency that had been more dictatorial than representative during most of the preceding fifteen years, filed as a candidate for the federal Senate from his home state of Rio Grande do Sul. On December 2, PSD Candidate Dutra was elected president of Brazil and many critics of Vargas in the major parties were sent to Congress. But the deposed dictator was elected a senator, proclaiming himself to be reformed into a commitment for representative government.

Nationally prominent newspapers in Rio de Janeiro and São Paulo had suffered enough under the censorship of Vargas. The new senator might get some space in his hometown of Porto Alegre, or even some mention on radio, but the big dailies and networks would now focus their attention on the incoming Dutra administration.

As inauguration time drew nearer in January 1946, even Luis Carlos Prestes, head of the Brazilian Communist Party (Partido Communista Brasileiro or PCB), received some newspaper space and air time coverage. Under a general amnesty and new Electoral Code, the PCB had emerged from underground into a legal party capturing 9 percent of the total congressional vote.[20] Rio and São Paulo newspapers were filled with comments and interviews involving President-elect Dutra and his PSD and opposition leaders of the PTB and UDN.

Senator-elect Vargas had a public relations agency flooding editor's desks with stories about his impending return to Rio but none of them was printed.

Vargas thereupon decided to advertise. He could not bribe or pressure his return to Rio into the news columns but he found he could purchase space for advertisements telling of his return. Stimulated to congregate by large display advertisements, a crowd of supporters met the flight from Porto Alegre to Rio carrying Vargas. Huckstering techniques had allowed Vargas to subvert the silent treatment from news editors through the advertising columns of their very own dailies. Similarly, radio stations that only recently had suffered under the Vargas-era censorship, enjoyed the newfound freedom to ignore his return to the capital. So Vargas purchased time on some Rio radio stations ostensibly to give weather bulletins from the airport, and to include, incidentally, a statement that the senator-elect had arrived back in the capital.[21]

In the October 1950 elections, Vargas, candidate of the PTB, only five years after being ousted as a mild dictator, won the presidency by popular ballot for a five-year term beginning in January 1951. He proclaimed his determination to practice democracy and during his new term did not resort to the censorship of the media he had employed in varying degrees from 1930 to 1945.

In fact, the open-society atmosphere engendered such severe press and broadcasting attacks on scandals in the Vargas administration in 1954, that Vargas ended up by taking his own life in August and his vice-president finished his term to 1956.

Early in 1954 the daily *Estado de São Paulo* led other major dailies in investigating irregularities in the Vargas administration. Despite the president's repeated promise to hold down inflation, the newspapers obtained the plan of Labor Minister João Goulart to increase the minimum wage 100 percent.[22]

Antigetulista congressmen uncovered the Vargas maneuvers that had resulted in irregular loan policies of the Bank of Brazil, including illegal subsidies to the newspaper *Ultima Hora,* a major spokesman for Vargas policies.[23]

Most of the big city dailies and the major radio commentators were antigetulista and steadily increased the daily criticism and investigative reporting into problems of the Vargas administration from February to August 1954. Brazilian coffee sales in the United States shrank drastically, sending the republic's dollar earnings to new lows in the midst of strikes and rising prices.

One of the most articulate and powerful critics was Carlos

Lacerda, publisher of the Rio daily *Tribuna da Imprensa* and a commentator on TI, the radio and television network with the largest audiences. Lacerda's printed attacks on Vargas became even more stinging when he voiced them in what was popularly regarded as the most authoritative broadcast voice in Brazil.

For television, Lacerda had his commentaries printed in large letters on cue cards with key words underlined, enabling him to ad-lib on occasion, adding a slightly conversational but authoritative tone to his delivery. After becoming governor of the state of Guanabara, which had been the Federal District surrounding Rio de Janeiro until the new Federal District was created around Brasília, he correctly predicted that by the mid-1970s the new state would vanish. In 1977 the state of Mato Grosso was divided into two states and the city of Rio de Janeiro was in the state of Rio de Janeiro again, giving the republic twenty-two states. In 1964, in an interview on NBC-TV in the United States, a reporter called Lacerda "the Brazilian Goldwater." To which Lacerda replied in clear English, "We are both anti-Communists. But I advocate public housing projects and similar welfare spending which the senator does not." When Lacerda died in 1977, longtime allies and opponents alike filled the Brazilian press with laudatory obituaries.[24]

Gregório Fortunato, chief of the presidential palace guard, hired a professional gunman to try to assassinate Lacerda. On August 5, 1954, that gunman opened fire on Lacerda in front of his apartment in Rio. Lacerda was only slightly wounded, but his companion, Air Force Major Rubens Vaz, was killed.

The mass media launched editorial attacks on Vargas more intense than those the North American media aimed at Richard Nixon after the Watergate scandal broke. Vargas protested that he personally had known nothing of the plotting by his staffers against his critic. Army and navy leaders closed ranks with the infuriated air force generals in demanding that the president resign.

On August 24, 1954, Vargas told his cabinet that public opinion had turned against him too much to permit his further effectiveness as president. He entered his office and killed himself with a pistol, ending weeks of intense attacks by the newspapers and broadcasting stations.

From Open to Closed Society

The presidency of Juscelino Kubitschek from 1956 to 1961 found Brazilian newspapers, magazines, and radio and television stations completely free to report or comment on anything in public life. With the dedication of the new federal capital at Brasília in April 1960, the government had a means for engendering a more favorable public opinion for the administration. With the new capital, it had opened up the midwestern frontiers for the adventuresome and ambitious.

Janio Quadros, former mayor of the city of São Paulo and then governor of the state of São Paulo, captured the presidency in the 1960 election for the UDN conservatives. Supported by many conservative publishers and broadcasters, Quadros remained a political enigma for many congressmen who blocked each of his new programs. In August 1961, after only seven months in office, Quadros resigned.

Under the existing constitution, the vice-president and president did not have to belong to the same party. Vice-president João Goulart, of the left wing of the PTB, became president of Brazil, causing panic among a majority of the members of Congress and the major newspaper publishers and broadcasting executives.

Even the setting for the presidential succession lent itself to sensational reporting. At the time Quadros resigned, Goulart was visiting the prime minister in the People's Republic of China and had to fly from Peking to Brasília to take the oath of office.

From August 1961 to April 1964, the news media's coverage of public life was based not as much on assigning reporters to cabinet ministries as previously but rather on spokesmen for the system of "barganha" or bargaining among power brokers. Labor leaders and leftist politicians steadily gained influence with the Goulart administration under what *Jornal do Brasil* and the *Globo* radio and television networks called "clientelismo." Leftist politicians obtained more and more preferential hiring at the federal level for their "client" groups.[25]

In 1963 and early 1964, Goulart tried to rally nationwide working-class support through the mass media. His proposals for land expropriations, increased government ownership of industry, and unionization in the armed forces had been rejected by Congress.

Seeking press support, Goulart utilized his control of government funds. Despite a still potent Congress, in the 1960s Brazil had a government system of executivism under which the chief executive could shift and augment budgetary categories and overspend authorized appropriations causing deficits totaling millions of dollars worth of cruzeiros. Through the government's Banco do Brasil, publishers received special low exchange rates of cruzeiros to the dollar for the importing of newsprint.[26] The 5 to 7 percent taxes publishers had paid for the imported newsprint was canceled by presidential decree. Similarly, managers of radio and television networks and stations suddenly found drastic reductions on import taxes for vital transmitter equipment.

Such inducements in 1963 found the following pattern of support and opposition for Goulart in Rio de Janeiro: on the far left the pro-Soviet Communist weekly *Novos Rumos;* and also the vigorously revolutionary weeklies *Semanário, Classe Operária,* and *Panfleto,* each of whose circulations centered in Rio and seven or eight other metropolitan areas. The most important daily newspaper supporting Goulart was the Rio daily *Ultima Hora,* originally subsidized by Vargas. Its circulation of 335,000 reached labor leaders and leftist politicians and administrators in seven major states of the republic. Its editorials either echoed Goulart's sentiments or on occasion even exceeded them in demanding changes toward a socialist Brazil.[27]

A more moderate image of Goulart came from the Rio daily *Diário Carioca,* which had been allowed to import 80 percent of its newsprint without paying even the interest on its government loans. Goulart's proposals to compromise a little with his opponents appeared in *Carioca,* often shortly after his aggressive demands in *Ultima Hora* had drawn severe criticism.

In the center of the political spectrum from 1961 to 1964 were two Rio dailies, *Diário de Notícias* and *Correio da Manhã,* which tried to balance moderate praise and criticism of the administration.

Spurning offers of tax rebates, low-interest government loans with long grace periods before any payments might be due, and similar favors were four Rio dailies: *O Jornal,* the flagship paper of the nationwide Diários Associados chain of dailies; *O Globo,* a circulation leader with 210,000 daily subscribers or street sales; *Jornal do Brasil,* a prestige paper read by civic leaders of various parties and affiliations; and *Tribuna da Imprensa,* published by radio-television commentator and conservative politician Carlos Lacerda, who had sparked the downfall of Vargas in 1954 and had gone on to become governor of the state of Guanabara and a presidential hopeful.

In São Paulo, the most influential and respected daily newspaper in the republic, *O Estado,* consistently revealed the detailed plans for collectivizing the economy that Goulart had privately circulated among his trusted key supporters but had carefully not mentioned in his own general press conferences and in broadcast interviews.

O Estado rejected offers of subsidies from the Goulart administration, receiving instead private bank loans in the United States so that Brazil's leading daily could buy new printing equipment. *Estado's* circulation from 1963 to 1969 increased from 180,000 weekdays to 201,000 and from 250,000 Sundays to 295,000. Publisher Julio de

Mesquita died on July 18, 1969, being succeeded by his son, Julio de Mesquita Neto, who has been equally as vigorous in striving to achieve freedom of the press.[28]

The weekly "National Hour" established by Vargas in 1936 was converted by Goulart into a nightly program. Every evening, the nation's radio stations had to hook into the special network to carry "Hora do Brasil," filled with government announcements of its accomplishments but not one word of any setbacks or delays in any programs nor any hint of any problems.

In 1963 a presidential decree promulgated a broadcasting regulation allowing the government to reply to any radio or television criticism of government programs for up to five times the amount of air time used in the original critical commentary. Such a weapon discouraged Brazilian broadcasters from airing extensive criticism of Goulart until the final weeks before his ouster.[29] Another regulation Goulart claimed to have devised to cope with "threats to national defense" required that formal political speeches on radio and television be approved by a government screening board three days before being broadcast.[30] As a result, from mid-1963 to early 1964, seven radio stations that refused to submit to prior censorship before air time were closed and their licenses suspended, and several others were threatened with similar fates if their managers again defied the decree.

Thus, in the final months of the Goulart regime, the president and his more ardent leftist administrators obtained considerable free radio and television time, whereas some of the administration's opposition obtained fewer and fewer chances for any air time.

The media corporation headed by Francisco de Assis Chateaubriand, Diários Associados—thirty-two newspapers, eighteen television stations, twenty-four radio stations, four magazines, and the DA news service—in 1963–1964 was at the peak of its financial power. After Assis Chateaubriand died in 1968, the media empire's longtime prosperity diminished and by 1978 the corporation had become as dependent on government subsidies as it had been independent of them twenty-five years before. Diários Associados radio and television news commentaries during the last six months in which Goulart was in power editorialized vigorously against his major declarations and plans.

Goulart in 1963 also appointed an aide to promote his political ideology in bookstores. Goulart's brother-in-law, Governor of the state of Rio Grande do Sul Leonel Brizola, drafted a list of books sympathetic to Marxism. The bookstore liaison then contacted the owners and managers of the major chains of book retailers. By early 1964

Brazilian bookstores abounded in volumes sympathetic to Fidel Castro, the Soviet Union, various socialist leaders in both Western and Eastern nations, and similar topics. In Rio de Janeiro alone, some 74,000 unsold biographies of Castro were returned to book wholesalers after the ouster of Goulart.[31]

On February 19, 1964, President Goulart addressed the nation concerning Brazil's financial problems via a radio-television network hooking up all the stations. He stated:

> I insist that our basic reforms in 1964 will bring economic emancipation and social justice. Valuable lands in the hands of the wealthy will become the people's through government action.[32]

Goulart was repeating his 1963 proposal, which Congress had rejected, to nationalize all privately owned properties fronting federal highways, railroad tracks, and rivers.

On March 2 a national radio-television network address was made by Governor Brizola. He stated:

> In our capitalistic society, the mass media constitute a monopoly of the dominant classes. But the wall posters and street meetings are powerful counter instruments in the fight of popular forces. . . . Our labor leaders and student organizations constitute a guarantee that the people will not have the wool pulled over their eyes. It is a duty of all popular organizations to attend, en masse, protest rallies, bringing banners with popular slogans, against those of conciliation.[33]

Goulart's favorite newspaper, *Ultima Hora,* sprang to the president's defense as unrest grew. One such editorial asserted:

> No one will snatch from the hands of Jango (Goulart) the banner of popular leadership. His policy will bring Brazil real economic emancipation against colonialism and imperialism. The firmness with which he is striving to liberate Brazil from feudalism confirms President Goulart's popular leadership.[34]

Diário Carioca defended Goulart in a different way:

> Mr. Goulart has exercised his constitutional mission within limits, fighting for basic reforms to keep on the peaceful road the revolution occurring in Brazil. . . . For this reason, he does not please those . . . favoring a coup, an infantile attitude.[35]

In March, Goulart, reacting to criticism from the generals and admirals, began organizing the soldiers and sailors into labor unions, a plan guaranteed to increase the military leaders' determination to pressure Goulart into resigning. The Communist party of Brazil spoke through *Novos Rumos:*

> We insist on the strengthening of the unity of the nationalist and popular forces. The solidity of this unity is a basic condition for the development of events favorable to the people. . . . mobilization of the great masses will bring a high point to the meeting of March 13 at the Central. Organized civilian and military workers and all other popular groups of the masses can influence decisively the political process.[36]

Thomas Skidmore, in *Politics in Brazil,* stated the Brazilian Communist party (Partido Communista Brasileiro or PCB) in 1945 openly declared for violent revolution, but by 1964 was hoping that PCB goals might be reached through momentum that Goulart reforms could engender.

On March 13 President Goulart appeared before television cameras, flanked on one side by Governor Brizola and a leader of the Communist party and on the other side by some of his cabinet ministers. He announced a decree expropriating Brazilian oil refineries and a decree to begin expropriating various private properties. Cameras slowly drew back to show all the speakers on the platform and then slowly moved among the assembled crowd, zooming in on clusters of enlisted men with the placards for the proposed sergeants, corporals, and petty officers enlisted-ranks unions.[37]

Less than a week earlier, a leading opposition daily had charged that Goulart not only intended to collectivize the economy and pit the enlisted ranks against the generals, but that he also had drawn up plans for extending his term of office beyond the constitutional deadline of January 1966. *O Jornal* quoted a constitutional reform proposed by the pro-Goulart National Student Union to change the presidential term from five to six years.[38]

After Goulart's March 13 proposals to expropriate the oil refineries and various properties, *O Jornal* and the other thirty-one dailies of the DA chain editorialized:

> If there were any political conscience in Brazil, there would be initiated today the impeachment process against the President, who went to a street meeting to foment subversion, insult the nation's political forces, and expose the Congress to the contempt of his followers.[39]

Estado de São Paulo, the prestige daily, tried to move the military into stopping Goulart:

In the life of a nation, there are moments when for the soldier, silence has the bitter taste of treason. If the armed forces keep quiet, we will have to arrive at the painful conclusion that they were not coerced into participating in the subversive meeting at Cristiano Otoni Square.[40]

General Humberto Castello Branco, then army chief of staff and later president of Brazil, felt that the March 13 televised rally constituted more than political propaganda for Goulart's programs. Rather, he stated, it was a direct challenge to all the civilian and military leaders who wished to preserve constitutional law and a republic in which conservatives and liberals would continue to be able to debate issues before they become government policies.[41]

In 1964 Good Friday came on March 27. Many of the nation's newspapers decided to skip Saturday editions and to print in advance Sunday editions filled with Easter features, giving editors and reporters a long-promised weekend holiday. Similarly, radio and television networks planned extra Easter features on tape, minimizing the number of live news reports for the long weekend. Thus the extraordinary gathering of army, navy, air force, and conservative civilian political leaders on Sunday, March 29, received abbreviated summary coverage on Monday, March 30. Rumors of an impending coup d'état were not matched by detailed reports of the various anti-Goulart meetings, even though the leaders at those gatherings did not attempt to shroud them in secrecy.

By the evening of March 30, most radio and television news programs contained stories hinting at political unrest that could force Goulart from office. That same night, Goulart, at a camp in the state of Minas Gerais, addressed a meeting of enlisted men and urged them to become insubordinate should their officers move against his administration. Some 20,000 soldiers had been invited by presidential aides but only 800 or 900 attended because officer-students at the Escola de Comando e Estado Maior do Exército (Army Command and Staff School) were especially sensitive to the Goulart challenge to chain-of-command discipline by which all armed forces function. Goulart's speech was tape recorded by the DA network and soon excerpts had reached rival networks and independent television and radio stations.[42]

Many factors were combining into what would become a coup, with broadcasting serving as a catalytic agent speeding up the political process.

By March 31, Goulart had arrayed against him most of the officer corps, the governors of the major states, and hundreds of key federal and state officials, plus most of the executives of the business and industrial sectors. Goulart went into exile in Uruguay and on April 1, the era of military government had come to Brazil.

The ouster of Goulart from the presidency by military leaders allied with key civilian state governors and conservative politicians provides an example of the functions of mass media during a political crisis in a developing nation.

Several of the papers that had been subsidized by Vargas eventually folded.

After deemphasizing general news in favor of sports features in 1965, *Diário Carioca* began to lose much of its circulation and advertising revenue and ceased publication on January 1, 1966.

After seventy-three years of publication, *Correio da Manhã* lost much of its circulation and stopped publishing June 10, 1974.

O Jornal closed on April 28, 1974, after a bitter struggle between the two factions that had inherited stock from the publisher, Assis Chateaubriand, in 1968.

In the 1970s again the "Hora do Brasil" was being aired on a special network of every radio station in the republic, produced by the agency Empresa Brasileira de Radiodifusão (Radiobrás) of the Ministério das Comunicações.

Censorship

Goulart had stretched constitutional limits beyond traditional legality, attempting to subvert the will of Congress through executive decrees. He did this while pressuring the opposition media but favoring and subsidizing the minority of mass media supporting his administration. Now military leaders would centralize power in their own way, without such subterfuge. Directly and openly, the generals suspended the Constitution of 1946 and the traditional political parties. They also substituted censorship of press and broadcasting for the indirect pressures of the era just ended.

During the first Vargas era, 1930–1945, Brazilian media had been restricted by censors. To prevent continuation of controls on the press and broadcasting, the Constitution of 1946 contained Article 141 guaranteeing the media independence from government controls whatever the news or information content. From 1964 to 1968, military leaders promulgated five institutional acts to serve as an interim substitute for the suspended constitution until a new charter could become fully operative. Institutional Act 5 especially concentrated power in the chief executive, permitting the president to suspend the writ of habeas corpus and the basic guarantees of free speech and free expression.[43] Although President Ernesto Geisel from 1975 to 1978 gradually reduced censorship and even suspended it for various periods, not until the approaching congressional elections of November 1978 did Congress repeal Institutional Act 5. The president ended press censorship in 1978.

The new Constitution of 1967, as amended in 1969, included a loosely worded article leaving to judicial interpretation the legal justification for the resumption of censorship when "national security and public order are threatened." Further, by *Decreto Lei 1077*, promulgated on January 26, 1970, the government was empowered to act should the media incite violence and prejudice against any race or religious group, or employ obscene materials to erode public morals.

After the Congress elected General Castello Branco as president of Brazil on April 11, 1964, the military junta supporting him issued Institutional Act 1, under which the new chief executive was mandated to suspend the political rights of Goulart supporters and those sympathetic to various Marxist and leftist groups aiding Goulart programs. Castello Branco responded by announcing his intention to mediate between the hardliners and the proconstitutionalists. Some editors, reporters, and broadcasters engaged in the self-censorship of silence or token criticism; some were in clear support of the new government; and some came out with bitter denunciations.

Soon a presidential decree created the Division of Censorship of Public Diversions (Divisão de Censura de Diversões Públicas or DCDP) as an agency of the Ministry of Justice. DCDP officers could prohibit publication or broadcast of any report that, in the opinion of the Justice Ministry, threatened the authority of the government. Regional offices of the DCDP in Rio de Janeiro, São Paulo, Porto Alegre, Brasília, Belo Horizonte, Salvador, and Recife issued guidelines that ostensibly anticipated different regional concerns, especially in the fine arts. That is, sexually suggestive songs and theatrical productions acceptable in Rio de Janeiro might not be acceptable in certain provincial cities.

Limited Freedom for the Media

The two major periods of censorship in Brazil this century were from the beginning of the *Estado Novo* in November 1937 to March 1945, and from the promulgation of the Fifth Institutional Act on December 13, 1968, under President Artur da Costa e Silva

(1967–1969) to the beginning of the presidential term of Ernesto Geisel (1974–1979). Geisel relaxed all guidelines for the 1974 elections and ended censorship for the 1978 federal congressional and state government elections. Technically the Law of National Security (Lei de Segurança Nacional or LSN) remained in force until January 1, 1979, when a new LSN took effect without the unpopular restrictions of Institutional Act 5.[44] Brief periods of censorship occurred after the 1964 ouster of Goulart and in 1961 when rightist forces questioned Goulart's succession to the presidency. By comparison, the media in 1978 were freer of restrictions than they had been for a decade.

Two political parties were certified for the ballot after Institutional Act 2 took effect in 1965: the military government's majority National Renovation Alliance (Aliança Renovadora Nacional or ARENA), and the civilian-dominated opposition party, the Brazilian Democratic Movement (Movimento Democrático Brasileiro or MDB). During the campaigns of 1974, with newspapers criticizing the government at all levels below the presidency itself, discussion of major issues returned to the front page. Both MDB and ARENA candidates received air time on radio and television.[45] As a result, in one-third of the states, the MDB won the majority position in the legislature and reduced the voting majority of the ARENA in the federal Congress in both the Deputies Chamber and the Senate.

Reflecting the government's concern over the reduced status of its party, the ARENA, in the federal and state legislative branches, a new broadcasting regulation was drafted by Minister of Justice Armando Falcão in 1976 and promulgated on July 1, setting the rules for the campaigns culminating in the 1978 elections.[46] Both political parties would continue to receive daily two free hours of air time at radio and television stations within the areas covered by the respective offices (statewide, congressional district, or municipal areas). Unlike the 1974 regulation, however, the new law specified that for the 1978 campaigns, a biographical sketch and platform summary statement for each candidate would be read by a staff announcer. Effective or charismatic voices among opposition MDB candidates aired in 1974 were missing in 1978.

On television in 1978, still photos or brief motion picture clips of each candidate were aired while announcers read the copy in neutral or dull tones. In some provincial cities, films of smiling MDB candidates remained on the air until one or two weeks before the November 15 balloting, but then were replaced by unsmiling still photographs exuding the grimness of passport photos.

Article I of the Lei Falcão specified that of the daily two hours of free time for political candidates of both parties, each radio and television station in Brazil had to air one of those hours between 8:00 P.M. and midnight, prime time for listening in many regions. Article V specified that the daily campaign broadcasts must begin thirty days before election day for municipal offices, and forty-five days before election day for state and federal offices.

Some of the restrictions on controversial dramas and other non-news television programs imposed by the DCDP from 1964 to 1974 ended upon a direct order in 1974 from President Geisel to the Ministry of Justice. Novelist Jorge Amado, a symbol of antiestablishment criticism and a leading literary figure of Brazil, had many of his stories converted into theatrical plays and motion pictures, but government pressures had kept Amado's most provocative works from becoming video programs. In the late 1970s that changed. The dramatic series "Gabriela," in 1971 had been rejected for television because the main characters complained about arbitrary government regulations. Now Amado's series could be aired, rewritten at a working-class level as a soap opera. In 1976, when "Gabriela" was broadcast in prime evening time, from 7:00 to 8:00 P.M., it captured the highest audience ratings of the year in almost every major Brazilian city.

By 1978, restrictions on television programming had further shrunk. Carnival sambas ridiculing bureaucracy found air time on both radio and television. Ironically, one statewide broadcasters group in Rio Grande do Sul, the Associação Gaúcha de Emissoras de Rádio e Televisão, even praised the Ministry of Communications for retaining some limitations on foreign programs that otherwise compete with Brazilian productions for video time. The regulation in question forced stations to air the detective series with Telly Savalas, "Kojak," and similar foreign dramas dealing with crime, after 10:00 P.M. That restriction had been designed to increase the number of Brazilian-produced dramatic series during prime time.

Audience surveys in 1978 showed clearly that in the major cities, after 7:00 P.M., radio lost millions of Brazilians to video. Yet the government continued to keep its nightly "National Hour" on radio from 7:00 to 8:00 P.M., despite requests from the producers at Radiobrás to move the nationwide hookup of all radio stations to a morning hour when radio still captures a large urban as well as a rural audience. Empresa Brasileira de Radiodifusão or "Radiobrás" is an agency of the Ministry of Communications, but the topics emphasized on the "Hora do Brasil" come from the office of the president and from the various cabinet ministries, through the Minister of Communications.[47]

Pressures on the Press

Censorship of newspapers, begun in 1968, went from stringent lists of banned topics into a twilight period, from 1972 to 1974, when the limitations often came after a controversial story was published or was already set in type but not yet circulated.

In October 1967, when some Brazilian dailies wanted to serialize the book *Revolution Within the Revolution* by French Marxist Regis Debray, the Ministry of Justice ruled that such daily excerpts would glamorize the Castro dictatorship in Cuba and the groups advocating violent overthrow of the Brazilian government.[48] The Debray book advocating armed insurrection, rather than being any domestic threat to the government, triggered the stationing in 1968 of censors in newspapers that previously had received only guidelines and printed instructions as to prohibited topics.

In 1969 the government-press conflicts receiving the most international attention involved two Rio de Janeiro dailies.

Correio da Manhã had been the last major daily in Brazil in 1968 to get censors stationed in its offices. When they were withdrawn on January 6, 1969, the editors assumed that the action meant that the paper was then free to publish whatever criticism it wished. Before dawn on January 7, *Correio's* front page was set in type under a large headline "Press Censorship Abolished." A printer informed the federal police, and agents of the Division of Censorship of Public Diversions (DCDP) quickly marched into the newspaper and confiscated that day's edition.

Mrs. Paulo Bittencourt, publisher of *Correio* and widow of the paper's longtime crusading editor, demanded that the DCDP circulate the confiscated press run. Instead police arrested her and detained her for two days.[49]

Alberto Dines, editor of the Rio daily *Jornal do Brasil*, wrote a lengthy factual account of how censors had moved into newspaper, radio, and television offices. Early in 1969 Dines was charged with attacking basic government policies and jailed to await trial. The Inter-American Press Association, and the trade publications *Editor & Publisher* and *Broadcasting* campaigned for the release of Dines, encouraging numerous editorials in dailies in the United States, Canada,

Britain, Mexico, France, Israel, and Sweden. DCDP charges were reduced to a misdemeanor and Dines received a token fine and his release.

Brazilian censors in May 1969 then began to utilize euphemisms, issuing a set of "recommendations" for press behavior to replace the list of banned topics in anticipation of New York Governor Nelson Rockefeller's fact-finding visit. The recommendations stressed these points: "Do not publish commentaries or criticisms of the government relating to the suspension of the political rights of extremists. Limit such news stories to official statements only. . . . Do not publish news or commentary that endanger the economic policy of the government. . . . Do not publish news of workers' disruption of public order through violent protest or guerrilla warfare. . . . Do not publish news of hostile acts against illustrious visitor Governor Rockefeller."[50]

During his visit, Governor Rockefeller and Brazilian President Costa e Silva politely debated the press restrictions. Rockefeller stressed the fact that in an open society, such as in the United States, even unfounded attacks can be refuted, with the truth being the ultimate yield of a media system based on unrestricted factual reporting. Costa e Silva retorted that Brazil was trying to regain its stability, which had eroded under extremists in the last months of the Goulart administration.

By mid-1969, again in place of direct censorship, the Justice Ministry had the DCDP issue lists of topics and data considered a threat to national security along with an invitation to newspaper editors to practice "self-censorship." In practical terms, a newspaper could avoid having a censor on its premises by toning down or eliminating severe criticism of major government policies.[51]

Two leading news correspondents covering Latin America, James Nelson Goodsell of the *Christian Science Monitor* and David F. Belnap of the *Los Angeles Times,* researched extensively among Brazilian officials to find the true impact of the 1969 "recommendations" and program of "self-censorship" replacing military censors. They found that the Ministry of Justice regularly offered specific suggestions to editors about avoiding commentary or reporting likely to provoke demonstrations.[52] Publishers who continued to ignore the government warnings then received fines or arrests and jail sentences ranging from days to weeks.

During the second half of 1969, the Justice Ministry tended to watch the big dailies of Rio de Janeiro, São Paulo, and Brasília closely for violations of guidelines, but became more permissive of provincial dailies until Sergio Costa Ramos was arrested for violating the

National Security Code. As editor of *O Estado* in Curitiba, capital of the state of Paraná, Costa Ramos wrote editorials strongly criticizing the federal government for having suspended the political rights of various opponents of the administration. He was indicted on a security charge and jailed. Vigorous protests by dozens of editors and publishers of the Inter-American Press Association, from the United States and from fifteen Latin American republics, prompted the Justice Ministry to drop the charges against Costa Ramos. As the controversy dragged on during July and August, several other provincial dailies, ranging from *O Povo* in Fortaleza to *Provincia* in Belém had reprinted the articles from Curitiba. The Justice Ministry did not want this provincial trend to spread further and moved to end the controversy.

Both losses and gains in press freedom multiplied during 1970 but the restrictions outnumbered the positive incidents. When federal police began preventing book distributors and retailers from featuring books from the Soviet Union and from Cuba, the DCDP did nothing to discourage press and broadcasting coverage of the restrictions. Then suddenly news about censorship of books disappeared from most media.

In October 1970 the Inter-American Press Association chose Nascimento Brito, publisher of the Rio daily *Jornal do Brasil,* as its 1970–1971 president. In deference to the symbolic and hemispheric importance of a Brazilian heading the IAPA, on December 22 the government authorized the resumption of publication of the satirical weekly *O Pasquim.*[53] It had been suspended in November after publishing numerous cartoons and articles depicting government officials in various guises ranging from circus clowns to ballet dancers balanced tiptoe on political trapezes.

O Pasquim in Portuguese means the "Broadside," indicating the type of humor emphasized in the magazine's political commentary. Cartoonist Ziraldo Alves Pinto, who had drawn Brazilian President Emilio Médici in a ballerina's tutu, was not permitted to rejoin the editorial staff. In late December the government had tapped the magazine's telephones while pretending to repair them and then had recorded a conversation in which Alves Pinto had suggested running a cartoon similar to one run in early 1970. That cartoon had quoted Médici's slogan "No one can hold this country back!" in a drawing of a general driving a wagon over a cliff with broken reins dangling in his hands.

When it resumed publication, *Pasquim* carried in its masthead this slogan: "A weekly of opposition to the Greek government," in a reference to the military junta then ruling Greece. Before its

November suspension, *Pasquim* had achieved a circulation of 900,000, approaching the success of the Portuguese language edition of *Reader's Digest* and the Brazilian news magazine *O Cruzeiro*. After the magazine resumed publication, its biting satire mellowed and its circulation never reached its former zenith.

O Cruzeiro was the second largest selling magazine in Latin America, adding 500,000 circulation of its Spanish language edition to its one million circulation in Portuguese. Owned by the Diários Associados media conglomerate of the Assis Chateaubriand family, the magazine suffered after the founder's death in 1968 as his sons and their rival groups of associates weakened the corporation internally. Like its format counterpart in the United States, the weekly picture news magazine *Life, Cruzeiro* succumbed in the 1970s to the combined pressures of inflationary rising production costs and declining revenues from advertising shifting to television. With the easing of government censorship in 1975–1976, *Cruzeiro* attempted a comeback but its revival was brief. *Cruzeiro's* revenues were insufficient to pay its taxes or even a token dividend to its stockholders.

William Montalbano, Latin American correspondent for the *Miami Herald,* found censorship of the Brazilian press more relaxed from 1971 to 1972 than it had been during 1969 to 1970. For weeks at a time, editors would receive an occasional telephone call from the federal police cautioning or recommending that specific stories threatened national security and should be avoided. But when guerrillas kidnapped a government official or a foreigner to gain publicity and ransom, police visited editorial offices to make sure news of the event did not appear.[54]

In 1971 a leftist group kidnapped the Swiss ambassador to Brazil, Giovanni Bucher. The Brazilian reporter for the Associated Press who broke the story received a jail sentence, but the newspaper and broadcasting editors who used the story received only warnings. Francois Pelou, chief of the Agence France Presse news service in Brazil, persisted in filing detailed follow-up stories about the Bucher kidnapping and was deported to Paris.[55]

Brazil's most prestigious and respected newspaper, *O Estado de São Paulo*—rated by foreign press specialist John C. Merrill as one of the elite dailies of the world because of accurate reporting and scope of coverage—in 1972 could no longer comfortably engage in self-censorship, even to insure a modest degree of freedom to criticize political events.[56] Thereupon a Justice Department censor returned to the news department, and *Estado* did not regain its journalistic flexibility until briefly in 1974 and then again in 1978.[57]

As federal officials began to realize that they remained ignorant of maladministration at the state and local level, they began to see the usefulness of allowing more grass roots investigatory reporting. The case triggering this limited easing of censorship erupted in the state of Bahia in October 1972. João Teixeira, editor of *Jornal de Bahia* in Salvador, reported that Governor Antonio Carlos Magalhães awarded state contracts to a company in which the governor had a substantial investment. The governor had Teixeira tried before an air force military court for violating national security. But from Brasília, the chief of the air force, upon the advice of the Minister of Justice, ordered the court to disqualify itself from hearing the case, inasmuch as "reporting of conflict of interest in no way threatened national security."[58]

The inconsistency of easing censorship over state and local politics while increasing it over national political and economic controversies in late 1972 puzzled veteran Latin Americanist Nathan Haverstock. He found that the government used pressure to try to curtail stories indicating that Brazil suffered from too much foreign indebtedness.[59] Top administrators indicated to him that they feared headlines stressing the foreign debts might trigger a demand among the officer corps for more economic nationalism just at a sensitive moment when foreign investors were helping further diversify the economy.

During the 1970s, even before President Geisel formally lifted censorship for the 1978 campaigns, the lyrics of the popular songs, especially the sambas written for Carnival week preceding Lent, continued to contain considerable social satire and commentary on issues of the day, as did the street poets who publish their own literary comments about all aspects of public and private life in *folhetos*. As Professor Mark Curran points out, a folheto carries advertisements for printing, rubber stamps, and horoscopes, giving the format a gaudy aspect censors might not consider journalism per se.[60]

In April 1973 Fernando Gasparian, publisher of the news weekly *Opinião*, flatly refused to follow directions of a censor. On April 15, he had his printers do his weekly press run before 6:00 A.M. Before the papers could be distributed to newsstands throughout Brazil, federal police confiscated them. A former professor at Oxford University, Gasparian previously had published with blank spaces to indicate censored material, much to the anger of the Justice Ministry. Gasparian was questioned at length but released.

Another weekly news magazine, *Veja*, began in 1973 and 1974 to test the limits to which the government might take criticism, utilizing irony, paradox, and analogies to criticize most major government programs. In 1973 *Veja* discovered a spy for the federal police on its editorial staff, who was alerting the Justice Ministry to pending anti-government commentary as pages were being laid out in page proof, prompting increased censorship.[61] From 1974 on, *Veja* became successfully bolder. *Manchete* had replaced *Cruzeiro* as the republic's leading photo news magazine but *Veja* became the most quoted anti-government publication.

By 1978, with restraints removed, *Veja* set a pattern for daily newspapers to try to emulate. Unlike the dailies, *Veja* only had to meet one deadline a week and could be much more selective in the stories it chose to cover, selecting topics its reporters might probe in depth. When the opposition MDB won almost as many seats in state legislatures and the federal Congress as the ARENA in the November 15, 1978, elections, MDB officials in Rio de Janeiro gave credit in part to the attitude of questioning the government as reflected in *Veja*.[62]

Women Use the Media

From 1976 to 1979, the women's movement in Brazil demonstrated a skill in utilizing the mass media, especially television and radio, to report on the movement's campaign for political amnesty, a topic the Brazilian government has suspected of being a device used by its most radical and leftwing opposition to encourage public criticism of the military government.

Late in 1976, Terezinha Zerbini founded and became president of the Feminine Movement for Amnesty in Brazil. She carefully explained in all news releases to the media that the word in the organization's name was "Feminine," indicating the movement consisted of female members, and not "Feminist," indicating a group seeking a more powerful status for women in public life.

With a core membership of approximately 300 in the handful of Brazilian cities with multimillion populations, the Zerbini movement soon indirectly involved thousands of other women in cities throughout the republic. The movement's demands centered in the goal of political amnesty for all Brazilians from left to right in the political spectrum. No mention was made of equal pay for women or abortions or similar topics heard in women's groups in the United States.

The repeated demands for a "spiritual amnesty" to bring all segments of society into civic participation from the local to the national level never used assertive or aggressive rhetoric but always stressed the traditional phrases associated with feminine charm. Yet

Mrs. Zerbini succeeded in constructing what she described as a vast "support network" of mainstream professional groups with overwhelmingly male memberships.[63]

She presented the Feminine Movement for Amnesty proclamation to the National Bar Association of Brazil, which endorsed the call for amnesty by acclamation. Other officers in the Zerbini movement then persuaded endorsement of the amnesty proclamation by the national associations of architects, psychologists, physicians, sociologists, and the Conference of Bishops of the Catholic Church.

All the while the movement steadfastly refused membership from male Brazilians seeking to join an organization with discernible momentum. Mrs. Zerbini felt that male members would invite pressures or even attacks by the government, whereas traditional Brazilian gallantry insured courteous treatment by the government. Radio and television news commentators, talk show hosts, and producers of homemaker daytime programs felt the same way, so during 1978 the movement received considerable mention on the air, but much less coverage in the print media. However, given the fact that more Brazilians get their daily information from broadcasting stations than from newspapers or magazines, the recognition on the air of the Zerbini movement added a new dimension to public life: an effective voice for political amnesty in a political system that had before discouraged or censored public debate of the topic. In August 1979 the government finally declared amnesty for all political dissidents. In July 1980 during the visit of Pope John Paul II, political dissidents attended various press conferences with the pontiff.

In an indirect relation to the Zerbini and other women's movements, an increase in news coverage of family planning in Brazil followed in-depth reporting in several newspapers about poor nutritional standards among the poor. On the very day in November 1978 when the Rede Globo television network carried an extensive report on increased family planning facilities available in the largest Brazilian cities, the network's affiliated newspaper, *O Globo,* reduced that story to a one-paragraph filler, overshadowed by a larger top-of-the-page story in large headline type proclaiming "Pope Condemns Abortion and Defends Christian Unity."[64]

Stepan's Analysis of Editorials

Political scientist Alfred Stepan of Yale accomplished the monumental task of reading and analyzing more than 1,000 editorials in nine leading Brazilian daily newspapers for periods preceding and following political crises or coups in 1945, 1954, 1955, 1961, and 1964.[65] Stepan's evaluations of these editorials as they related to Brazilian politics are invaluable for any study of Brazilian government-media relations.

Stepan studied editorials from the conservative dailies *Estado de São Paulo, Tribuna da Imprensa,* and *O Globo;* the leftist *Ultima Hora;* and the relatively nonideological newspapers *Correio da Manhã, Jornal do Brasil, Diário Carioca, O Jornal,* and *Diário de Notícias.* In addition, he found that editorials in four provincial dailies—*Estado de Minas* in Belo Horizonte, *Correio do Povo* in Porto Alegre, *A Tarde* in Salvador, and *Jornal do Comércio* in Recife—followed the editorial opinion of a majority of the newspapers in Rio de Janeiro and in São Paulo. Two provincial exceptions occurred. In 1961 *Correio do Povo,* in the capital of the state of Rio Grande do Sul, supported native son Goulart's right to be president. And in 1964 *Jornal do Comércio* reflected the fears of leaders in the northeast with an early strong stand against Goulart.

Stepan explored these hundreds of editorials during the crises in five pivotal years to test his hypotheses relating executive legitimacy to military intervention. He saw that Brazilian military activism has been congruent with civilian political elite attitudes. Stepan has therefore concluded that successful military coups against the presidency correlate with a prior low legitimacy accorded to the president by civilian political elites and a high legitimacy accorded by these civilians to military leaders to perform their moderating role by removing the executive. His converse hypothesis followed: unsuccessful military attempts to remove the executive correlate with prior high legitimacy accorded to the executive and low legitimacy to the military.[66]

Exploring almost 1,000 editorials, Stepan found that his hypotheses were supported. In each of the five crises, he found debate reaching the level of editorial concern weeks or months before the actual coup succeeded or failed to materialize. Except for the 1964 ouster of Goulart, the crises had been very public affairs, widely discussed in all the major newspapers before any action erupted.

In this most extensive, profound, and useful political analysis of the Brazilian press ever attempted, Stepan found civilian leaders and their journalistic spokesmen, when sanctioning military intervention to head off an anticipated national disaster, did not necessarily give the military carte blanche to decide by themselves what action to take. Editorial demands often were quite specific as to the limits of intervention in politics, depending on the crisis in question.

In 1945, editorials in general worried that Vargas might postpone the presidential elections and therefore the military must supervise free elections. Stepan cites a typical editorial two and a half weeks before the military removed Vargas from office:

> Nothing is more right and legitimate than that the political parties should ask the army, navy, and air force to intervene in the sense of guaranteeing the election laws already designated, and to impede them from being modified.[67]

In 1954, when the assassination of an air force officer led to the Vargas suicide, Stepan found editorials not only demanding military intervention but condemning some of the military for allowing President Vargas to continue in office during the crisis. *Estado de São Paulo* commented:

> There continues . . . a civilian movement urging the armed forces to convince the chief of the nation to vacate his office. The armed forces however are unfortunately not unanimous in this respect. If the armed forces believe they are serving Brazil . . . by maintaining in the presidential office a completely discredited citizen, they will in fact be giving *carte blanche* to new immorality and even to new crimes.[68]

Stepan found numerous editorials from 1945 through 1961 that assured civilians that the military, after intervening to end a crisis, had always returned power to civilian hands. With the ouster of Goulart in 1964, that was no longer true.

Recent Editorial Trends

Inspired by the perspective derived by the Stepan analysis of editorials from 1945 to 1964, I began collecting Brazilian editorials in 1978, but having to cover several other Latin American nations as to both print and electronic media for the scope of this volume, the sample had to be only a fraction of the Stepan compilation.

With censorship removed, how candid are Brazilian dailies in reporting on sensitive relations between Brazil and foreign nations? Sometimes the same newspaper can range from specific detailed commentary to vague generalities, depending on how much information government sources reveal. Consider two samples from the same Rio de Janeiro daily, *Jornal do Brasil*, on two consecutive days in August 1978.

The first story concerned the proposal of the Brazilian Petroleum

Corporation, Petrobrás, to prospect for oil in the North Sea. Officials in Brasília did not want to talk about the proposal until a trade deal had been completed for Norway to sell Brazil oil. *Jornal do Brasil* broke the silence in Brasília by interviewing Bjartmar Gjerde, Norway's Minister of Oil and Energy, who stated flatly Norway would allow Petrobrás to prospect in the North Sea.[69]

The day before, *Jornal do Brasil,* after a week of trying, admitted in print it could not find out why a top diplomat was visiting the Soviet Union:

> João Paulo do Rio Branco, chief of the Foreign Ministry's European Department, went on a secret mission to Moscow last weekend and will stay there until Thursday. Although the ministry declined to disclose the purpose of this visit, it is known that he will hold talks regarding the housing problems Brazilian diplomats are having in Moscow as a result of increased rents, which have reached intolerable levels. The housing difficulties Brazilian families are facing in Moscow might mean retaliatory actions against Soviet personnel in Brasília on the part of the Brazilian Foreign Ministry.[70]

In early October 1978, the São Paulo daily *Jornal da Tarde,* afternoon affiliate of the more famous morning *Estado de São Paulo,* ran an editorial as vigorously critical of the government as could be found since the ending of censorship. It summarized that "the military regime is in gangrenous agony and its death is just a matter of time."[71] The editorial dealt with the government's own investigations into misuse of public funds. The paper and its morning affiliate published by the Mesquita family had been reporting in its news columns about a large-scale theft from the Brazilian embassy in Paris by Brazilian foreign ministry employees. Both papers had also been reporting in detail the investigations of the Court of Accounts of the Union (Tribunal de Contas da União) into misuse of funds of the federal savings bank, the Caixa Econômica Federal.[72]

Not only these two dailies, but most other major Brazilian dailies in Rio de Janeiro and in the republic's largest cities, also had been persistent in reporting on the federal savings bank investigations, despite efforts of several high-ranking administrators in Brasília to have the Justice Ministry curtail such reporting. Both the Justice Ministry and the office of the president refused to reinstate censorship and the probing reporting continued.

The publisher of the daily *Folha de São Paulo,* Octavio Oliveira, early in the presidential campaign of 1978, editorially began supporting MDB candidate Euler Bentes Monteiro, who ran against victorious ARENA candidate General João Figueiredo. In September, *Folha* commented that:

> Figueiredo has increased rapidly irritating statements and used up the margin of error a man in public life has. Each new declaration of his reveals the preoccupation of the power elite which contributes to national problems.[73]

Also early in September, in a campaign that ended with the presidential election on October 15, *O Estado de São Paulo* published numerous reports of high-ranking military leaders who favored Bentes Monteiro over Figueiredo. Such reports circulated freely throughout the republic without engendering any return of censorship. The election results from the Electoral College showed 355 votes for Figueiredo and 226 votes for Bentes Monteiro. The government's ARENA, while more vulnerable in the popular balloting on November 15 for members of state Legislatures and the federal Congress, knew that it could not lose the presidential election, which is indirect. That is, citizens had previously chosen the incumbent Congress, which together with representatives from the state governments, sat as the 581 voting members of the Colégio Eleitoral.[74] Therefore, campaign oratory at the presidential level could reach limits of militancy that orators and writers at the congressional and state levels often did not approach.

Beginning for Independent Media

In September 1978, *O Estado de São Paulo* and *Correio Brasiliense* of Brasília began daily reports claiming that the Army Ministry had been sounding out various high-ranking officers on their attitudes toward the presidential succession. That topic, which would have been considered too sensitive to continue without guidelines or censorship by the government in power from 1968 to 1974, in 1978 went unchallenged except for one mild ministry denial.[75]

During 1979 the play "Highirte" vigorously attacked the concept of military dictatorships before full theater audiences and received favorable press reviews.

As Brazil prepared to enter the 1980s, more of its citizens were watching television or listening to radio than were regularly reading daily newspapers or magazines. And even though the networks slowly but steadily increased the amount of air time devoted to serious coverage of public events through news or panel or talk shows, the fact remained that the largest audiences tuned in to hear soap operas, comedies, and music.

The television soap opera "O Astro" ("The Star") for eight consecutive months during 1978 enjoyed the highest audience ratings in the history of Brazilian television, capturing 92 percent of the sets in use, even in the largest cities where as many as six competing television programs vied for viewers.[76] During the diplomatic banquet honoring visiting Henry and Nancy Kissinger, at 8:00 P.M. dozens of guests left the banquet hall for the nearest television sets to watch "Astro."

The series chronicled the career of a character named Terculano Quintanilha, who, through dirty tricks, rose from his job as a nightclub magician to become a nationally powerful business executive. Millions of Brazilians, ranging from manual laborers and homemakers to teachers and clerks, were fascinated with the theme of upward mobility. It is only fair to point out that in dozens of other nations, including the United States, more people are aware of television entertainers and their fictional adventures than they are aware of national and world leaders and issues.

Economist Albert Fishlow, director of the Concilium on International and Area Studies at Yale, and former deputy assistant secretary of state for Inter-American Affairs, perhaps best summed up the profound changes under way in Brazil:

> Relative democracy, as President-elect Figueiredo has described the Brazilian political system, shows signs of more vitality . . . in the emergence of an opposition military candidate for the presidency . . . and a consequently broadened scope for debate. As that debate has proceeded, military and civilian views have begun to coalesce on the need for a more open society . . . censorship of the press has been lifted . . .[77]

Brazilian media have begun to articulate national problems and to report candidly on the gains and losses in government and the economy. The repression of recent years has yielded on many basic points and even the device of indirect election of the president now faces the diminished legitimacy found in public opinion nurtured by information-prone mass media. During 1980 the Communist Party newspaper *Voz* and other leftist papers circulated freely.

In July 1980 Pope John Paul II visited thirteen Brazilian cities. His criticism of social conditions afflicting the poor and his demands for increased welfare were fully reported by the Brazilian media. The government's acceptance of these press reports critical of domestic conditions further decreased its guidance of the media.

References

Agence France Presse. "Brazil Overview," *Agence France Presse*, Apr. 2, 1964, and Feb. 9, 1971, dispatches.

Alisky, Marvin. "Early Mexican Broadcasting," *Hispanic American Historical Review* 34 (November 1954): 515–16.

Almeida, José, Américo de. *Ocasos de Sangue* (Rio de Janeiro: Livraria Olympio, 1954).

Amaral Peixoto, Alzira Vargas do. *Getúlio Vargas, Meu Pai* (Rio de Janeiro: AP, 1967).

Associated Press. "Advertisements Used by Vargas," *Associated Press Review of Brazil*, Dec. 30, 1945, Dispatch A 101.

———. "Astro's Highest Rating," *Associated Press Review of Brazil*, Aug. 1, 1978.

Banco do Brasil. "The Dynamic Growth of Industry in Brazil," *Brazilian Bulletin* 10 (November 1977): 2–4.

———. *1963–1978 Cacex* (Brasília: Carteira de Comércio Exterior, 1978).

Baer, Werner. *Industrialization and Economic Development in Brazil* (Homewood, Ill.: Richard D. Irwin, 1965).

Belnap, David F. "How Brazil Muzzles the Press," *Los Angeles Times*, Aug. 2, 1969, p. 7.

Campos, Roberto de Oliveira. *Do Outro Lado da Cêrca* (Rio de Janeiro: APEC editora, 1967).

Chaves Paz, Horacio. Historian of pioneer Brazilian broadcasting records, correspondence to Marvin Alisky, March 29, 1970.

Conselho Nacional de Comunicações. "Comunicações," *Decreto Lei 568*, May 18, 1963, pp. 1–2.

Curran, Mark J. "The 'Journalistic Page' of the Brazilian Popular Poet," *Revista Brasileira de Folclore*, Apr. 1972, pp. 3–4.

Dulles, John W. F. *Castello Branco: The Making of a Brazilian President* (College Station, Tex.: Texas A&M University Press, 1978).

———. *Vargas of Brazil: A Political Biography* (Austin, Tex.: University of Texas Press, 1967).

———. *Unrest in Brazil* (Austin, Tex.: University of Texas Press, 1970).

Ferreira, Oliveiros S. *As Forças Armadas* (Rio de Janeiro: Editora GRD, 1964).

———. "Uma Caracterização do Sistema," *O Estado de São Paulo*, Oct. 17, 1965, p. 4.

Fishlow, Albert. "Flying Down to Rio: Perspectives on U.S.Brazil Relations," *Foreign Affairs* 57 (Winter 1978–79): 387–405.

Fundação Instituto Brasileiro de Geografia e Estatística. *Sinopse Estatística do Brasil 1977* (Rio de Janeiro: Instituto Brasileiro de Geografia e Estatística, 1977).

Gandini, Alceu. Assistant publisher of *Estado de São Paulo;* correspondence to Marvin Alisky, January 5, 1977.

Geyer, Georgie, Anne. "Women Set New Political Tactics," *Phoenix Gazette*, Dec. 7, 1978, p. 7.

Goodsell, James Nelson. "Brazil's Military Regime Tightens Press Muzzle," *Christian Science Monitor*, June 11, 1969, p. 12.

Harris, Mel. "Brazilian Broadcasting" (Paper at the International Communication Associaton in Phoenix, Arizona, April 1971).

Haverstock, Nathan A. "Censorship in Brazil Baffling," *Times of the Americas*, Oct. 25, 1972, p. 10.

Horowitz, Irving Louis, ed. *Revolution in Brazil: Politics and Society in a Developing Nation* (New York, 1964).

Instituto de Direito Público e Ciência Política. *Centro de Documentação de História Contemporanea do Brasil: Ultima Hora* (Rio de Janeiro: Fundação Getúlio Vargas, 1957).

Inter-American Development Bank. *Economic and Social Progress in Latin America: 1977 Report* (Washington, D.C.: IADB, 1977).

Inter-American Press Association. "1971 Is Designated by Brito as Year of Freedom of Information," *IAPA News*, Jan. 1971, p. 1.

Johnson, Peter T. "Academic Press Censorship Under Military and Civilian Regimes:

The Argentine and Brazilian Cases, 1964–1975," *Luso-Brazilian Review* 12 (Summer 1978): 6–7.

Jobim, Danton. *Espírito do Jornalismo* (Rio de Janeiro: Libraria São José, 1960).

Lane, Jonathan P. "Functions of the Mass Media in Brazil's 1964 Crisis," *Journalism Quarterly* 44 (Summer 1967): 297–306.

Leite Filho, Barreto. "Campanha," *Diário de Noticias,* Mar. 25, 1945, p. 3.

Lowenstein, Karl. *Brazil under Vargas* (New York: Columbia University, 1942).

Medio Rio de Janeiro. *Radiómetro 1978* (Rio de Janeiro: Medio, 1978), volume of bimonthly reports.

Merrill, John C. *The Elite Press: Great Newspapers of the World* (New York: Pitman Publishing Company, 1968).

Ministério das Comunicações. "Radiobras," *Perfil Federal* (Brasília: Ministério das Comunicações, 1977), pp. 36–38.

———. "Regulamento dos Serviços de Radiodifusão," *Codigo Brasileiro de Telecomunicações* (Brasília: Ministério das Comunicações, 1973), pp. 1884–85.

Ministério da Educação e Saúde. *A Radiodifusão Educativa No Brasil* (Rio de Janeiro: Serviço de Documentação, 1946).

Ministério do Exército. "Estatuto: Jornalismo," *Decreto Lei 1077,* Jan. 26, 1970, pp. 2–10.

Montalbano, William. "Press Freedom in Brazil," *Miami Herald,* Feb. 11, 1971, p. 3-B.

Packenham, Robert A. "Yankee Impressions and Brazilian Realities," *Wilson Quarterly* 2 (Autumn 1976):65.

Parker, Phyllis. "Separate but Equal? U.S. Policy toward Brazil, 1961–1964," (Independent Research Project, Lyndon B. Johnson School of Public Affairs, University of Texas at Austin, May 1976) pp. 2–97.

Poder Legislativo. "Lei Falcão, No. 6.339," *Atos do Poder Legislativo* (Brasília: Atos Complementares, July 1977), IV, 15–16.

Reis, Edgardo. Correspondent for *O Globo* interviewed by Marvin Alisky in Washington, D.C., on November 16, 1978.

Roett, Riordan, ed. *Brazil in the Seventies* (Washington, D.C.: American Enterprise Institute, 1976).

Skidmore, Thomas E. *Politics in Brazil, 1930–1964* (New York: Oxford University Press, 1967).

Soares, Glaucio Ary Dillon. "The Political Sociology of Uneven Development in Brazil," in Irving L. Horowitz, ed., *Revolution in Brazil: Politics and Society in a Developing Nation* (New York, 1964), pp. 164–95.

Stepan, Alfred. *The Military in Politics: Changing Patterns in Brazil* (Princeton, N.J.: Princeton University Press, 1971).

———, ed. *Authoritarian Brazil* (New Haven, Conn.: Yale University Press, 1973).

Wirth, John D. "Brazilian Economic Nationalism: Trade and Steel under Vargas," (Ph.D. diss., Stanford University, Stanford, California, 1966).

Worldmark Encyclopedia, eds. "Brazil: Industry," *Worldmark Encyclopedia of Nations.* Vol. 3 (New York: Harper and Row, 1971),.pp. 33–48.

Young, Jordan. *The Brazilian Revolution of 1930 and the Aftermath* (New Brunswick, N.J.: Rutgers University Press, 1967).

Newspapers and Periodicals: *Arizona Republic; Christian Science Monitor; Correio Brasiliense,* Brasília; *Correio da Manhã,* Rio de Janeiro; *Diário Carioca,* Rio de Janeiro; *Diário de Noticias,* Rio de Janeiro; *Estado de São Paulo,* São Paulo; *Folha de São Paulo,* São Paulo; *Jornal de Bahia,* Salvador; *Jornal do Brasil,* Rio de Janeiro; *Jornal da Tarde,* São Paulo; *Latin America,* London; *Manchete,* Rio de Janeiro; *Miami Herald; New York Times; Novos Rumos,* Rio de Janeiro; *O Cruzeiro,* Rio de Janeiro; *O Globo,* Rio de Janeiro; *O Jornal,* Rio de Janeiro; *Operária,* São Paulo; *Opinião,* Rio de Janeiro; *Pasquim,* Rio de Janeiro; *Phoenix Gazette; Rede Globo Tv,* Rio de Janeiro; *Rede Tupi,* Rio de Janeiro; *The News,* Mexico City; *Times of the Americas,* Washington, D.C.; *Tribuna da Imprensa,* Rio de Janeiro; *Ultima Hora,* Rio de Janeiro; *Veja,* Rio de Janeiro.

Nations with Media Freedom

THIS section deals with two democracies, Venezuela and Colombia. Costa Rica also qualifies as a republic with complete freedom from government interference. At various times, press freedom also recurs in the Dominican Republic and Ecuador, then alternate periods of censorship or guidance resume. Mexico technically could qualify for this section also, but, in practice, the institutional pressures resulting in bandwagon journalism keep it in the category of nations with institutionalized guidance from the political establishment. In the 1980s, should the return of civilian government in Peru become stabilized into a pluralistic, left-center political spectrum, that republic might again forego its governmental guidance and return to a policy of press freedom.

6

Venezuela: Oil Rich and Media Conscious

VENEZUELA is among the handful of Latin American nations—also Costa Rica and Colombia—with a free press and genuinely free and independent broadcast media. Economically, Venezuela is Latin America's wealthiest nation, in terms of annual income, because it is one of the world's four biggest producers and exporters of petroleum. In 1979 Venezuela's per capita income reached $2,357, the highest in any Latin American nation.[1]

Venezuela's land area covers 353,000 square miles, the size of Texas and Oklahoma combined. Yet its 14 million citizens have crowded into a small portion of the national territory, giving it a demographic disequilibrium as unbalanced as that of Argentina or Chile. The northern mountain area, only 12 percent of the national territory, contains 66 percent of the total population.[2] More than 75 percent urban and 88 percent literate, Venezuelans tend to live within cities served by the republic's newspapers, magazines, radio stations, and television stations.[3] And those media are free of government restraints.

The petroleum and iron ore industries provide three-fourths of the government's revenues and more than one-third of the gross national product. Agriculture contributes only 7 percent of the GNP but employs one-third of the work force. The working class, which makes up 75 percent of the population, has some upward mobility, but its meager income contrasts sharply with the purchasing power of the upper and middle classes.

A 1978 *Washington Post* survey told of upper-class Venezuelans frequently flying into Miami, Florida, to shop in surroundings totally staffed by Spanish-speaking personnel.[4] Venezuelan leaders learn about U.S. culture first hand. This factor reinforces the tendency of Venezuela's government administrators and mass media executives to adopt for their country certain norms in U.S. public life, especially the use of public relations and broadcasting in political campaigns, and in government efforts to engender widespread support for national programs.

From Dictatorship to Democracy

Venezuela represents one of the few genuine democracies in Latin America, with competitive political parties each going through periods of being in or out of power. Also, the Venezuelan press exercises a vigorous watch on the political, economic, and social life of the nation much in the manner of the United States, Canada, or Western European nations.

This era of representative government and press freedom began in 1958. Honest, open elections from the office of president on down to municipal officials have been held every five years, in December of 1958, 1963, 1968, 1973, and 1978. In each case, campaigns were waged freely without any government intervention. The newspapers and the radio and television stations and networks covered each campaign without any government restrictions.

This period of press freedom of the past two decades contrasts with much of Venezuela's earlier political history, which had been pockmarked by dictatorship and political repression, complete with press censorship. Spain's power ended in Venezuela in 1821, beginning the era of the *Gran* Colombia federation in which Venezuela shared a political union with Colombia and Ecuador until 1830. Then, as an independent republic, Venezuela suffered nineteenth-century dictatorships when generals governed, with the facade of a Congress and judicial branch exercising token counterbalances.

In 1908, while the president underwent medical treatment in Europe, Vice-President Juan Vicente Gómez seized power and for twenty-seven years ruled as dictator. Political parties and elections disappeared, and the press rubberstamped government announcements as the news of the nation. No violence or revolution ended the lengthy despotism. In December 1935 Gómez died a natural death. Under the Constitution of 1936 there followed a period of centralized administration in Caracas in the form of federalism, though states' rights remained more cosmetic than substantive. A degree of press freedom did ensue, though bribery and political patronage often insured that newspapers would not report corruption in high places.

The anti-Marxist left-of-center reform party, Acción Democrática (AD), came to power in a 1945 revolution and in 1947 won an open and honest election. But in November 1948, a military junta seized power and developed the dictatorship of General Marcos Pérez Jiménez, who instituted severe censorship of the press and broadcasting stations. He made no pretense of maintaining token democratic procedures: "I give Venezuelans the kind of government adapted to them. . . . We are still in our infant years and we still need halters. . . . There must be a leader who shows the way without being perturbed by the necessity of winning demogogic popularity."[5]

Broadcasters and newspaper editors and reporters who on occasion did manage to evade censors and circulate news of the arbitrariness of the dictatorship often met with torture and prison terms.

A rigged, fraudulent, and unconstitutional plebiscite on December 15, 1957, supposedly authorized the continuation of Pérez Jiménez for another five years. Widespread resentment building beneath the surface during years of dictatorship erupted over this flagrant attempt to legitimatize the government in power. On January 21, 1958, a general strike brought retail commerce, industrial activities, and public transportation to a halt. Neither government nor the private sector could function during a national work stoppage. Pérez Jiménez resigned and went into exile. Years later he would be extradited from the United States and convicted of embezzling millions of dollars from the Venezuelan treasury.

After a period of a caretaker government, elections in December 1958 found AD candidate Rómulo Betancourt the new president. Acción Democrática retained control of the presidency with the victory of Raúl Leoni in the 1963 elections. With newspapers and broadcasting stations free to report on government mistakes as well as successes, and with a vigorous debating of the issues confronting the nation, the political "ins" then became the political "outs."[6] In December 1968 the candidate of the Social Christian party (COPEI), Rafael Caldera, won the presidency. Then in December 1973 the AD regained the presidency with candidate Carlos Andrés Pérez. And in December 1978 again power shifted. The COPEI candidate, Luis Herrera Campins, won over his AD candidate by a margin of 200,000 votes out of a total of 5 million.[7]

A More Open Society

Fundamental prerequisites for an informed public, capable of making realistic judgments about political leaders and the rival programs proposed by the major parties, would include a substantially literate population and a press free of censorship or various indirect pressures or "guidance." Only within the past two decades has Venezuela achieved those fundamental bases for a more open society than existed during much of its history.

Beginning in 1959 President Betancourt's administration launched a massive assault on adult illiteracy. Both the AD and its opposition COPEI made literacy campaigns major items in their campaign programs. In less than twenty years, the literacy rate rose from 52 to 88 percent.

In an atmosphere of democratic, representative government, various pressure groups throughout the 1960s and 1970s learned to engage in ongoing public debates without frightening the government into imposing restrictions, as has so often happened in other Latin American republics attempting to change a closed society into an open one.

Until the 1960s, public dialogue between management and labor usually degenerated into name calling. But the Venezuelan Federation of Labor discovered it could receive accurate coverage in the newspapers and on broadcasts, and began to use some of the phraseology found in North American contract negotiations. Managerial groups, eager to avoid work stoppages during a period of unprecedented economic growth that was spurred by the rising price of petroleum in world markets, responded in kind.

Despite this dialogue in a more open society, violence was still used as a political action during the 1960s. Professor Robert J. Alexander, a noted scholar on the activities of the Venezuelan Communist party (Partido Comunista de Venezuela or PCV), observed that the PCV was one of three Communist parties in Latin America that openly resorted to force during the 1960s while trying to gain power.[8]

Alexander noted that the PCV, encouraged by the establishment of the Castro regime in Cuba, in 1962 committed itself to a campaign of urban terrorism, ranging from guerrilla attacks on army barracks to bank robberies and political kidnappings.

Thanks to the AD and COPEI commitments to social reforms and economic development, financed in part by the steadily increasing oil income of the government, the PCV found by 1965 its tactics had failed.

Fortunately for the democratic processes in Venezuela, during the escalation of PCV violence and that of the allied Revolutionary Leftist Movement (Movimiento de Izquierda Revolucionaria or MIR), the government did not attempt to hamper the newspaper and broadcasting reporting of the violence. As a consequence, the institutionalizing of a free press tradition within the social and political systems of Venezuela, begun in 1958, enjoyed uninterrupted growth for two decades, into the 1980s.

Foreign correspondents for the news services and the networks found Caracas as convenient a city to file stories from as any city in North America or Western Europe. Interference with mail and long distance telephone calls or telegrams ended in 1958. During the fall of the Marcos Pérez Jiménez dictatorship in January 1958, censors monitored the telephone calls from Caracas to the United States. If adverse stories began in Spanish, Portuguese, French, or English, the line went dead. Brazilian-born U.S. citizen Tad Szulc, then a correspondent for the *New York Times,* had parents who had migrated to Brazil from Poland, enabling him to learn Polish as a child. Szulc simply telephoned a Polish-speaking rewrite editor in New York and dictated his dispatches in Polish while censors, who were multilingual only in the Latin languages, remained confused.[9] Throughout the 1960s and 1970s, no such subterfuge was necessary.

A Television Election Campaign

At least three other Latin American republics—Brazil, Mexico, and Argentina—are large enough in population and land area, substantial enough in GNP and domestic retail sales, and developed enough in terms of households with television and radio in use to support elaborate television and radio advertising campaigns. However, as noted in Chapter 5, Brazil has suffered from media censorship. Until recently it was without a political system geared to aggressive political broadcasting. Mexico, like Brazil, in recent years has permitted some free air time to political parties, with regulatory abridgements not conducive to full-fledged broadcast campaigning. And Argentina has suffered the Perón dictatorship and military censorship from 1966 to 1973 and again since the ouster of Isabelita Perón in 1976. Thus, of the Latin American republics large enough to support privately operated television networks reaching national audiences and with enough potential revenues to finance costly video campaigning, only oil-rich Venezuela, with its democracy of recent years, has had the combination of genuine freedom of information and an economy able to underwrite television campaigning.

The campaign of 1978 found Venezuelan politicians emulating U.S. candidates in utilizing prime time television and techniques perfected by U.S. advertising agencies. In Venezuela, better than seven out of every ten households have television sets, prompting both major presidential candidates, winner Luis Herrera Campins of COPEI and runner-up Luis Piñerua Ordaz of AD, to break the record in Latin American history for campaign spending.[10] Each of them spent $8 million for television time.[11] For that sum, unprecedented even in affluent Venezuela, Herrera received 47 percent of the vote, Piñerua received 43 percent, and eight minor-party candidates received the remaining 10 percent.

Both the COPEI and the AD candidate depended heavily on professional campaign strategists from the United States. Victorious Herrera hired David Garth, who had helped manage the election victories of New York Governor Hugh Carey and New York City Mayor Edward Koch. Piñerua hired Clifton White, a former campaign manager for U.S. Senator Barry Goldwater, and Joseph Napolitan, who authored *The Election Game and How to Win It* and managed the successful 1973 campaign of Venezuelan President Carlos Andrés Pérez.

At the National Autonomous University of Mexico in 1950, Professor Ladzslo Radvanyi pioneered public opinion polls in Latin American cities. These polls were forerunners of the extensive radio audience surveys throughout Mexico by Joe Belden of Dallas, through his Mexican subsidiary Radiómetro. By 1958 extensive public opinion polling had been established in Uruguay, Chile, Brazil, Colombia, Costa Rica, and Cuba. Curtailment of surveys came in Cuba in 1959, and in Uruguay and Chile in 1973. In none of these nations except Costa Rica, however, were voter surveys during election campaigns extensive or significant in the sense such polls are in the United States and Canada. But during each week of the 1978 Venezuelan campaign, a nationwide survey was given of the cross sections of all registered voters in every major urban area. After nine polls had pinpointed voter concerns, Garth tailored Herrera's final campaign programs accordingly. Herrera emphasized that AD, under incumbent President Pérez, had not accomplished enough with the increased government revenues resulting from the rise in world oil prices after 1973. Such revenues enabled the Pérez administration to triple government spending during the five-year term to $10.7 billion during 1978. Yet the annual inflation rate persisted at 13 percent.

Herrera's television talks bluntly reminded voters that although unemployment had dwindled among the highly skilled, within sight of the Caracas highrise skyline hundreds of thousands of peasants lived in shantytowns without running water.

Incumbent President Pérez, hoping to get his party's candidate,

Piñerua, into office, circumvented the federal law barring an incumbent chief executive from running for a second consecutive term or actively campaigning on the air. He merely engaged in the most extensive "administrative tours" in the republic's modern history, spending $15 million to contact leaders in dozens of cities in every state, having each such speech or discussion of government programs filmed or videotaped for later broadcasts.[12]

Results late in the campaign polls indicated that COPEI was ahead not only in the presidential race but also in congressional races. Thereupon, the AD resorted to announcements attempting to make candidate Herrera appear to be pro-Communist. One television spot announcement compared him to a watermelon: "Green on the outside, but red on the inside." The barb carried an extra meaning, because green is the party color of COPEI.

Herrera effectively answered that blast by stressing his career record as a firm anti-Communist liberal, citing the endorsements he received from the anti-Marxist Christian Democratic parties throughout Europe when the dictatorship had sent him into exile from 1952 to 1958.

Perhaps the most dramatic television announcement of the 1978 campaign involved bipartisan appeal of the Herrera family. Herrera pointed out that he had served a term as a senator while a COPEI member, whereas his own brother had served a term as a senator while an AD member. The presidential candidate hoped that his brother's affiliation would encourage AD members to vote a COPEI member into the presidency, and reportedly, it helped.

In November a water shortage in the Caracas metropolitan area hurt the incumbent AD government and helped COPEI challengers. Right after an AD campaign program on television, audience pollsters found large numbers of viewers irritated because the incumbent president had been claiming a rise in living standards on one of the very days bathrooms were without enough water to shower.[13]

Emphasizing the paradox of affluence among the shortages in Venezuela a few days after the December 3, 1978, election, the Associated Press reported more than 500,000 color television receivers in use, despite a government ban on the manufacture or importing of color sets. The government policy was designed to limit luxury spending as part of an antiinflation program.[14] Domestically produced television sets are black-and-white receivers, but imported models are color sets with anticolor filters technically complying with the letter of the law. In 1978 and 1979, programs were still being telecast in color without interference from the government.

Confidential News Sources

More than three out of every four Venezuelans live in cities or towns with competing local radio and television stations and network programs. Television news commentator Carlos Rangel in Caracas is almost as well known in provincial cities as are national government leaders.[15] The fact that better than eight out of every ten Venezuelan adults read and write has not kept the broadcasting media from reaching many more citizens with news than do the newspapers and magazines. This is parallel to a U.S. trend in the 1970s.

Therefore, it may have been appropriate that Venezuela's celebrated case involving confidential news sources concerned a broadcast news editor rather than a newspaper editor or reporter. Although all the media have been relatively free from government interference since 1958, in the late 1970s Caracas had a few instances of judges trying to put limits on what reporters made public about court cases that were in progress.

On August 30, 1978, José Campos Suárez, director of news for the Radio Continente network, was sentenced by a judge in Caracas to serve five days in jail for contempt of court. Campos Suárez had revealed the contents of a recording that a court considered prime evidence in the murder of attorney José Carmona Vásquez.[16] The news commentator chose the brief jail term rather than reveal to the court the confidential sources that had made the recording available.

Hundreds of listeners in Caracas and in provincial cities signed petitions, wrote letters, or made telephone calls to the network's affiliates or to the government, expressing support or sympathy for the news commentator and opposition to the court's questioning of a reporter's right to protect a news source. Many Venezuelans could remember when government censors or police, before 1958, threatened or physically abused reporters for making public stories the government wanted quashed.

Investigatory Reporting

The case of the broadcast news editor being jailed for protecting his news source does not in any way typify Venezuelan government-media relations. Throughout the 1970s, Caracas daily newspapers in particular investigated various errors or malfunctions in government agencies without any serious obstructions or penalties. And in the case of a few large robberies, reporters moved ahead of the police in tracking down culprits.

On December 27, 1978, at Bolívar International Airport in Caracas, thieves broke into a storage room of the Dutch airline KLM and stole $2 million in foreign currency, watch parts, and other valuables. The Caracas daily *El Universal* asked reporters on Christmas and New Year's vacations to voluntarily work on the case. These reporters, after a week's research, determined that the crime constituted the largest cash burglary in Venezuelan history. Newspaper staffers painstakingly pieced together, from numerous sources, the denominations of the missing currency and turned the vital data over to the police, who used the newspaper's investigations to recover some of the stolen money.[17]

Founded in 1901, *El Universal* for decades featured the essays and short stories of the nation's top writers, including novelist Rómulo Betancourt, who later became president of Venezuela. The daily introduced the political philosophy of reformer Arturo Uslar Pietri to the nation before it became a popular topic on university campuses. In 1960, under the editorship of Pascual Venegas, *El Universal* began to strengthen its investigatory prowess instead of relying mostly on its brilliant literary columnists to maintain its position as the leading newspaper in the republic.

On June 21, 1980, the Caracas television station RCT broadcast a documentary about children receiving psychiatric treatment at a government health center. The government ordered the station not to repeat the documentary because it violated the right of privacy of the young patients. The station reluctantly accepted the official view that the privacy of the individuals in the story took precedence over the right of broadcast journalists to investigate a social problem in depth.

The Challenge of *Resumen*

The most influential magazine in Venezuelan national life is *Resumen*—read by most of the leaders of both major political parties; most of the nation's newspaper, radio, and television editors and reporters; and civic leaders. The British correspondents from the weekly *Latin America Political Report,* searching for the factors that allowed the COPEI to oust the AD from power in the December 1978 elections, recognized the powerful impact of the COPEI television campaign at the popular level. But at the leadership level among those who help shape public trends, the LAPR felt that

> . . . the ferocious campaign against alleged government corruption and malpractice waged by the influential magazine *Resumen* chimed well

with (winning candidate) Herrera's promises to wield a new broom, and clearly rattled the ruling party.[18]

The last issue of *Resumen* to be circulated before the elections were held on December 3, 1978, was partially confiscated. The magazine carried charges of corruption in high government offices that outgoing incumbent President Carlos A. Pérez had failed to end. On December 4 President Pérez announced that he would file a libel suit against the publisher of *Resumen,* Jorge Olavarría.

The federal attorney general's office assumed it could confiscate all copies of that issue of the magazine until the libel litigation could be initiated. Several experts on constitutional law disputed this assumption, and some 6,000 impounded copies of *Resumen* were released after the election, but 100,000 other subscribers had already received and read their own copies. In 1979 Olavarría was exonerated.

The action by the attorney general's staff proved to be a minor exception in the general atmosphere of genuine press freedom established in Venezuela since 1958.

One case of an attempt to abridge freedom of information did occur at the end of 1977. The Communications Ministry suspended for one week the program "Renny on Your Radio" after commentator Renny Ottolina used some rude words to describe top government leaders. A similar radio talk program on a rival Caracas station picked up the controversy and broadcast the disputed words alleged to be offensive in polite circles. For that effort, the second station also received a one-week suspension for its talk show. In response to protests from the Inter-American Broadcasters Association and the Inter-American Press Association, the minister of communications claimed that the issue was not political censorship but regulations against foul language.[19]

In most other Latin American nations, suffering either governmental guidelines for the media or outright censorship, the penalties against the two radio programs and *Resumen* would not have themselves been news. But in Venezuela, striving to maintain genuine press freedom, the hint of an abridgement did itself become news.

A majority of the working editors and reporters of Venezuela's mass media seem to practice professional dedication to nonpolemic journalism. Many of them are graduates of the Central University School of Journalism, among whose professors is Héctor Múgica, who was the 1978 presidential candidate of the Venezuelan Communist party.[20] Despite his lectures of leftist advocacy journalism, most of the graduates of the Central Journalism School go on to practice nonideological journalism, with few exceptions.

Film Industry

The major motion picture industries of Latin America, producing feature-length films for theaters, center in the three largest nations, Brazil, Mexico, and Argentina. However, with the political climate of constitutional democracy, and an economy invigorated by petroleum wealth, Venezuela in 1975 began to develop a sizeable film production industry. In less than two years, studios in Caracas were completing twenty-one feature-length motion pictures annually.[21]

The government acknowledged that film production was a privately owned and privately operated industry, but the Ministry of Tourism did possess its own Bureau of Cinematography. In 1977 the Ministry of Development established its own film division, to loan $2.5 million to independent producers to encourage the growth of the industry.[22] So far, no government restrictions of film content have surfaced, the conditions for loans presumably being the marketing factors themselves.

References

Alexander, Robert J. *The Communist Party of Venezuela* (Stanford, Calif.: Hoover Institution Press, 1969).
_____. *The Venezuelan Democratic Revolution* (New Brunswick, N.J.: Rutgers University Press, 1964).
Alisky, Marvin. "Public Opinion under Dictatorship," *Nieman Reports* 16 (April 1962): 12–14.
Bell, John. "Venezuelan Elections," *Associated Press,* Dec. 10, 1978.
Bétancourt, Rómulo. *Venezuela's Oil* (London: George Allen and Unwin, 1978).
Bonilla, Frank, and José Michelana, eds. *The Politics of Change in Venezuela* (Cambridge, Mass.: MIT Press, 1967).
Dirección General de Estadística y Censos Nacionales. *Indicadores Socioeconómicos y de Coyuntura,* vol. 3 (Caracas: DGE, July 1978).
Hayes, Monte. "Venezuela: Color Its People Determined," *Arizona Republic,* Dec. 10, 1978, p. M-7.
International Monetary Fund. *International Financial Statistics* (Washington, D.C.: International Monetary Fund, 1978).
Latin America Daily Report. "Radio Continente News Director Given 5 Days," *Foreign Broadcast Information Service* 6 (Aug. 31, 1978): L-1.
Lott, Leo B. *Venezuela and Paraguay* (New York: Holt, Rinehart, and Winston, 1972).
_____. "Venezuela," in Martin C. Needler, ed., *Political Systems of Latin America,* 2nd ed. (New York: Van Nostrand Reinhold, 1970), pp. 272–98.
Martz, John D. *Acción Democrática: Evolution of a Modern Political Party in Venezuela* (Princeton, N.J.: Princeton University Press, 1966).
Ministerio de Hacienda. "Introducción," *Memoria* (Caracas: Ministerio de Hacienda, April 1978), pp. 2–17.
Needler, Martin C., ed. *Political Systems of Latin America,* 2nd ed. (New York: Van Nostrand Reinhold, 1970).
Penzini Fleury, Pedro. "Peligro: Radio," *El Nacional,* Dec. 23, 1977, pp. 1, 7.
Saleta, Marianela. "Venezuela Cinema Digging into Government," *Variety,* Apr. 6, 1977, pp. 66–67.

_____. "Venezuela's Film Policy," *Variety,* Apr. 6, 1977, p. 66.

_____. "Venezuela's Well-Oiled Democracy: Film Production Industry," *Variety,* Apr. 6, 1977, pp. 64–66.

Tad Szulc. News correspondent, *New York Times;* correspondence to Marvin Alisky, January 2, 1959.

Washington Post correspondents. "Latin Americans Flocking to Miami on Spending Spree," *Arizona Republic,* Dec. 17, 1978, p. C-31.

Newspapers and Periodicals: *Arizona Republic; El Nacional,* Caracas; *El Universal,* Caracas; *Latin America Political Report,* London; *New York Times; San Francisco Chronicle; Time; Times of the Americas,* Washington, D.C.

7

Colombia: Class Publications and Mass Broadcasting

LIKE its neighbor Venezuela, Colombia enjoys a constitutional democracy with two major competing political parties and genuine freedom of the press. From the beginning of its independence as a republic through the remainder of the nineteenth century, Colombia suffered periodical violence in its political system, with arbitrary presidents often resorting to press censorship. From 1899 to 1902 a civil war between the Conservative and Liberal parties ended in a negotiated peace, marking the beginning of forty-five years of relative political peace. Localized violence did recur at election time, and following the transfer of power from a Conservative to a Liberal administration in 1930, extensive rural violence erupted briefly. However, no forcible overthrow of the government occurred from 1902 to 1948, and peaceful transfer of power between the two traditional parties took place twice, in 1930 and in 1946, as the result of free elections.[1]

Colombia became an aristocrat-led republic in the style of Athens, in which Liberals and Conservatives quarreled over the separation of church and state and the place of the Catholic church in politics and in national life more than about economic issues.[2] The challenge of modernization grew slowly. From 1948 to 1957 a disastrous decade of civil war included the dictatorship of General Gustavo Rojas Pinilla, 1953–1957, with its strict censorship of the press and broadcasting.

Since 1957, however, Colombia's modernizing elite leadership has broadened the political base while adhering to public discussion and debate, flexibility of action, and a system of mass media that remains independent of the government.[3]

The Setting

In recent decades, the death rate has plunged because of disease control while the birth rate has remained high, giving Colombia an annual increase in population of 3.2 percent. In less than twenty-five years, the population doubled, and only in the 1970s was the yearly net increase reduced to 2.9 percent, through vigorous private efforts to promote family planning. In 1977 the population totaled 24.5 million—putting Colombia in fourth place among Latin American republics, and in a position to overtake third-place Argentina in the early 1980s.[4]

Half the population lives in cities with more than 20,000 inhabitants, with migration to the cities proceeding in steps, from rural areas to small towns to larger cities. Thus the rapid urbanization in Colombia has been widely distributed across the country.[5] The greater metropolitan area of the capital, Bogotá, with its 3 million inhabitants, is followed by the largest provincial city, Medellín, with 1.5 million.

Approximately two-thirds of all Colombians are *mestizos,* with less than one-fifth the population being European ethnically, with smaller groups of mulattoes and Indians. The poorest 40 percent of the population remains illiterate, living predominantly in rural areas beyond modern education and good land transportation.[6]

In 1970 the wealthiest 20 percent of the population received 61 percent of the national income, with the poorest 40 percent receiving only 9 percent. Only 20 percent of the population over seven years of age had completed primary school but another 40 percent of the people had attained functional literacy.

The national territory covers 440,000 square miles, which equals the combined areas of France, Spain, and Portugal, or a combined Texas and California. But the rugged terrain divides into mountainous regions and the plains, with Colombians concentrating their cities and towns at the higher altitudes, leaving two-thirds of the national territory relatively empty.

Colombia's upper and middle classes buy most of the 1.6 million daily newspapers circulated, whereas the 5 million radios in daily use, especially the tiny transistors, are distributed throughout the population.[7] The 1.9 million television receivers are found mainly in city households and public gathering sites.

The Parties and the Press

Two major parties, the Liberal and the Conservative, have long dominated the political system of Colombia. Each party, however, in various time periods, has developed militant and moderate wings.

In the 1930s and 1940s, the publisher of Colombia's leading newspaper, *El Tiempo,* Eduardo Santos, led the moderate wing of the Liberal party. His newspaper gave both news and editorial space to both factions of that party, and less space and emphasis to the Conservative party.

Alfonso López, as president of the republic from 1934 to 1938 and leader of the progressive wing of the Liberal party, attempted reforms to bring welfare benefits to the working class. *El Tiempo* chronicled all the government actions and debates, but also featured ideas from the Employers National Economic Association on the need to expand business.[8]

Newspaper publisher Santos then was elected as the Liberal party candidate and served as president of Colombia from 1938 to 1942. The constitution prohibits two successive terms by the same chief executive. To further his 1942 campaign and to promote reform measures in the Congress, López in 1938 established his own Bogotá daily newspaper, *El Liberal,* which was published successfully until 1951, when heavy advertising revenue losses curtailed its operations.[9] López did win a second term in 1942, but ill health forced his resignation in 1945.

El Tiempo, not only in the 1940s but continuing throughout the 1970s, stressed editorially Liberal party pledges for individual political freedoms and economic development that encompassed both the private sector and some government investment.

Still another newspaper publisher went on to become president of Colombia. Laureano Gómez, leader of the right wing of the Conservative party, established the Bogotá daily *El Siglo* in 1936. From the late 1930s through the 1940s, Gómez had *Siglo* editorially oppose all social reforms, and until Colombia joined the Allies in declaring war on Germany in 1943, its editorials also expressed sympathy for Franco in Spain and fascist ideas. Since the 1960s, *El Siglo* has become more moderate or temperate in its editorials. Like its rival *El Tiempo,* today *El Siglo* still serves not only a readership in the capital but also its party leaders in key provincial cities. Gómez was elected president of Colombia for the 1950–1954 term but a military coup by General Rojas Pinilla ousted him in June 1953.

Mariano Ospina, president of Colombia from 1946 to 1949 and a Conservative party leader, had the support of the Bogotá daily *La República* and the daily *El Colombiano* in the largest provincial city, Medellín.

Liberal party leaders, Alberto Lleras Camargo, president of
Colombia from 1958 to 1962, and his cousin, Carlos Lleras Restrepo,
president of Colombia from 1966 to 1970, were involved in various professional and financial activities. But they were also journalists writing
for the Liberal party newspapers and for magazines, including the internationally circulated news periodical *Visión*.

Laureano's Editorial Intemperance

From 1938 through the 1940s, the editorial debates between *El
Tiempo* and *El Liberal* not only factionalized the Liberal party, but also
encouraged Laureano Gómez to attack both factions in his paper, *El
Siglo*.[10] Journalists and politicians following his lead took their label
from his first name and became Laureanistas.

From 1937 to 1943, *Siglo's* editorials shifted from conservative to
reactionary. Editor José de la Vega began to emphasize news stories
that paralleled the Gómez editorials.

Francisco Franco's Spain became a Laureanista model, and the
many moderate Conservatives had to wait for this phase to pass. One
1940 editorial in *El Siglo* asserted:

> We were born Spanish. The twenty cowardly governments of Latin
> America have put themselves into the hands of masonic, atheistic
> democracy. Each day the yoke of Anglo-Saxon Americana is drawn
> tighter around our throats. Sometimes the yoke is of steel, sometimes of
> silk . . .
>
> But all is not lost. There is still heard the voice of Laureano Gómez to
> tell the truth about the future, to direct us to the road of tomorrow, the
> Catholic Hispanic Empire.
>
> And we will go back to Spain. The five arrows of Ferdinand and
> Isabella, the symbol of Catholic unity, will be our symbol also . . .[11]

In 1943 a political scandal hurt the Liberal party, giving *El Siglo* an
opportunity to launch an inflammatory editorial campaign. The scandal arose when a prizefighter was knifed to death in a Bogotá park. He
had published a radical weekly newspaper called *La Voz del Pueblo*. A
police official confessed to the killing and linked some Liberal party
members to the plot to eliminate the radical leftist journalist. Even
though Gómez himself opposed all leftists, his newspaper took up the
case and made unsubstantiated editorial charges, such as the accusation that the minister of the Interior of the López cabinet had known
about the murder but had tried to block the investigation. Before

Siglo's editorial campaign ended, it had provoked rioting in the streets.[12] In some editorials in *El Siglo,* the leftist fighter had even been identified as a Conservative party member without later corrections being made.

Despite such intemperate and irresponsible journalism on the part of Laureanista writers, the government of President López never even contemplated any pressures or any tampering with Colombia's traditional press freedom. From 1937 through 1943, Gómez had *El Siglo* editorials continue to hold up Franco's Spain as the model defender of Hispanic Christian civilization without many angry replies from other Conservative or from the Liberal party papers.[13] In fact, during the 1946 campaign that resulted in Conservative party candidate Ospina winning the presidency, the Liberal daily *El Tiempo* and the Conservative daily *La República* both reported on some of the major issues with professional restraint.

The 1948 Riots or "Bogotazo"

Extensive bloodshed and property damage from riots in April 1948, with extremists capturing radio stations to announce fictional attacks, strained the dedication to constitutional government on the part of the Ospina administration. But the government did not resort to censorship of the mass media.

The riots themselves put a new word in the Colombian political dictionary, a "bogotazo" or rioting of massive proportions and gigantic destruction.

Jorge Gaitán—a law professor, social reformer, and leader of the left wing of the Liberal party—was a spellbinding orator who had built up a large following among peasant farmers and urban workers. With the victory of the Conservative party in the 1946 elections, Gaitán shifted from being leader of the underprivileged to supporter of the entire Liberal party, trying to encourage both progressives and moderates within his party not to take positions in the Ospina administration.[14]

President Ospina's job became even more difficult when Gómez was able to increase the Laureanista dominance within the chief executive's own Conservative party. Even before the April 1948 assassination of Gaitán, banditry and numerous outbreaks of violence erupted in several parts of the hinterland.

Gaitán's charismatic oratory had aroused the masses against the elite leadership of both parties for the first time in Colombian history. The republic may have been closer to a prerevolutionary situation from 1946 to 1948 than it had ever been before. Gaitán's assassination not only ignited the "bogotazo" but also engendered a Liberal-Conservative civil war in the countryside, which erupted on and off until 1957.

On April 9, 1948, the twenty-one republics of the Western Hemisphere assembled in Bogotá for the Ninth Inter-American Conference. Two blocks away, in the early afternoon, Gaitán left his office and walked through a plaza, where a gunman, later identified as a mystic named Juan Roa, shot him. As Gaitán slumped to the sidewalk, an outraged mob kicked the killer to death, preventing subsequent investigation about conspiracy.

By word of mouth all over Bogotá, rumors spread that Laureano Gómez, object of hate of the Liberals, had ordered the killing of their party leader. A crowd pushed guards aside in the Capitol and destroyed furniture, records, paintings, and then set the building on fire. Looting and gunfire soon spread to the other government buildings and to private offices.

After the announcement came that Gaitán had died, howling mobs broke into hardware, liquor, and other retail stores, then raced through the streets with dynamite, machetes, torches, and guns.[15]

Dynamite destroyed Gómez's newspaper, *El Siglo,* which burned to the ground. Later its entire plant and press had to be replaced before the daily could resume publishing.

Radical agitators seized the *Radio Nacional* and broadcast fictional reports that priests and bishops were commanding troops from the churches and ordering the troops to fire on the protesting mobs. The rioting, burning, and shooting had begun on a Friday afternoon. By Saturday evening, Bogotá, according to foreign correspondents covering the Inter-American Conference, looked like London's destruction after the Nazi blitz during World War II.[16] Forty-seven buildings had been burned to the ground and dozens of others severely damaged. Some historic churches and museums had also been either destroyed or damaged. Some 2,000 bodies were stacked in morgues or remained in the streets awaiting disposal. Hundreds of others remained missing.

Later that month, Enrique Santos, political writer and editor for *El Tiempo,* and the brother of former President and publisher Eduardo Santos, summed up the tragedy:

> Jorge E. Gaitán was the first and most illustrious victim of the Communist Politburo's policy. . . . The unchained multitudes, mad with grief

and rage, might have limited themselves to protests but never would have thrown themselves into the destruction of stores, sacking . . . demolishing the pride of the city . . . looting the Colonial Museum where mementos of Bolívar are kept. . . . Anyone who observed them, saw in Bogotá the functioning of the classical Communist action plan. They seized the radio stations, spread terror, directed teams of dynamiters, incendiarists and looters. To spread terror, to create panic, are fundamentals of the Communist offensive strategy. . . . Why throw workers and modest employees out of work? Because all of this enters into the Communist plan: creation of desperation, or disorientation . . .

On the radio we heard them urging on the incendiarists. And we saw them at the head of the mobs which set the torch to the government palace . . . the jails were thrown open, bringing 6,000 more malefactors into the wild melee and the wild hordes.

Is it possible to doubt the Communist direction of the uprising? Whoever listened on the radio would have been sufficiently convinced. They had everything ready and were prepared. They called over the radio to cities and towns, to specific individuals in those places to whom they gave specific orders and directions; and on the radio appeared the name of the mysterious "Doctor X," as head of the operation.[17]

The Santos report came after most of the Liberal party and Conservative party leaders had investigated the tragedy and had conferred as separate groups and together. To bind the wounds of the nation, leaders of both parties pushed the government into hiring Scotland Yard detectives from London to sift through all the evidence.[18] Laureano Gómez had certainly been intemperate in his editorials. And no detailed probe ever fully linked the assassin Juan Roa to any specific group. But the wholesale and widespread carnage and destruction had gone beyond any likely spontaneity. Many of the building-burnings and attacks on the churches had been orchestrated and rehearsed and certainly did not come from Catholic-oriented Liberal or Conservative Colombians. All the mass media investigated thoroughly and most of the reports tended to agree with the Santos summary.

United States Secretary of State George C. Marshall, representing the United States at the Inter-American Conference, called the *bogotazo* a Communist operation.[19]

Reporters for United Press, International News Service, and Reuters reported that Communist agents had directed the attacks on the churches. Given Colombia's Catholic traditions, such attacks were without precedence. In Barranquilla, priests were beaten and dragged through the streets and stoned to death. In some provincial cities, convents were burned to the ground and some nuns were insulted verbally.

Julio Hernández, editor of *El Colombiano* of Medellín, the most prominent of the provincial newspapers, reported:

> Without doubt, the Communists were the instigators and organizers of the rioting mobs . . . agents coming from Cuba, Chile, Mexico, to take a genuinely frustrating situation which justified deep anger . . . to try to start a revolution which would overthrow constitutional government and destroy both traditional parties.[20]

With the help of President Ospina, and the leaders of both the Conservative and Liberal parties, the editors of *El Colombiano* purchased from the assistant to Guatemalan diplomat Luis Cardoza, a letter the Guatemalan had received from Blas Roca, of the Communist party of Cuba. Cardoza was a leader of the Guatemalan Labor party, the name the Communist party of his country had taken at the time. The Medellín newspaper published the letter in June 1948, along with evidence of its authenticity.[21]

In the letter published in *El Colombiano,* Roca said that Latin American Communist parties wanted the Inter-American Conference wrecked and the Colombian establishment discredited. The letter was dated April 4, 1948. Roca stated: "We have entered upon the month of trial, the period of our plans. If luck is with us, we will triumph." The Roca message was on stationery with a letterhead of the University Students Federation (Federación Estudiantil Universitaria) of the University of Havana, where Roca, at the time, maintained the headquarters of the Communist party of Cuba.

In the Liberal Bogotá daily *El Espectador,* in July 1948, the head of the Bogotá Stock Exchange, Gonzálo Restrepo, stressed the economic and social problems that had engendered the widespread discontent and frustration upon which the riot instigators had depended. He stated: "Economic causes helped create a situation favorable to insurgency and to directing it towards abnormal goals."[22]

As bitterness over the rioting lingered in memories, outbursts of violence recurred between Conservatives and Liberals, between splinter groups, and between feuding families and communities periodically caught up in the general negative atmosphere until 1957, with 200,000 killed during the years of the era of *violencia.*[23]

Despite the civil warfare in the countryside, the Colombian mass media managed to remain free of government censorship until 1952, when Laureano Gómez began preventing by force the publishing of stories about the sporadic violence. The president's police and civilian agents intervened in August 1952 at *El Tiempo* and *El Espectador* and then at the other dailies and broadcasting stations, ignoring the protests of the Inter-American Press Association.

The Dictatorship

For most of this century, Colombia's government has managed to remain popularly elected and constitutional. However, the violence of the 1948–1953 period, with the underlying stresses of economic problems, did give Colombia a full-fledged dictatorship before constitutional government was restored.

In November 1949 the militant Laureano Gómez, as candidate of the Conservative party, was elected president of Colombia for the 1950–1954 term. His administration worked against organized labor's independent Federation of Labor of Colombia and tried to build up a rival federation under Jesuit auspices to strengthen the position of management in strikes and contract disputes. Gómez began pressuring Congress for decree powers to meet economic problems; another Laureanista proposal favored censoring radio news. A majority of the deputies and senators postponed or rejected such measures.[24]

In 1953 Gómez directed the drafting of a new constitution based on corporative, fascistic principles. That arrogant move, coupled with the lingering violent outbursts in the countryside, prompted military leaders under General Gustavo Rojas Pinilla to intervene in a bloodless coup.

On June 13, 1953, the armed forces ousted Gómez and his entire administration, and installed Rojas Pinilla as president of Colombia. With civilian political and government activities now under military direction, civil liberties were suspended. This misfortune had happened many times in most other Latin American republics but was a rarity for Colombia.

The ideology of the Rojas Pinilla government remained vague except for its programs to reduce and eventually end the strife and violence between Liberals and Conservatives throughout the countryside. The army did round up guerrilla bands and disarm thousands of peasants throughout rural Colombia.

Rojas Pinilla created a National Press Directorate (Directorio Nacional de Prensa or DINAPE). For the first time in many decades, Colombian newspaper editors and broadcasters found censors from the DINAPE entering their offices to prevent the publication of news stories that might threaten the dictatorship. In addition to prohibiting certain stories, DINAPE demanded that other reports be published or aired as top priority news and even furnished photographs to the newspapers and magazines. At the time, Colombia had only one television station airing news, but every radio station and network had a government agent assigned to direct the newscasts.

The cabinet ministries and other government entities, as sources of the official news that constituted the most important stories of the day, had orders to use caution. Inasmuch as the newspapers and broadcasting stations had been brought under DINAPE control against their will, management of official news sources became especially important in shaping and controlling each day's budget of national news.[25]

In August 1955 the nation's leading newspaper, *El Tiempo,* was ordered closed down for allegedly insulting President Rojas Pinilla in various news stories.[26] Despite such vague charges, the newspaper had to suspend operations. Rojas Pinilla did not want the international uproar that Juan Perón had encountered when he closed the world famous Buenos Aires daily, *La Prensa.* As journalism professor John C. Merrill of Louisiana State University has pointed out, various surveys of media experts in the 1960s found *El Tiempo* to be one of the best edited and journalistically professional daily newspapers in the world.[27] *El Tiempo's* forty to sixty pages included news from around the world, reports on economics, science, music, theater, film, sports, book reviews, and on Sunday, literary essays and supplements. So the government worked out a compromise to let the Santos family reopen the newspaper. The professional staff and the publisher, however, did not want to use the proud name of *Tiempo* as long as censorship prevailed, so that newspaper was allowed to resume publication in 1956 under the name *Intermedio.*

Intermedio continued to publish until the Rojas Pinilla regime was ousted by a coup in May 1957, when the newspaper again resumed its honored name of *El Tiempo.* False tax claims that Rojas Pinilla had made against the paper were dropped after his ouster.

In August 1953, *El Siglo* ran an editorial criticizing the Rojas Pinilla government, whereupon Minister of the Interior Lucio Pabón Núñez in a nationwide radio broadcast attacked the newspaper for not cooperating with the government and for being irresponsible. When *Siglo* did not run the minister's attack in full text in a prominent place, the daily was suspended until August 22, when it did give its front page to the minister's speech.[28]

In his radio broadcast, the Interior Minister had warned:

> Since press censorship exists in Colombia, its function is not only to forbid but also to indicate to the newspapers the form in which to conduct themselves with the state. . . . The speech of the Minister of the Interior must be published with the same typographical display used in publishing the . . . message of the former president . . . as a rectification of charges made there.[29]

Later in the year, when *El Siglo* published another critical comment, it received a thirty-day suspension. For failure to print government analyses of the national trends, *El Colombiano* in Medellín and *El Liberal* of Popayán received periods of suspension.

On March 6, 1954, a presidential decree ordered all newspapers not to insult government authorities. Even stating "it is rumored" would question the authority of officials. Conviction could bring up to two years in prison and fines up to 50,000 pesos.[30]

One week later the Bogotá weekly *La Unidad* published a politician's charge that the Rojas Pinilla regime was unconstitutional, whereupon the government closed down the periodical under the anti-insulting decree. Thus, by the time *El Tiempo* was closed in 1955, both Liberal and Conservative publications of lesser status had been suspended, fined, or closed over a two-year period.

In March 1955 a presidential decree ordered all radio stations in Colombia, most of whom were privately owned, to provide free air time for government news programs whenever they might be scheduled.[31]

During 1955 *La República* of Bogotá received a suspension for reporting on an insurrection in Tolima and *El Litoral* in Barranquilla was similarly suspended, and *El Crisol* in Cali was heavily fined.[32]

A presidential decree of August 23, 1955, created the National Publications Enterprise (Empresa Nacional de Publicaciones or ENP) to control the importing of newsprint needed by newspapers and magazines. Periodicals that cooperated with the government could buy newsprint at the official rate of 2.50 pesos to the dollar, but those without government permits had to buy newsprint at 4 pesos to the dollar plus a 30 percent tax. As a result, the Liberal *El Espectador* dropped its Sunday edition and the Conservative *El Diario* reduced the number of pages of each edition.[33]

The Inter-American Press Association and the leading dailies of the hemisphere that belong to the IAPA condemned the Colombian government's action. Rojas Pinilla reacted by issuing a new decree forbidding the publication of any news disrespectful to the president. At that time, in addition to DINAPE, press censorship had been coming from the Office of Information and Propaganda, assisted by the Colombian Intelligence Service. Now the ENP newsprint office, directed by General Rafael Calderón, also issued censorship orders.[34]

In August 1956 the government took its Ministry of the Interior journal that published laws and regulations, the *Diario Oficial,* and added regular pages of news. The government then began circulating it as a newspaper to the public. After the fall of the dictatorship, the *DO* returned to its status as a legal journal.

Rojas Pinilla hoped to end or reduce criticism from foreign nations by allowing suspended newspapers to reappear. *El Tiempo* temporarily reappeared with the name *El Intermedio.* Also in 1956 *El Espectador* resumed publishing under the name *El Independiente* and *El Diario* resumed as *Información.*

A group of journalists connected with the dictatorship established a National Press Federation, secretly tied to personnel in DINAPE, to "cooperate" with the government in solving national problems.

Encouraged and supported by civilians from every walk of life, the armed forces staged a coup on May 10, 1957, and ousted the Rojas Pinilla dictatorship. On May 15 the governing junta announced the abolishment of all censorship of press and broadcasting, the elimination of the DINAPE, and equal treatment in releasing news about the government to all mass media.[35]

The Liberal and Conservative parties could function freely again, and a campaign and election in 1958 restored constitutional democracy to Colombia.

National Front

Radio Bucaramanga, Radio Cauca, Voz de Medellín, and stations in Antioquia and throughout the republic began airing complete news roundups from whatever uncensored newspapers or news agency reports they could obtain or buy during 1958. With a return to press freedom, provincial Colombians who previously had not purchased radios began buying them. Radio listening grew substantially.

In an attempt to avoid the violence between Conservatives and Liberals that had cost lives and had given Rojas Pinilla an excuse for establishing a dictatorship, leaders of the two traditional parties in 1957 signed an agreement to adhere to a National Front. In a plebiscite, voters overwhelmingly endorsed constitutional amendments that created a system of sharing the government from 1958 to 1974, a period of sixteen years.

Under the National Front plan, the Liberal and Conservative parties alternated in the presidency every four years, and each party received half the seats in the Congress and in the Municipal Councils. Liberal President Alberto Lleras Camargo (1958–1962) was followed by Conservative President Guillermo Valencia (1962–1966), then by Liberal President Carlos Lleras Restrepo (1966–1970), then by Conservative President Misael Pastrana (1970–1974).

The necessity of securing bipartisan agreement on policies led to occasional stalemates and the creation of the anti-National Front third party, the National Popular Alliance (ANAPO), supported by former dictator Rojas Pinilla. ANAPO's campaigning in the 1970 and 1974 elections proved that traditional Colombian tolerance for and understanding of dissident opinions and a free press and broadcasting system were firmly rooted in the national culture.

In January 1961 Laureano Gómez blasted the National Front, stating in the Cali newspaper *La Unidad* that Colombia had fallen into moral decay by the Liberal-Conservative cooperation.[36] Similar editorial criticism from ANAPO spokesmen up to the 1974 election drew no pressures from the governments involved.

From the Marxist left the National Front was challenged by the National Liberation Army (Ejército de Liberación Nacional or ELN), a guerrilla group established in July 1964. Camilo Torres gave up the orders of priesthood to join the ELN in 1965 and arranged to circulate news of the organization around the world through the New China News Agency of the People's Republic in Peking.[37]

The Cuban news agency, Prensa Latina, throughout the late 1960s ran stories of the activities of the ELN, of the United Front for Revolutionary Action, the Colombian Communist party, and other leftist groups. It remained, however, for the Bogotá dailies to put the guerrilla violence into the perspective of attacking National Front efforts to restore constitutional democracy. *El Tiempo, La República, El Espectador,* and *El Siglo* each interviewed numerous former guerrillas who had returned to the mainstream of public life, to give readers from both major parties that perspective.[38]

After serving as president of Colombia from 1958 to 1962, Alberto Lleras Camargo became chairman of the board of the international weekly news magazine, *Visión,* which maintains offices in Bogotá, New York, Mexico City, and Buenos Aires. *Visión* encouraged Colombian news magazines, such as *Semana,* to remain nonpartisan rather than report from the editorial stance of either the Liberal or the Conservative party. *Visión* had been founded in 1950 to give Latin America a nonpartisan Spanish-language news magazine. Well into 1978 Lleras Camargo directly contributed to its editorials and to the formulating of its policies and coverage.

Mass Broadcasting

Although some newspapers—*El Crisol* in Cali, *Diario* in Cucuta, *El Correo* in Medellín, *El Heraldo* in Barranquilla—have become independent or nonpartisan, the Bogotá dailies have been affiliated with either the Liberal or Conservative party and have had the leadership elite and upper middle class as core readerships.

Contrasting with this trend for the press to be class media, radio and television stations have now developed as nonparty mass media.

The twenty-nine television stations grouped into two video networks serving the republic are government owned. These stations do sell commercial time to earn advertising income. Broadcasting regulations prohibit politically partisan commentary and give an agency of the Ministry of Communications supervisory authority over news programs.[39]

The government operates its own *Radio Nacional* stations in Bogotá and in the principal provincial cities. The telecommunications law requires RN news programs to be nonpartisan.

Of the 380 commercial radio stations in Colombia in 1978, 280 of them aired daily news programs.[40] In every basic listening area of the republic, one of these stations has affiliated with the *Radio Cadena Nacional* (National Radio Network). RCN audiences receive newscasts at various times of the day from headquarters in both Bogotá and in Medellín. Network commercials for nationwide audiences encourage local stations to be nonpartisan.

Since 1949, through a Catholic organization, radio has been a vital means of education in rural Colombia. In that year in provincial Sutatenza, a young priest, Joaquín Salcedo, established his first full-time educational radio station.[41] *Radio Sutatenza* began teaching reading, writing, and basic arithmetic on a daily basis. And in dozens of villages and small towns, group leaders would help adult and young audiences alike follow the broadcast lessons.

The bishop of Tunja began working with laical fund raisers and broadcasters in Tunja and in Bogotá, and soon the movement Popular Cultural Action (Acción Cultural Popular or ACP) was incorporated as a nonprofit foundation with contributors and supporters from throughout the republic. In 1953 the Ministry of Education officially accredited the radio classes of the *Radio Sutatenza* network. A new 25,000-watt transmitter carried public health, vocational, and literacy courses for six hours each day, plus news and music and dramatic offerings.

In the 1960s, eight other 10,000-watt transmitters in key locations throughout the republic expanded the *Radio Sutatenza* network.

From 1954 through 1960, some 154,000 Colombians completed the sixth-grade equivalent reading tests based on the radio lessons. In 1962 classes were meeting in 891 municipalities throughout Colombia for the radio lessons in literacy, hygiene, and basic trades.[42] By then, 220,000 Colombians each year registered for one or more series aired on *Radio Sutatenza.*

Popular Cultural Action began giving away 43,000 transistor radios per year, each of them constructed so that they only could tune in the stations with frequencies of the *Radio Sutatenza* network. In addition, every three years some 100,000 all-channel transistors have been sold at cost by the ACP.[43]

Geography, history, and civics courses were added at certain hours during most of the 1970s, and proved to be almost as popular as the longtime series on land use and crop cultivation. With the addition of courses on nutrition, recreation and housing repair, by 1978 more than 500,000 rural Colombians were listening to *Radio Sutatenza* stations each day or evening. On a once-a-week contact, in recent years, as many as 3 million rural listeners in groups have been reached by one or more *Sutatenza* programs.[44] Lesson plans and self-help booklets coordinate with various radio series ranging from carpentry to auto mechanics fundamentals.

At the end of his term, on July 3, 1970, President Carlos Lleras Restrepo agreed with the Congress that a government information officer, Eduardo Camargo Gámez, could edit out of radio news programs congressional testimony from closed hearings and confidential reports. Somehow such reports were being regularly broadcast by *Radio Sultana* in Cali. When station manager Hugo Velasco refused to stop airing these reports, on July 23, the station received a suspension from the Ministry of Communications for several weeks.[45]

In December 1970, Channel 7 in Bogotá, and video Network One, aired a series of debates that Colombian army troops while policing remote jungle areas had mistreated Indians in the eastern region. Father Gustavo Pérez, a sociologist who headed the Institute of Social Development, debated Colonel Juan Rodríguez, commander of the brigade that patrolled the eastern jungles. No government action resulted against either the army or the television officials who aired the controversy but the public affairs series did emphasize that considerable freedom existed in broadcast information programs.[46]

In 1971 the Congress enacted legislation so that the Ministry of Communications would have an agency, the National Institute of Radio and Television, to oversee the programming content of broadcasting in Colombia, to prevent obscene or libelous materials, and to enforce restrictions on advertising harmful to health. Luis Eduardo Fonseca, director of the Institute, banned cigarette advertising on television before 9:30 P.M.[47]

The National Front's alternating of the presidency with two Conservative and two Liberal chief executives during the 1958–1974 period ended with the term of Conservative President Misael Pastrana in 1974. Since then two more Liberals were elected in 1974 and 1978. President Alfonso López-Michelsen in 1975 became the first of these chief executives to threaten radio with censorship.

On November 7, 1975, a general transportation strike of bus and train employees stranded Colombians in the major cities. As radio stations in the capital and the major provincial cities continued to report in detail the clashes between strikers and the army and police, President López-Michelsen announced he was ready to decree a state of siege and to suspend any radio stations continuing to broadcast commentaries or reports that encouraged a breakdown of law and order.[48]

The Association of Broadcasters offered its services to solve the crisis and the radio stations engaged in self-restraint, avoiding the possibility of suspensions or even expropriations. The crisis ended before any such threats could materialize.

Julio César Turbay was inaugurated as president of Colombia on August 7, 1978, for a four-year term. His only broadcasting policy was to urge that more funds be appropriated for educational radio and television programs.

On January 12, 1979, Minister of Communications José Arias Carrizosa announced that cultural programs would be expanded and that new repeater transmitters guaranteed that almost the entire nation would be within range of reception for the two television networks.[49]

The Communications Ministry's Institute of Radio and Television, known as Inravisión, directed by Germán Vargas, also on January 12, 1979, announced that the two television networks and their principal anchor stations, Channels 7 and 9 in Bogotá, would receive news and information programs that would be nonpartisan and balanced as to interests among the general public.[50]

Whereas the newspapers of Colombia remain free of government, television news does have a degree of governmental guidance.

Temporary Censorship Lifted

In 1978 and early 1979, a presidential decree authorized the Minister of Communications to prohibit radio and television news about far-left guerrilla attacks on provincial government sites. On February 10, 1979, the government ended the emergency security statute against airing such news after the army and the police reported the restoration of order in the countryside.[51] During 1980 radio and television stations freely reported on the government's difficulty in fighting narcotics smugglers.

References

Arciniegas, Germán. *The State of Latin America* (New York: Alfred A. Knopf, 1952).
Associated Press correspondents. "Secretary of State George Marshall at Inter-American Conference," *Associated Press*, Apr. 13, 1948.
Azula Barrera, Rafael. *De la Revolución al Orden Nuevo* (Bogotá: Editorial Kelly, 1956).
Belnap, David F. "Colombia Regains Press Freedom," *Editor & Publisher* 90 (May 25, 1957): 11, 90.
Bernstein, Harry. *Venezuela and Colombia* (Englewood Cliffs, N.J.: Prentice-Hall, 1964).
Carty, James W., Jr. "Colombia's El Campesino," *Grassroots Editor* 8 (September–October 1967): 20–21.
Dix, Robert H. *Colombia: The Political Dimensions of Change* (New Haven: Yale University Press, 1967).
Editor and Publisher, eds. *Editor and Publisher International Yearbook 1978* (New York: Editor & Publisher, 1978), pp. III 42–43.
Fluharty, Vernon L. *Dance of the Millions: Military Rule and Social Revolution in Colombia, 1930–1956* (Pittsburgh, Pa.: University of Pittsburgh Press, 1957).
Latin America Daily Report. "Government Lifts News Broadcasting Restrictions," *Foreign Broadcast Information Service* 6 (Feb. 12, 1979): F-3.
Lleras, Alberto. "Rojas Pinilla y la Libertad de Prensa," *Visión*, Oct. 14, 1955, p. 14.
MacDonald, Austin F. *Latin American Politics and Government* (New York: Thomas Y. Crowell, 1949).
Martz, John D. *Colombia: A Contemporary Survey* (Chapel Hill, N.C.: University of North Carolina Press, 1962).
Maullin, Richard. *Soldiers, Guerrillas, and Politics in Colombia* (Lexington, Mass.: Lexington Books, 1973).
Merrill, John C. *The Elite Press: Great Newspapers of the World* (New York: Pitman, 1968).
Ministerio de Comunicaciones. *Memoria al Congreso Nacional 1978* (Bogotá: Congreso Nacional, 1978).
Ministerio de Relaciones Exteriores. "Colombia Basic Data," *Colombia Today* 13, no. 10 (1978): 6.
———. "Colombia Pioneers in the Use of Radio for Rural Education," *Colombia Today* 5 (July 1970): 4.
Scully, Michael. "Adventure in Inspiration," *Reader's Digest* 64 (September 1954): 25–28.
United Press International, eds. "López-Michelsen: Estricta Censura a la Radio," *Diario de las Américas*, Nov. 8, 1975, p. 1.
———. "Radio Sultana," *United Press International*, July 25, 1970.
Zschock, Dieter K. "Inequality in Colombia," *Current History* 72 (February 1977): 68–69.

Newspapers and Periodicals: *Chicago Tribune; El Colombiano,* Medellín; *El Espectador,* Bogotá; *El Siglo,* Bogotá; *El Tiempo,* Bogotá; *La Prensa,* Buenos Aires, Argentina; *La República,* Bogotá; *La Unidad,* Bogotá; *New York Times; Semana,* Bogotá; *Times of London,* London; *Times of the Americas,* Washington, D.C.

Nations with Censorship

BEFORE the 1970s, Uruguay and Chile were among the minority of Latin American republics with genuine press freedom, but they now suffer severe censorship. Since 1976 Argentina's military government has imposed strict censorship on all mass media.

Cuba, with an institutionalized Communist government, does not allow rival political points of view nor any serious criticism of the government or the Communist party, following the views of Lenin that the mass media should be arms of the government in building a Marxist state.

Guatemala, El Salvador, Honduras, Nicaragua, and Panama all suffer government press censorship. In addition, in the Caribbean, the republic of Haiti has had press censorship for almost all of its existence as an independent nation. In South America censorship has remained unbroken and unchallenged in Paraguay since the beginning of the era of General Stroessner in 1954. Given the efforts of the military governments of Ecuador and Bolivia in 1979 to try to revive elected civilian governments, hope continues for ending or reducing censorship in those republics in the 1980s.

8

Cuba: Conformity and Communism

WITH the promulgation of a constitution in 1975, Fidel Castro formally completed the institutionalization of a Communist government in Cuba, and explained to foreign correspondents that no rival political parties, ideologies, or media criticism would be allowed to undermine the Marxist state.

As scholars Jorge I. Domínguez, Edward González, Maurice Halperin, and Jaime Suchlicki have observed, the Communist Party of Cuba (Partido Comunista de Cuba or PCC) remains the dominant power in Cuban public life, more so than the structure of government, which, as in the Soviet Union, carries out the policies formulated by the PCC.[1] Therefore, the mass medium setting the standards for reporting and commentary for all other Cuban media, the Havana daily *Granma,* appropriately enough, is the official organ, not of the government but of the PCC. The two television networks, each anchored in a Havana station, and the three radio networks are owned and operated by the government's Cuban Institute of Radio and Television.

Radio Havana operates a domestic standard-band service and an international shortwave service. *Radio Reloj* provides multi-interest programming, with the Havana station coordinating what provincial stations air for regional audiences, such as *Radio Oriente,* which serves the five provinces that formerly made up Oriente Province.

(Cuba's six large traditional provinces were reorganized into fourteen smaller provinces with the promulgation of the 1975 Constitution.)

When Castro came to power on January 1, 1959, Cuba already had the highest ratio of television receivers per 1,000 population in Latin America and more than one million radios in daily use for a population then 75 percent literate. Cuba is now 90 percent literate.[2] Given Castro's charismatic personality and his style of building support with the masses through frequent speeches, television and radio soon became his means for reaching most of the population quickly. Some 95 percent of all dwellings have radios and every public gathering site and neighborhood in the nation provides television for viewing by crowds or small groups.[3]

Besides the morning daily *Granma* of the PCC, the other nationally circulated daily newspaper is the afternoon *Juventud Rebelde,* published by the Union of Cuban Youth (UJC) of the PCC. In addition, the party publishes provincial newspapers in nine of the fourteen provinces, such as *Guerrillero* in both eastern and western regions, but these circulate only within a province. The Cuban Federation of Labor or CTC (Confederación de Trabajadores de Cuba) also publishes a daily circulated among unions. The army publishes a weekly news magazine *Verde Olivo,* and the Federation of Cuban Women or FMC (Federación de Mujeres de Cuba) publishes the magazine *Mujeres.* Staffed by editors from the government and the party is the weekly news magazine *Bohemia.*

After the fidelistas and the 26th of July Movement came to power in 1959, the veteran magazine *Bohemia* began publishing in exile in both San Juan, Puerto Rico, and in Mexico City. After the consolidation of the Communist state in the early 1960s, the PCC encouraged a group of journalists in Havana to revive a progovernment version of *Bohemia,* already a household name for a news magazine in Cuba.

The Committees for the Defense of the Revolution, after organizing in 200,000 neighborhoods to guard against counter-revolutionaries, decided to publish a national magazine. The CDR journal is *Con la Guardia en Alto.*

Because of a continuing newsprint shortage, with paper having to be imported, *Granma's* circulation has been kept to 600,000, whereas as early as 1965, Cuba had more than 700,000 television receivers well distributed throughout the island. Given Castro's effective use of television and radio, the broadcast media have continued to be more prominent than the press as channels of political socialization, along with schools and peer groups.[4] Fidel and Raúl Castro and others of the PCC Central Committee have noted that the party and government leadership must be reached by printed organs and that eventually the print media role in public life must be more prominent.[5]

Other than control of the armed forces, no factor is more essential to an authoritarian government than mass media control. Marxist ideology warns that the media cannot function outside the society from which they spring, and in a Communist state, the media serve the government and the party, their primary function *not* the factual reporting of news. Unlike some leaders in non-Communist developing nations, Cuban leaders offer no apologies for state and party control of press and broadcasting, and make no pretense of guaranteeing the right of dissidents to challenge in rival media their social order.

The final official declaration of the 1971 Cuban Education Congress stated:

> Radio, television, cinema, and press are powerful instruments of ideological education for creation of a collective conscience. Mass media cannot be left to chance or used without direction.[6]

Functions of the Media

In many developing nations, governments use censorship to prevent the political opposition from gaining power. In Cuba the direction of the media goes beyond authorities indicating what not to print or air. Party leaders dictate what should be published to mobilize support for the government and create within the public an identification with the administration and the party.

The first obligation of Cuban media is to make nationally known the official positions and programs of the government. The government news service, Prensa Latina, distributes all major national news stories to all newspapers, magazines, and broadcasting entities. Editors are able to determine the importance of a story often by the person or agency used as its source. An announcement by Fidel Castro carries more weight than one by a deputy cabinet minister or even another member of the PCC Central Committee. A statement by Vice-President and veteran PCC Vice-Chairman Carlos Rafael Rodríguez becomes more important news than statements by the foreign minister, the provincial or municipal authorities, or directors of decentralized agencies.

Official statements may be phrased in direct, clear language. Or the message may contain hidden meanings that only PCC or foreign Communist leaders will understand in a dual-level communication. During 1978 and 1979, Cuba publicly disputed with Yugoslavia over the so-called Non-Aligned Movement, with Belgrade periodically warning about hegemony, a term denoting distrust of Soviet Union domination of the foreign policies of other Communist nations, and Havana rejecting that warning.[7]

The second function of Cuban media is to help the government make its foreign positions known internationally and understood by specific foreign governments. Often Cuban leaders will use harsher language than their counterparts in the Soviet Union or the People's Republic of China, both of which must consider worldwide implications of their statements. In February 1979, during China's invasion of Vietnam, in a mass rally in Havana, Castro denounced Teng Chiao-ping as an impudent traitor to socialism, leading a clique of fascists.[8] Rarely has a leader of the USSR, China, or other Communist nation used such language against another Communist country's leaders, nor have the media of other Communist nations used as many violently blunt phrases as the international broadcasting service of *Radio Havana* periodically airs.

Some news events are not published or broadcast inside Cuba for weeks after they occur, until the government or the party has finalized a position and Castro himself makes an announcement. Yet the Cuban government feels the pressure to provide some bare mention of top foreign news because of the accessibility of foreign radio broadcasts in the Caribbean from Mexico, Puerto Rico, Florida, and the Voice of America.

Batista's Bribery

Cuba now suffers from a lack of divergent viewpoints and media independent of the government that can report in a nonpartisan manner. But in the pre-Castro period, Cuban journalism suffered from alternate periods of censorship and bribery, genuine press freedom being rare. From 1925 to 1933, dictator Gerardo Machado simply used overt censorship to control the press.[9]

During the first Batista era of fronting presidents and the Batista presidential term (1940–1944), censorship alternated with controls through bribes and subsidies. From 1944 to 1952, the presidencies of Ramón Grau San Martín and Carlos Prío allowed some legitimate press criticism by the Ortodoxo party against these two leaders of the Auténtico party, with the two administrations able to purchase considerable favorable press and broadcasting coverage. Ortodoxo leader Senator Eduardo Chibás, at the time Cuba's most popular radio commentator, was able to exercise considerable criticism of the government over the CMQ Radio Network and over CMQ-TV until he killed himself in 1951.[10] Given the political history of Cuba since it first became a republic in 1902, the 1949–1951 period of freedom to criticize was a high point in press freedom.[11]

Returning to power in a coup in March 1952, President Fulgencio Batista decided to employ subsidies and bribes more than censorship, and his system flourished as painless control until his ouster on December 31, 1958. During this period, Havana had a population of 1 million and Cuba some 8 million. Yet Havana had twenty-one daily newspapers, whereas New York at the time with nine times as many inhabitants, could only support five large dailies. Similarly, London, with more than nine times the population of Havana, could only support a handful of dailies, which also were national in circulation throughout the United Kingdom. London newspapers had no advertising competition from the three BBC radio networks and advertising competition from only one television network.

By contrast, Havana during the 1952–1958 period had the most competitive broadcasting market of any city in the world: thirty-two commercial standard-band radio stations and five television stations. With so much competition, no one medium could deliver a large enough audience or readership to guarantee very high advertising rates. The Havana newspapers and stations all had low rates and depended on government subsidies.[12]

Two of the twenty-one dailies were small Chinese-language newspapers and two were small-circulation English-language papers, though the *Havana Times* did have some Cuban subscribers.

The "big three" were the *Diario de la Marina, El Mundo,* and *Información,* with the bulk of the daily sales circulations and the major advertising. The fourteen small dailies existed on government subsidies. But even the three large dailies received government subsidies in the name of culture, so that they could publish rotogravure sections and maintain fine arts critics. Such government funding, however, muted their editorial page criticism. No press censorship was needed, for Batista had substituted the big carrot for the big stick.

Cuban reporters had a closed shop. The only way to get a job as a journalist was to graduate from a journalism school, and the number of graduates was limited.[13]

A reporter assigned to cover the Ministry of Education worked a five-day week. On Saturdays he would moonlight as a public relations counsel for the Education Ministry for a freelance salary. The chances of his writing adverse stories about the ministry he advised were zero.

In 1957 and 1958, when the Castro "26th of July" rebels made a few successful attacks on the Cuban army, the government did resort to direct censorship.[14]

When Herbert L. Matthews of the *New York Times* interviewed Fidel Castro in eastern Cuba, his paper ran the first of a three-part series on the front page on February 24, 1957, launching a campaign that glamorized Castro as a nonideological reformer fighting for the poor.[15] Even with some censorship and the bribery system at the time, *Bohemia* magazine was allowed to carry summaries of the Matthews interviews. Without explanation, Cuban censorship ended and other media carried news of Castro.[16]

In 1960 a new type of press guidance came to Cuba. Printers began to wield the editor's pencil instead of sticking to their linotype machines. Editorials in the conservative *Diario de la Marina* critical of the Castro government had notes added from the pro-Castro printers giving the fidelista views.[17] The printers union, led by Communists of the Popular Socialist party kept up the offensive against the anti-Castro editorial staffs of *Diario, Avance,* and any other remaining opposition paper until the Ministry for Recovery of Stolen Property could confiscate these dailies in the name of the Cuban nation.

Meantime, the Communist daily *Hoy* and Castro's "26th of July Movement" daily *Revolución* debated editorially over whether the revolution should organize along Marxist or democratic socialist lines. Prime Minister Castro and his cabinet ministers time and again intervened to take power from those in the movement who claimed an independent role for their organization. In October 1959 *Revolución* pushed its own movement slate for leaders in the Cuban Labor federation (CTC) until Castro forced acceptance of his own "unity" slate.[18] By 1961 *Revolución* was echoing *Hoy,* guided by the Integrated Revolutionary Organizations or ORI, leading to the reorganized Communist party in 1965 and the establishment of *Granma,* named after the ship in which Castro returned from exile in Mexico to Cuba in 1956.

Aníbal Escalante became ORI organization secretary. On December 1, 1961, Castro proclaimed to the world that Cuba was henceforth a Communist state. When Escalante tried to assert some positions rivaling those of Castro in the mass media, the prime minister met the challenge by sending Escalante into exile in Czechoslovakia. The PCC was restructured to oust oldline Communists attempting to increase their own power. Rival Marxist factions disappeared from the press.

Political Socialization by the Media

The Cuban revolution was institutionalized not only by Fidel Castro's charisma, the reorganizing of all groups in public life, and the PCC's restructuring of government, but also by the mass media. Messages for social justice and the redistribution of income and the nation's resources were repeated in broadcasts and newspaper articles, warning that the alternative would be violence and corruption. In 1960 Lloyd Free conducted a nationwide survey that indicated Cubans felt they had been saved from the problems of the past.[19] Even in that early stage they had been saturated with the propaganda of the revolution, aimed at mobilizing their support.

Professor Michael Sewell did a content analysis of *Granma* based on one randomly selected issue from each month of thirteen months from January 1968 through January 1969, including a designated issue of July 28, 1968. That issue was used as a standard of comparison for the six issues preceding and the six following it.[20] In addition, Sewell took two issues of *Granma* from 1966 and two randomly selected sample issues from 1972 to compare the frequency of usage of symbol words in those years with frequencies in the 1968 samples. Sports stories and articles on other topics not related to the politico-economic affairs of Cuba were excluded from the analysis.

Sewell found in a "moral incentives emphasis" category the symbol words "sacrifice" and "consciousness" most frequently used in articles, far more than the runner-up symbol words "dedication" and "commitment" or "duty." In his "material incentives" category, he found the symbol words "extraordinary hours" and "salary" and "pay" recurred more often than the words "wealth" or "promotion."[21] The emphasis in *Granma* continued to shift from material to moral incentives.

After Castro's July 26, 1968, speech setting long-range goals, the Labor Ministry proposed new social security benefits. Compensation for sick leave and maternity would be at 100 percent of a worker's salary if he or she took no overtime pay and worked a forty-four instead of a forty-hour week, surpassed production quotas without a bonus, and engaged in unpaid voluntary work. The symbolism tried to promote raised consciousness instead of material reward. With a shortage of consumer goods, there would be little to buy with increased wages.

Edward González points out that Castro's shift from material to moral incentives in 1966 was not dictated by ideology but by economic necessity. The regime had to devote an ever increasing share of the gross domestic product to investments, reducing the availability of goods and services for personal consumption.[22] The government's own limitations were reflected in the changed emphasis in the themes in *Granma*. Fidelistas feared that the masses might revert to consumer market relationships spontaneously, threatening the socialist state. In 1968 the Castro government again faced the problem of which strategy and set of symbols to stress. Emphasis on moral incentives in *Granma* increased progressively into 1972, as the Sewell analysis indicated.

The media encourage readers and listeners to identify the regime with the values of the nation. Frequent repetition of the titles of leaders identifies them with their roles. In a first reference in a story about Fidel Castro, *Granma* will list his titles of first secretary of the PCC and president of the Council of State and Council of Ministers. That citation is not to impart information inasmuch as the titles are well known. The intention is to reinforce his position within an aura of legitimacy.

Slogans are also used to make the revolution part of the Cuban national consciousness. Every year is dedicated to a goal or the celebration of an event. During 1979 each issue of *Granma* carried the slogan: "1979—20th Year of the Victory."

Professor James W. Carty has examined not only *Granma,* but *Juventud Rebelde* (circulation 193,000), and *Los Trabajadores* (issued three times a week, circulation 300,000), and nine provincial dailies (with a total circulation of 122,000).[23] He has found media mobilization efforts highlighting behavior desired by the government. Each brigade of sugarcane harvesters who meet quotas is pictured in the press as heroes. Various groups meeting their production quotas in every field become newsworthy.

In 1978 Carty found 500 full-time journalists studying Communist ideology as in-service training, and another 500 students were studying journalism hoping to enter mass media work. The emphasis was more on political socialization than newsgathering techniques. The Union of Journalists of Cuba (Unión de Periodistas de Cuba or UPEC), headed by Ernesto Vera, has also developed a Latin American Federation of Journalists, designed to spread Cuban influence among journalists throughout Latin America.

Carty found political socialization in the school press, ranging from *Vida Universitaria* at the University of Havana to *Juventud de Acero* at Lenin Vocational School. The large book publisher for Cuba, *Casa de las Américas,* coordinates textbooks, novels, and critical essays with the curricular goals of the schools.[24]

The medium Fidel Castro has used most effectively has been television. In the early years of the revolution, his frequent, lively, lengthy speeches were broadcast live, with most of the population becoming an extension of his political rallies. Castro was the first Communist leader coming to power in the age of television, and he found he had a very effective delivery and a nation in which almost every citizen could be reached by broadcasts. The Latin American tradition of personalism in politics also helped him utilize television and radio in institutionalizing his government.

International Efforts

Directed by Alfredo Viñas, *Radio Havana Cuba* (RHC) has become a major means of promoting Cuba's foreign policies. RHC broadcasts in eight languages on three frequencies some forty-seven hours a week. RHC broadcasts twenty-two hours a week in Spanish, eleven hours in English, five in French, three in Portuguese, two each in Quechua (to Peru and Bolivia) and Creole (to Haiti), and one hour each in Arabic and in Guaraní (to Paraguay). Programming stresses news programs giving the Cuban position in international affairs and claims of achievements by the government inside Cuba.[25]

Tricontinental is a magazine published by the Organization of Solidarity of the Peoples of Africa, Asia, and Latin America, in Havana, with some 500,000 copies distributed globally three times a year. Articles stress Communist and Socialist bloc policies and anti-U.S. themes. In 1978 the themes stressed the growing Marxist influence in Africa and Asia.

Oclae is a journal of the Latin American Continental Students Organization in Havana, distributed to university student leaders throughout Latin America, stressing socialist student federation activities.

Cuba Internacional is a photo magazine stressing tourist attractions in Cuba, sporting events, and human interest features.

Casa de las Américas, a journal of the publishing company, stresses problems in the Latin American nations under conservative governments. The same company publishes a bimonthly, *Conjunto,* about theater in Latin America.

Best known of all is the *Granma Weekly Review,* based on the *Granma* daily editions, published each Sunday in Spanish, English, and French, with 100,000 copies distributed abroad.

Use of the Media

Fidel Castro often grants interviews to foreign correspondents, from both western democracies and Communist nations. To encourage lifting of economic pressures on Cuba by the United States, on October 22, 1974, Castro had a lengthy interview with Dan Rather of CBS-TV, insuring that his views would reach a large audience in the United States. Castro's lengthy interviews with Barbara Walters on ABC-TV during June 6, 7, 8, and 9, 1977, gave him a major and lengthy platform to explain his policies and goals not only to the United States, but to a bonus worldwide audience getting news service summaries of these interviews.

Castro makes distinctions between what he says to the foreign and domestic audiences. He can test Cuban policies abroad while avoiding domestic media discussions of highly sensitive topics.[26] The Cuban government can judge foreign reaction to these topics, and if it should be severely negative, Castro can assert that he was misquoted or quoted out of context. For example, during the massive buildup of Cuban troops in Angola's war in 1975–1976, Castro announced to foreign correspondents that Cuba was fighting in Angola two months before the Cuban mass media told about it. Until the Cuban media use such a story, officially the event has not taken place.

When Castro decided to reverse his policy of twenty years of denouncing the Cuban exile community as counter-revolutionary worms, he spoke with U.S. correspondents about the release of political prisoners, anticipating that the Cuban "community abroad" would respond positively and help improve his relations with the United States. After getting such a response from Florida, he then made his statements on political prisoners and exiles in the Cuban press and on Cuban radio and television. The Cuban Institute of Cinematographic Art and Industry (ICAIC) hopes to use Cuban films to bridge the gap with exiles in Florida, but so far, political documentaries, rather than entertainment features, have dominated production.[27]

The New York Times found in late 1978 that Cuban television was attempting to add some lighter variety to its programming to relieve the image of ideological preaching. The popular new program series was "Ara Bailar" ("To Dance"), featuring teenage dancers and American popular music, which can easily be picked up directly by Cuban radio listeners from U.S. stations.[28]

Also in 1978 the army's weekly news magazine Verde Olivo tried to add more variety. A September issue included an article favorable to Mozambique, one denouncing Nicaragua, some articles on science, new aircraft, reports on world affairs from the PCC's viewpoint, plus three articles on sports about boxing, wrestling, and gymnastics.[29]

In the same year a Cuban radio series featured commentator Guido García Inclán with a "Letter from Freddy." Freddy is a fictional Cuban living in the United States. García Inclán read fictional letters to promote the idea that Cuban relations with the United States had improved.

With conformity built into the mass media system, and non-Marxists and even Marxists who challenged Castro's authority prohibited from editing or reporting, the government has considered the difficulty of getting a sense of the public mood concerning various problems and crises, other than through the use of surveys. The answer has been to allow criticism of local government entities to appear in the press.[30]

By allowing some critical aspects of local government to be reported, the national administration can divert frustrations that might otherwise be felt towards the central government to the local level. And with the information obtained from such reports, the national government can correct maladministration at the local level, the basic daily contact for a majority of the citizens who must deal with government. When such criticism begins to reach upward to the regional or national level, then censorship or constraints can quickly be applied. The net effect has been an improvement since 1977 in the flow of information upward to the real decision makers, without any basic alteration in the control over public life by the PCC and the government.

Among the local government criticism that has been allowed into the newspapers since 1977 are reports about long waiting lines to purchase basic consumer goods, municipal officials being unaware of changes in national programs, lack of instructions for citizens trying to use local public facilities, delays in getting errors in local records corrected, and inquiries and letters to local offices remaining unanswered.[31]

Satire and humor are handled at the popular level through the weekly magazine *Palante*, distributed nationally from Havana. With color cartoons and captions, *Palante* attacks American capitalists, multinational corporations, certain successful Cuban exiles in Florida, unpopular Cuban and foreign athletes, rock music, the scarcity of taxicabs in Havana, high-fashion clothing from abroad, unskilled auto drivers, and students who use flattery in trying for better grades.[32]

The humorous stories in *Palante* contrast sharply with the preaching and opinionizing that crowd out spot news in *Granma*. For example, in February 1978, before getting some data on the government's having invested 800 million pesos in electric power generators since 1959, and having completed plans for a 440-megawatt nuclear power plant near Cienfuegos, the reader had to wade through this introduction:

What great moral significance work has for us today. How gratifying and stimulating it is to work today building these thermoelectric plants. And for whom are these plants built? For the workers themselves, for the people.

Commander in Chief Fidel Castro, first secretary of the Central Committee of the Party and president of the Council of State and of the Government, attended a ceremony on February 15 in Mariel, Havana Province, to put into operation on a trial basis 100,000-kilowatt generator No. 6 of the Maximo Gómez power plant.[33]

A high degree of social mobilization in Cuba has been achieved by the PCC and by the government. But mass participation in the various programs does not mean that citizens can ever amend laws, vote against them, or propose strong alternatives. They must try to persuade PCC leaders or those in the National Assembly sounding board. The true opposition elite was exported to Florida among 800,000 Cubans in exile. And control of the mass media by the PCC and the government prevents popularizing any political movements to change the system of government.

References

Aguilar, Luis E. *Cuba 1933: Prologue to Revolution* (Ithaca, N.Y.: Cornell University Press, 1972).

Alisky, Marvin. "Cuba Press: Censorship Replaces Bribery," *Nieman Reports* 11 (April 1957): 17–18.

_____. "Confused Cuba: Printers Who Edit—Government by Television," *Nieman Reports* 14 (April 1960): 12–14.

_____. "Havana Havoc: Too Many Dailies," *Nieman Reports* 10 (April 1956): 16–18.

Azicri, Max. "A Study of the Structure of Exercising Power in Cuba, 1959–1968," (Ph.D. diss., University of Southern California, Costa Mesa, California, 1975).

Baklanoff, Eric N. "International Economic Relations," in Carmelo Mesa-Lago, ed., *Revolutionary Change in Cuba* (Pittsburgh, Pa.: University of Pittsburgh Press, 1971).

Bernardo, Robert M. *The Theory of Moral Incentives in Cuba* (University, Ala.: University of Alabama Press, 1971).

Canales, Serio. "La Casa Central de las FAR," *Verde Olivo*, July 27, 1975, pp. 17, 30.

Carty, James W., Jr. "Castro Prefers Foreign Journalists," *Times of the Americas*, Oct. 4, 1978, p. 16.

_____. "Cuban Communicators," *Caribbean Quarterly* 22 (December 1976): 59–67.

_____. *Cuban Communications* (Bethany, West Va.: Bethany College, 1978).

Center for Cuban Studies, New York. *Constitution of the Republic of Cuba* (New York: Center for Cuban Studies, 1975).

Comité Central del Partido Comunista de Cuba. *Estatutos del Partido Comunista de Cuba* (Havana: Imprenta Engels, 1976).

Domínguez, Jorge I. *Cuba: Order and Revolution* (Cambridge, Mass.: Harvard University Press, 1978).

_____. "Institutionalization and Civil-Military Relations in Cuba," *Cuban Studies,* Jan. 1976.

_____. "Sectoral Clashes in Cuban Politics and Development," *Latin American Research Review* 6 (Fall 1971): 7–29.

Draper, Theodore. *Castroism: Theory and Practice* (New York: Praeger, 1965).

Escalona, Juan. "Las FAR y los Reservistas," *Verde Olivo,* Apr. 25, 1976, p. 18.

Fagen, Richard. *The Transformation of Political Culture in Cuba* (Stanford, Calif.: Stanford University Press, 1969).

Foreign Broadcast Information Service, eds. *Trends in Communist Media* 6 (July 19, 1978, and Aug. 2, 1978).

Free, Lloyd A. *Attitudes of the Cuban People toward the Castro Regime* (Princeton, N.J.: Institute for International Social Research, 1960).

García Márquez, Gabriel. "Cuba in Africa," *Washington Post,* Jan. 12, 1977, p. A-12.

González, Edward. *Cuba under Castro: The Limits of Charisma* (Boston: Houghton Mifflin, 1974).

_____ and David Ronfeldt. *Post-Revolutionary Cuba in a Changing World* (Santa Monica, Calif.: Rand Corporation, 1975).

Halperin, Maurice. *The Rise and Decline of Fidel Castro* (Berkeley: University of California Press, 1972).

Jenks, Leland H. *Our Cuban Colony* (New York: Vanguard Press, 1928).

Junta Central de Planificación, *Anuario Estadístico de Cuba 1957* (Havana: Dirección Central de Estadística, 1958).

_____. *Compendio Estadístico de Cuba* (Havana: Juceplan, 1975).

_____. *Censo de Población y Viviendas, Septiembre de 1970* (Havana: Juceplan, Dirección General de Estadística, 1971).

Knudson, Jerry W. *Herbert L. Matthews and the Cuban Story* (Minneapolis, Minn.: Association for Education in Journalism, Monograph 52, 1978).

Latin American Daily Report. "Cuba," *Foreign Broadcast Information Service* 6 (Feb. 23, 1979): 4–6.

Márquez Sterling, Carlos. *Historia de Cuba* (New York: Las Americas, 1969).

Mesa-Lago, Carmelo, ed. *Revolutionary Change in Cuba* (Pittsburgh, Pa.: University of Pittsburgh Press, 1971).

Nordheimer, Jon. "20 Years with Fidel," *New York Times Sunday Magazine,* Dec. 31, 1978, pp. 16, 28.

Padula, Alfred L. "The Fall of the Bourgeoisie: Cuba, 1959–1961," (Ph.D. diss., University of New Mexico, Albuquerque, New Mexico, 1974).

Ratliff, William E. *Castroism and Communism in Latin America, 1959–1976* (Stanford, Calif.: Hoover Institution, 1976).

Rodríguez, Carlos Rafael. "La Revolución Cubana," *Cuba Socialista,* Jan. 1966, p. 53.

Sewell, Michael. "Some Themes of Politico-Economic Socialization in Cuba's *Granma,*" *South Eastern Latin Americanist* 21 (September 1977): 1–7.

Suárez, Andrés. *Cuba, Castroism and Communism* (Cambridge, Mass.: MIT Press, 1967).

Suchlicki, Jaime, ed. *Cuba, Castro, and Revolution* (Coral Gables, Fla.: University of Miami Press, 1972).

Szulc, Tad. "Cuban Television's One-Man Show," in R. L. Shayon, ed. *The Eighth Art* (New York: Holt, Rinehart, and Winston, 1962).

Terzian, Philip. "Cuba in Panavision," *Harper's* 258 (January 1979): 28–30.

Ward, Fred. "Inside Cuba Today," *National Geographic* 151 (January 1977): 32–69.

Newspapers and Periodicals: *Avance,* Havana; *Bohemia,* Havana; *Casa de las Americas,* Havana; *Con la Guardia en Alto,* Havana, Matanzas, and Santiago; *Cuba Internacional,* Havana; *Diario de la Marina,* Havana; *El Mundo,* Havana; *Granma,* Havana; *Granma Weekly Review,* Havana; *Hoy,* Havana; *Juventud Rebelde,* Havana; *Mujeres,* Havana; *New York Times; Palante,* Havana; *Revolución,* Havana: *Times of the Americas,* Washington, D.C.; *Verde Olivo,* Havana; *Vida Universitaria,* Havana.

9

Argentina: Perón's Legacy
of Censorship

ONE leader, Juan D. Perón, left a negative imprint upon the public life of Argentina both politically and journalistically. Prior to the seizure of power by his "Colonels' Clique" in 1943, Argentina for decades had enjoyed press and broadcasting freedom and the luster of two of the world's outstanding daily newspapers, *La Prensa* and *La Nación*.[1] With the 1955 ouster of Perón, a period of media independence from government began, but the surrounding economic and political chaos inhibited editors into degrees of self-censorship. The military government era made censorship official from 1966 to 1973, with few exceptions. With the return to power of Perón, and then his widow from 1973 to 1976, again technically free mass media struggled along with most other entities of society to communicate clearly amid violence. And since 1976 the military government has stifled press freedom in a nation that has never fully regained the open society elements it had before Perón's dictatorship.

Argentina from the 1880s to the 1940s prided itself on being Latin America's most literate nation, with 90 percent adult literacy, surpassed in the 1950s only by Uruguay's 92 percent. With a national territory covering one million square miles, Argentina's 26 million citizens bunch together in the greater metropolitan Buenos Aires area encompassing the city, its federal district and surrounding suburbs in adjacent states, and in a relatively few provincial cities. With 12 million people living within seventy miles of downtown Buenos Aires, its mass media are national in scope and impact.

Argentines are mostly of Spanish, Italian, or other European origin, with almost no Indian minority nor any other minority not speaking Spanish. Thus the mass media are relieved of a problem of communication that confronts Peru, Bolivia, Ecuador, and Guatemala.

166

Despite the economic ills that have plagued Argentina since the 1950s, a cultural carry-over from earlier times still gives the republic one of Latin America's best ratios of radio and television receivers, telephones, daily newspaper sales, and automobiles per 1,000 population, among all the region's nations.[2]

The Perón Era

The Radical Civic Union (Unión Cívica Radical or UCR) had been founded as a progressive political party of reform in 1890 and the rival Conservative party traced its beginnings back to 1860. Until the 1912 Electoral Law brought Argentina the secret ballot and honest vote counting supervised by all parties on the ballot, fraudulent tabulations had often blemished elections. The press had been free to investigate but stopped short of hounding aristocratic national leaders until 1916, when vigorous candid reporting became the norm for major newspapers and magazines.[3]

During World War I, Argentina remained technically neutral but pro-German in sympathy. Although among non-Hispanic Argentines, those of English origin almost matched the number of German origin, the armed forces by the 1930s had developed an officer corps trained and influenced by Hitler's Nazi war machine and by Mussolini's Fascist regime. Although one-third of all Argentines had Italian ancestors, mostly the military, not the civilian, leaders of the republic seemed attuned to Mussolini's philosophy and to a lesser extent to Franco's Falangist Spain as reservoirs of Latin culture and Catholic traditions.

During World War II, Argentina's chief exports, beef and wheat, sold at high prices, benefiting the landed aristocracy while the working class wrestled with rapidly rising inflation. The civilian Conservative party majority in Congress and the presidency became popular hate targets.

Before dawn on June 4, 1943, a military junta of generals and colonels seized the government, as well as telephone, telegraph, and radio facilities. General Pedro P. Ramírez became president of Argentina but it soon became apparent that the real power centered in a junta of colonels dominated by Juan D. Perón, a sympathizer of Europe's fascists and perhaps the most charismatic orator in Latin America until the rise of Fidel Castro. Perón contented himself with the office of vice-president and minister of labor after creating the republic's first full-fledged labor ministry.[4] Ramírez served Perón's purposes as a symbolic lightning rod, drawing the cross fire of rival groups within the ruling military until Perón could consolidate his own power.

The difference between the Perón dictatorship and those of other Latin American nations could be measured in the pressures the junta applied to all walks of life, imitating the Third Reich in banning certain motion pictures, radio programs, and musical recordings. Argentina's most popular comedian, Luis Sandrini, had the largest radio audience in the nation for his Radio Belgrano network weekly program. Sandrini joked that the political signs "P.P.R.," which stood for Pedro P. Ramírez, the president, really stood for "presidente para rato," that is, "president for a little while." He was fired from the network and blacklisted by the film studios. Sandrini appeared in movies in Mexico until the post-Perón era, when he resumed his career in Argentina. Culture control had come to a nation saddled with a dictatorship without a sense of humor.[5]

The election of Perón as president in early 1946 technically constituted a genuine contest, for the ballots were tabulated according to law. But the campaign leading up to election day brought Argentina fraudulent practices and demagogic pressures previously unknown in its public life. Perón was the candidate of the Peronista party. His opponent was José Tamborini of the UCR. A colorless, honest, former senator, Tamborini could not buy prime time on radio, could not find billboard space, could not hire desirable auditoriums for rallies, or even receive token police protection against peronista gangs who broke up UCR gatherings.[6]

Perón monopolized parades, popular broadcasts, much of the radio time devoted to the campaign, and theater newsreels. Even the bus and trolley transfers in Buenos Aires carried his name and slogan. Most of the Argentine newspapers and magazines by then had come under peronista control. Prestige papers, such as *La Prensa* and *La Nación* bravely chronicled the erosion of political freedoms in Argentina and provide us with valuable documentation of the era.[7]

Perón's demagogic speeches during his campaign and during his presidency lent themselves to dramatic presentation on radio, on television, and even in those newspapers not yet under peronista control. The base of his power became the labor unions of the meat packing industry, the steel mills, and most other Argentine industries. Perón would whip off his coat and cry "You're dirty and shirtless. We're all workers together." Tens of thousands of "descamisados" or "shirtless ones" would respond.[8]

The dictator invented a vaguely defined ideology for his Peronista party called "Justicialismo," a social justice in which urban workers would receive preference for welfare benefits and whatever else the government could provide. His program of labor politics paralleled his campaign to end the power of the landed aristocrats. His foreign policy stressed an anti-U.S. position, which the government repeated in periodic statements to the press.

Impressed with the device of a scapegoat utilized by Hitler, Perón realized that Argentina also had a handy minority that could become the focus of public anger, solidifying his power. Of the one million Jews throughout Latin America, almost half of them resided in greater Buenos Aires. Anti-Semitism became a policy of the peronista government, filling the media with anti-Semitic propaganda at a time when that tactic had been discredited and ended in Europe.[9]

Perón's second wife, Evita, a former actress, also proved to be a powerful political asset. A beautiful blonde, her dramatic appearance and voice became the basis of a cult, thanks to mass media glamorization. Not that Evita had to rely solely on charm, for she possessed a natural ability as a politician and organizer, developing a nationwide women's movement within the Peronista party. She publicly expressed a desire to be vice-president of Argentina, but the age of woman's liberation had not dawned when Evita died of cancer in July 1952. Perón's third wife, Isabelita, in the 1970s would enjoy for a while the status Evita had sought.[10]

Evita also helped her husband control the mass media. The most distinguished motion picture and theater actress and singer, Libertad Lamarque, was banished to Mexico by Evita for criticizing the dictatorship. Not until the post-Perón era could Miss Lamarque resume her career in Argentina. Dozens of other less prominent entertainers, writers, producers, novelists, and directors suffered the same fate.

La Prensa's Struggle

The Buenos Aires daily *La Prensa* managed to operate independently for a time after most other Argentine mass media had already come under peronista control. Its status as one of the world's leading quality newspapers gave it advertising and other support rival papers could not receive.[11] Over a five-year period, *La Prensa* became the most celebrated symbol in the world of an entity struggling against dictatorial supression. This daily was confiscated by the government on January 26, 1951, and did not resume independent publication until February 3, 1956. In the late 1970s, *La Prensa* lost some of its illustrious staff and some of its longtime reputation as one of the best newspapers in the world.[12]

Founded by José C. Paz on October 18, 1869, *La Prensa* under the founder's son, Ezequiel, and then for decades under his nephew, Alberto Gainza Paz, utilized the family fortune to purchase all the world news services from American, British, French, and other sources; maintained its own correspondents in key capitals of the world; contracted with famous authors for columns and essays; and maintained the largest reporting corps in South America. The newspaper maintained its own clinic for health services for its employees and paid the highest wages of any Argentine newspaper, which helped it resist the peronista unions replacing the antiperonista unions of its printers and journalists.

In 1943 President Ramírez issued a state-of-emergency decree suspending the press freedom article of the constitution, countersigned by members of the junta. In 1944 most official advertising funded in the federal budget was placed with pro-Axis newspapers such as *La Fronda* and *Clarinda*. Argentine government subsidies matched those from the German Embassy for the daily *El Pampero,* whose editorial staff had more German citizens than Argentines. Large Argentine government subsidies went to the pro-Axis peronista daily *El Crisol,* which editiorially attacked President Franklin D. Roosevelt and Secretary of State Cordell Hull.[13]

During 1946 and 1947, President Perón ordered the closing of dailies that editorially criticized his government's actions and programs, including *La Tribuna Demócrata,* published by the Conservative party; *El Hombre Libre,* a liberal daily; *Provincias Unidas,* of the UCR; *Qué,* a politically independent weekly news magazine; and twenty other daily newspapers in the capital and the five largest provincial cities.

After the Socialist newspaper *La Vanguardia* published political cartoons critical of Juan and Evita Perón, in 1946, its supply of newsprint was impounded for "import tax irregularities." In 1947 it attempted to publish as a four-page daily, then a four-page weekly, but it finally had to cease publication as its paper reserves vanished.

In 1948 the Ministry of Press and Propaganda—Argentina actually had that title for the ministry—budgeted $7 million for subsidies to the mass media, the largest such expenditure openly earmarked for such purposes ever made public to that time.[14]

Peronista newspapers such as *Democracia, La Epoca,* and *La Tribuna* were summoned for press conferences by the president, and for major announcements from key cabinet ministers, whereas *La Prensa* and *La Nación* remained uninvited and had to obtain several major government reports late and sometimes second hand.

La Prensa was restricted to twelve pages per edition, whereas peronista dailies could purchase enough paper for 40-page editions or more.[15]

Peronista gangs periodically would throw bricks through the windows of *La Prensa* at night, and the next morning police would promptly impose a fine for violation of safety and health regulations. Building inspectors shut off the newspaper's press-room ventilators and then health inspectors would quickly appear to impose fines for inadequate ventilation.[16]

The new Penal Code of 1949 became an effective control over the press. Its Article 244 dealt with "desacato," or disrespect for public authority leading to a threat to law and order. If the federal attorney general's office declared that a newspaper had violated the code, the editor of the paper was held accountable unless the reporter who did the writing signed a confession.

The code went into effect in early October, and within ten days the Ministry of the Interior carried out one of its provisions, to register every news editor in the republic. No change of editorship could then take place without reregistration. The existence of a Registry of Editors itself constituted a symbolic deterrent to all but the most intrepid editors against engaging the government in any challenge to authority.

Numerous possibilities of press intimidation arose from Article 219 of the code:

> He who by hostile acts, not approved by the national government, should give rise to the danger of a declaration of war against the nation, should expose its inhabitants to reprisals, or should disturb the friendly relations of the Argentine Government with a foreign government, shall be punished with imprisonment for from one to six years.[17]

During 1950, as a consequence of that article, the only Argentine newspapers initiating any contact with the United States Embassy were *La Prensa* and *La Nación,* and the only newspaper in the nation to publish announcements from that embassy was *La Prensa.*[18]

Also during 1950 the Committee on Anti-Argentine Activities of the federal Congress, chaired by Deputy José Emilio Visca, suspended more than sixty newspapers for unspecified seditious editorial opinions, including *La Hora* in Buenos Aires, *El Intransigente* in Salta, *La Nueva Provincia* in Bahía Blanca, and *Democracia* in Junín. The public learned of the actions through the brief reports of the closures appearing in *La Prensa.*

To ensure impartiality in covering the activities of government, *La*

Prensa had always prohibited its staff members to hold any official appointment.[19] The peronista government charged that this rule was unpatriotic.

La Prensa was the only daily newspaper in Latin America to allow veteran employees to retire at age sixty-five on a pension equal to full salary.[20] After the peronista government pressured longtime advertisers and *La Prensa* began to lose some of its advertising revenue, the pension plan had to be curtailed.

For decades there had been no import tax on newsprint. In 1950, after Deputy Visca's congressional committee finished a three-month investigation of the financial records of *La Prensa,* tax inspectors took their turn and filed a suit for back payment to 1939 of customs duty on newsprint that had been free of tax when originally imported.

In March 1950 the government expropriated nearly 6,000 tons of *La Prensa's* newsprint supplies as part of a penalty for the import tax conviction, and then proceeded to sell back small amounts of the paper to *La Prensa* at 100 percent profit for the government.[21]

Shortly thereafter, the only other newspaper in the nation to print even mildly critical stories about the government, *La Nación,* published a speech by a UCR leader who asserted that Perón had come into office a relatively poor man and would leave the government service as a millionaire. All *Nación* elevators were shut down as unsafe and the paper began to omit such reports. Of all the modern, successful media that had functioned independently when Perón came to power, only *La Prensa* remained as a vehicle for criticism.

In late 1950 and early 1951, Buenos Aires was plastered with posters denouncing *La Prensa* as an enemy of the nation and of the programs for the workers of the nation. Government radio broadcasts editorially attacked *La Prensa* three times a day for twenty-eight days in succession.[22]

The Visca congressional investigating committee took from the telegraph office copies of all cabled news which *La Prensa* had received containing unfavorable comments about the economic policies of the Argentine government.

On January 26, 1951, peronista unions of printers and news vendors affiliated with the progovernment General Federation of Labor (Confederación General de Trabajadores or CGT), began a boycott of *La Prensa* after the newspaper's management refused the vendors' demands for sole distribution rights plus a guaranteed percentage of classified advertising revenues. The CGT pickets prevented *La Prensa's* own printers from going to work and the newspaper's appeal for police protection went ignored.

On February 27 the 1,300 news and printing employees voted to return to work in the face of violent threats. One printer was killed trying to enter the printing plant and then 79 other employees were severely beaten. The Ministry of the Interior ordered the police to seize the newspaper building, arrested 205 employees for holding a public meeting without permission, confiscated cameras and other equipment, and failed to arrest or even question any of the club-swinging CGT pickets.[23]

La Prensa ceased publishing on January 26, but the government did not take formal possession of the newspaper's buildings and other properties until March 20, 1951, after a special session of the federal Congress voted for expropriation of the paper without compensation in punishment for alleged violations of labor laws in which "the vendors had been victimized."[24]

When formal censorship failed to silence a prestigious newspaper having worldwide sympathy for its defense of press freedom, a determined dictatorship utilized other pressures. These attempts at suppression were: violence against the paper's employees and property, impoundment of its supply of newsprint, legalistic harassment over tax interpretations, and exaggerated demands by unions organized by the government itself. The peronista government's campaign against *La Prensa* became a famous case of government suppression of press freedom in Latin America because of the attention that major foreign newspapers gave to it.

A Civilian Era of Freedom and Chaos

From the ouster of Juan Perón from power in September 1955 to the taking of power by military leaders in June 1966, Argentina experienced almost eleven years of political and journalistic freedom made perplexing by a weak economy. Adding to the confusion was the absence of a majority consensus on policies to replace the preperonista social standards that had been eradicated by twelve years of dictatorship control of the entire culture.

Even though two-thirds of the voters displayed dismay and anger over what the peronista era had done to them and their traditions, one-third of the voters remained loyal peronistas. These urban unionized workers, who had benefited at the expense of other sectors of society when Perón had been in power, remained a cohesive political force, whereas the Conservative party had vanished and the UCR had splintered from a majority party into rival parties—the Intransigent

Radical Civic Union (Unión Cívica Radical Intransigente or UCRI) and the People's Radical Civic Union (Unión Cívica Radical del Pueblo or UCRP).

UCRI candidate Arturo Frondizi was elected president in 1958 with peronista support even though the Peronista party was barred from the ballot. Frondizi attempted to lead a nation divided into several mutually hostile groups, presiding over an almost bankrupt economy, and simultaneously pressured by antiperonista military leaders and peronista labor leaders.[25]

Large sums of the national budget had been spent on industries that required increasingly more expensive imported petroleum since domestic oil production was small.

Peronista victories in the March 1962 elections in ten of the provinces (states), including Buenos Aires, capturing a large bloc of congressional seats, prompted the military to oust Frondizi before he could form a coalition government with the peronistas. In 1963 UCRP candidate Arturo Illia was elected president, but soon Congress had fractured into twenty-four political parties and both the legislative and executive branches bogged down into a swamp of incoherence and inaction.

A volume of erratic information helped spread confusion among citizens as to whether or not events actually were taking place or merely consisted of rumors. By 1966, except for *La Prensa* and *La Nación*, most Argentine newspapers were mixing views and news in unprofessional jumbles.

News magazines such as *Mayoría, Esto Es, Qué,* and *Norte* from 1958 to 1966 published various charges and claims by peronistas without any sources cited for the information, and these sensational reports frequently were reprinted by daily newspapers trying out the press freedom that had long been denied them. *La Prensa* tried to make the public aware that the flow of news was being poisoned with unsubstantiated gossip, but the readership of the irresponsible papers far exceeded that of the few responsible dailies. *La Prensa, La Nación,* and the *Buenos Aires Herald* during 1964 managed to publish large numbers of objective stories about world news.[26]

In June 1966 a military junta deposed President Illia and installed General Juan Onganía as chief executive. Neither the general nor his cabinet ministers distinguished between responsible and irresponsible journalistic criticism and reporting. The Onganía government moved against the polemic *Trinchera,* published by the Peronista Youth movement, and *Liberación* published by the National Liberation movement

Marxist guerrillas. But the government moved as forcefully and swiftly against establishment media and journalistically professional papers.

On July 20, 1966, Onganía banned the widely respected magazine of satire, *Tía Vicente*. On April 26, 1967, he ended the current affairs discussion panels on Channels 9, 11, and 13. On October 27, 1967, he closed the moderately conservative magazine *Azul y Blanco*. A new age of censorship of the media had descended upon Argentina, and would not be lifted until the military leaders under General Alejandro Lanusse handed power over to elected civilians in 1973.

Censorship by the Generals

From 1966 to 1973, despite the presence of government censors, *La Prensa* and *La Nación,* as well as the provincial dailies *La Capital, Crónica,* and *La Tribuna,* managed to report with great care many of the problems and crises in public life by exercising selective self-censorship, conjuring a facade of neutralism toward the government that permitted reporting leeway other media did not have.[27]

The troubled Argentine economy, beset with inflation, underemployment, huge trade deficits, and production stagnation throughout the 1950s, 1960s, and 1970s, brought hardship to journalists and broadcasters, as well as most other workers. Real purchasing power continued to slip. From 1955 to 1960, the average Argentine reporter's salary rose from only $50 to $98 per month, less than half of what middle-class workers needed for basic necessities.[28] A nationally accepted practice of moonlighting thereupon became established, whereby most newspaper reporters and editors and radio and television broadcasters regularly held two jobs in order to subsist. Newspaper reporters could also work as public relations or advertising writers, as broadcasters, as magazine editors, or in any variety of combinations. This pattern of journalistic moonlighting was set in the late 1950s and in 1979 remained a standard practice for Argentina's mass media work force.[29]

The factor of moonlighting has built into the Argentine mass media system potential conflicts of interest at almost every publication and broadcasting station. This journalistic vulnerability has been exploited in turn by the military leaders in power from 1966 to 1973 and those in power after 1976. Argentine military government administrators during both periods did not hesitate to use censorship to control the content of the news but also, when convenient, utilized as media control consultant fees to working reporters in the vaguely defined area of public relations.

The military governments during the 1966–1973 period also discovered that a majority of reporters and editors were no longer veteran journalists who had learned their profession in the pre-peronista days before 1943. Such professionals, dedicated to objectivity in writing the news and intensive efforts in seeking the facts and checking them for accuracy, were beginning to be outnumbered by younger reporters who were products of the Argentine educational system during the Perón era. Retirements, deaths, and emigration had taken a toll.

In addition to the obstacles presented by the economy, the training of mass media personnel, and government censorship, working conditions themselves in the late 1960s discouraged journalistic initiative. Argentina's once modern telephone system had aged into disrepair. Trunk line overloads caused frequent busy signals. Often an hour of dialing did not complete a call. Cameras and printing presses were wearing out and replacements were not being manufactured or imported.

The Perón dictatorship's legacy to Argentina newspapers and broadcasting stations involved more than government censorship. It also imposed on the reporters and editors the psychological posture of caution. Once the Argentine journalistic tradition had centered in vigorous investigation. In the 1960s reporters tended to soften highly critical stories to avoid trouble. Even without censorship, the military governments of 1966–1973 might not have suffered as severe criticism as they feared. The Buenos Aires daily *La Razón* acquired the largest circulation in the nation, and did not even carry an editorial page. Its emphasis on sports, entertainment, and human interest trivia may have reflected the nation's apprehensions more than the serious content found in *La Prensa* and *La Nación*.[30]

Despite such inhibiting factors as poor working conditions and political caution, many Argentine news editors and reporters in the late 1960s continued to try to discover the negative as well as the positive facts about public events, and military censorship continued to prevent much in-depth reporting from reaching the public.

Publisher Victorio Dalle Nogare founded the weekly news magazine *Primera Plana* in 1960, and by 1967 its nationwide readership had come to expect reliable, nonpartisan coverage of the economy, world affairs, and as much of national government activities as official pressures would allow. During the second half of 1967,

Primera Plana in weekly installments, ran the "History of Peronismo" series in moderate, impartial style. Provincial newspapers ranging from *Los Principios* of Códoba to *La Capital* of Rosario contracted to reprint its weekly news summaries. No other Argentine magazine had so mastered the art of presenting reports and analyses of economic trends with a bare minimum of political commentary except for the veteran periodical *Veritas,* the respected magazine still being published by Francisco A. Rizzuto.[31] *Veritas* has long been respected throughout Latin America for its nonpartisan, nonemotional chronicling of the economic trends in Argentina.

In August 1967 *Primera Plana* angered the government by reporting at length on meetings between former President Illia and spokesmen for Juan Perón, living in exile in Spain.[32] The magazine had alerted its nationwide readership that the seemingly inactive opponents of the military government already were planning long-range cooperation.

On August 5, 1969, the Ministry of the Interior closed *Primera Plana,* and the magazine did not resume publication until September 8, 1970, by which time General Roberto Levingston had replaced General Juan Onganía as president.

On March 21, 1971, the ruling junta replaced General Levingston with General Alejandro Lanusse as president of the republic.

In addition to the foreign news services—Associated Press, United Press International, Reuters, Agence France Presse—the Argentine news agency, Saporiti, founded in 1900 and the oldest continuing such service in Latin America, had managed to survive the republic's periods of dictatorship. To promote a news service more in sympathy with the military regime, in May 1968 the government bought the Telenoticiosa Americana news agency (better known as Telam) and awarded it a monopoly in administering all government advertising.[33] Thereby the government acquired still another mechanism of media control. Telam could cripple numerous newspapers, magazines, and broadcasting stations by removing the profitable government advertising until critical editorial policies changed.

Like the two military chief executives before him, President Lanusse objected to the portrayal of Argentine politics and government in *Primera Plana* and on several occasions had the magazine's editors and reporters taken to court and fined for "inciting violence" by running stories that guerrillas were operating in the country. The stories were true but the government objected to any mention of such activities for fear of lending legitimacy to the guerrilla operations. After the September 16, 1972, edition of *Primera Plana* was confiscated by the government, other publications became more reluctant to mention the existence of guerrillas in Argentina.

The National Security Council (Consejo Nacional de Seguridad or CONASE) from 1966 to 1973 served as the formulator for the president and the ministry of the interior of policies, laws, and regulations defining subversion and the related crime of publishing or broadcasting seditious information. CONASE's Anti-Communism Law of August 25, 1967, provided penalties for being judged subversive, including loss of civil rights, being ineligible for government jobs, and being ineligible for any appearances or interviews on television and radio programs. Violators could receive up to eight years in prison.[34]

President Lanusse restored political party activity, recognizing that his nation was fragmented into several political groups within a unique atmosphere in which everyone had come to invoke the term "peronismo" for whatever rival solutions they had for bettering the economic continuing crisis. Originally, under General Perón himself before 1955, peronismo had been classified as fascist, but by the 1970s, peronista groups ranged from Marxist to quasi-socialist. Lanusse sensed that the now aged former dictator could provide a cosmetic symbol of national unity without much substance to back it up. But the military leaders were weary of an ongoing losing battle against inflation, underemployment, and stagnant productivity. Elections were held in March 1973, with Héctor Cámpora as a stand-in presidential candidate bringing civilian government back to Argentina.

The Second Perón Era

Censorship and most government controls of the mass media ended with the termination of military government. After eighteen years in exile, Juan D. Perón returned to Buenos Aires, and Argentina held a second 1973 election, choosing Perón as president and his third wife, Isabelita, as vice-president.

Newspapers and broadcasting stations and networks were free to report anything in public life, but sorting out truth from fiction and significance from trivia during the 1973–1976 period became as difficult for the mass media as during the earlier civilian government period of 1955–1966. An ambiguous peronista identification inside and outside government was now shared by such dissimilar groups as right-wing Catholics, socialists, leftist intellectuals, student sympathizers of Fidel Castro, unreconstructed fascists, and labor boss opportunists.

On July 1, 1974, Perón died and his wife became the first woman president of any Latin American nation. That novelty alone prompted most of the newspapers and broadcasting stations to report about government with care for a time. But soon the media dropped the posture of gallantry when they discovered that Minister of Welfare José López Rega was the nation's de facto chief executive and policy formulator. Kidnappings and attacks on the army and police by the Montoneros and other Marxist guerrilla groups continued, giving the newspapers and broadcasting stations a steady daily budget of violence as the major stories in the nation.[35] Especially in the news was the People's Revolutionary Army (Ejército Revolucionario del Pueblo or ERP).

La Prensa, La Nación, and a few other dailies and magazines from 1973 to 1976 carried the burden of investigatory reporting. The status of broadcasting had changed from private to government ownership. Channel 7 in Buenos Aires had been the republic's first video station in 1951 and had always been owned by the government. The privately owned commercial television stations of Buenos Aires, Channels 9, 11, and 13, on October 9, 1973, were defendants in legal action by the Federal Radio and Television Commission for nonpayment of back taxes, and consequently were expropriated by the government.[36] Similarly, the government acquired Channel 8 in Mar del Plata and Channel 7 in Mendoza.

Presidential Decree 587 in late 1973 ordered newspapers to work towards a quota goal for news categories. Papers should publish 50 percent Argentine news, 30 percent Latin American news, and 20 percent news from the remainder of the world. When the proposal was first discussed in public, news editors warned that no practical way existed for guaranteeing that each day's total of news could be edited by category percentages.[37] By late 1974 the government had not been able to devise any specific means for implementing the arbitrary news category percentages nor for finding the manpower to classify and check each daily newspaper's stories. The decree quietly slumped into disuse because it remained unworkable and unenforceable unless all papers were to be shut down or reduced to slim bulletins.

In March 1974 the Buenos Aires station *Radio Ciudad* began daily news commentaries using slogans that had been popular in Nazi Germany in 1939, ranging from anti-Semitic stereotypes to accusations that the United States wanted to end by force the status of Latin American nations as independent republics. Some of the radio commentaries were excerpted in the far right newspaper *El Caudillo.*[38] After Juan Perón refused to let the Ministry of the Interior even investigate the station's editorials, protest groups gave up. After his death, Isabelita Perón, as president, allowed the federal attorney general's office to consult with the station's management and two former broadcast writers for Germany's Ministry of Propaganda in 1939 were then dropped from the station's news staff.[39]

Montonero Marxist guerrillas kidnapped the publisher of the daily *El Día* of La Plata on June 25, 1974. Local officials and federal police from Buenos Aires announced that they could not bring the Montoneros to justice at that time. The publisher was released after the group received nationwide publicity in most of the mass media, which was the ransom asked. In the aftermath of the candid admission by the government that it could not contain terrorists, most Argentine newspaper and broadcasting officials began to hire full-time private bodyguards.

As public protests over the government's inability to stop guerrilla operations mounted, Isabelita Perón issued Presidential Decree 630 on August 27, 1974, closing the newspaper *Noticias,* the official organ of the Montoneros.[40] Arrested editors then startled the government by testifying under oath that the Peronista Youth movement had collected funds for *Noticias.* The inconsistency and variety of groups within Argentina still using a peronista label while attacking a government headed by Isabelita Perón became clear.

On September 6, 1974, she issued Decree 770 that abolished the magazine *La Causa Peronista,* successor to the more traditional peronista periodical *El Descamisado.* The magazine was banned for publishing a detailed account of the kidnapping of former Interim President of Argentina (during 1955–1958) General Pedro Aramburu. Aramburu had been kidnapped in May 1970 by the Montoneros led by Fernando Abal Medina. His body was found with a Montonero note claiming vengeance for Aramburu's antiperonista politics.[41]

On December 20, 1974, Mrs. Perón issued Decree 1961 that closed the large circulation morning and afternoon newspaper *Crónica* (total circulation 792,000 for three daily editions). The paper was charged with sedition because of its editorial campaign to raise a volunteer army to invade the Falkland Islands. These islands have been occupied since 1833 by Britain. Despite Argentina's longtime claim to them, the government felt *Crónica's* attempt to raise a private army constituted an illegal attempt by a private entity to conduct the foreign policy of the nation, thereby endangering trade relations between Argentina and Britain.

On April 25, 1975, on a public affairs program on Channel 11 in Buenos Aires, Enrique Llamas de Madariaga interviewed Ismael Haiek, public relations consultant for the Argentine embassies of Arab nations. Haiek switched from negative commentary about Israel to criticism of Jewish citizens of Argentina. Shortly after the program concluded, the extremist Argentine Anti-Imperialist Alliance distributed leaflets charging César and Carlos Civita, publishers of the periodical *Editorial Abril,* and playwright Roberto Cossa with being "Jewish enemies of Argentina" and threatening them with death if they did not leave the country.

The Argentine Newspaper Publishers' Association (Asociación de Directores de Periódicos de Argentina or ADEPA) condemned the broadcast as irresponsible and the death threats as barbaric.[42] On April 29 Minister of the Interior Alberto Rocamora announced an investigation of the death threats. Later Haiek was arrested and convicted of printing publications for the Montoneros and sentenced to jail.

In February 1976 a traditional peronista newspaper, *Mayoría,* criticized the government for the practices of its news and advertising agency Telam. The paper charged that Telam made no effort to pay the backlog of debts for advertising it had placed in many publications over a long period of time. The paper's editorial asserted that the non-payment constituted a maneuver by the government "to strangle the press in general but especially newspapers which publish critical commentary or views about government."[43] The next day the paper published an even stronger editorial, but the government chose to ignore the challenge.

The government did not ignore, however, the front page of the February 13 issue of the daily *La Opinión.* It contained a headline across the top of the page reading "Congress Starts Action To Prevent the Total Breakdown of the Constitutional System."[44] The story quoted various members of Congress who were concerned with what they perceived as unconstitutional and arbitrary actions by the president, her advisors, cabinet ministers, and administrators of various agencies. Isabelita Perón issued Presidential Decree 619, closing the newspaper for ten days and accusing *La Opinión* of publishing "false news."

Videla's Military Government

Several Marxist guerrilla bands were terrorizing the dozen largest provincial cities as well as the Buenos Aires suburbs. By early 1976 political kidnappings had become so commonplace they no longer commanded the largest headlines in newspapers nor the lead position in radio and television newscasts.

In dollar value, Argentina was exporting less than one-third the amount it was importing annually. Runaway inflation since Isabel Perón had become chief executive had forced five devaluations of the peso in one and a half years. Both left-wing and right-wing guerrillas seemed to roam the countryside at will and both the police and the armed forces seemed paralyzed. Unrest seemed an almost institutionalized standard of Argentine public life.[45]

An armed forces junta on March 24, 1976, removed Mrs. Perón from power and designated General Jorge Videla as president of the republic. Decrees by the junta suspended Congress and activities of the political parties. Strict censorship for all newspapers, magazines, radio stations, television stations, broadcasting networks, book publishers, theatrical and motion picture productions, billboards, posters, and even comic books was promulgated. In terms of media control, Argentina had returned to the despotic days of 1946.

The Videla government claimed that the censorship would not be carried out by military officers sitting at editors' desks. Rather, publishers and broadcasters were told to show that they "patriotically cooperated" with the new regime by practicing self-censorship in a set of rulings for mass media.

The Ministry of Press and Broadcasting (Secretaría de Estado de Prensa y Difusión or SEPYD) issued a fourteen-point document called *Principles and Procedures*.[46] The "Principles" section gave the media seven points to remember:

1. Foster the restitution of fundamental values which contribute to the integrity of society: order, work, hierarchy, responsibility, national identity, and honesty within the context of Christian morals.
2. Preserve the defense of the family institution.
3. Tend towards informative elements which contribute to the nation's cultural enrichment.
4. Promote for youth social models which stress the values mentioned in (1) to replace and eradicate present values.
5. Strictly respect the dignity, private life, honor, and reputation of people.
6. Work towards the eradication of stimulants based on sexual stimulation and criminal violence.
7. Take firm and consistent action against vice in all its manifestations.

The "Procedure" section gave the media seven other points to follow:

8. Publish information checked at its source and never sensational information.
9. Do not investigate fields which are not for public debate because

of their effect on audiences which are unprepared (for such topics) or because such topics are foreign to their physical and mental age.

10. Eliminate all obscene words and images which are vulgar, shocking, or have double meanings.

11. Eradicate stories which are truculent in the use of words or image portrayed.

12. Tend towards the grammatically correct use of the national language.

13. Eliminate publicizing among the masses the opinion of persons not qualified or without specific authority to give opinions on subjects of public issue. This includes interviews and public opinion surveys and polls.

14. No advertisements (commercial announcements) are to be aired within radio and television news programs.

This remarkably arrogant pontification about what Argentines were entitled to know about the public life of their own country was signed by Navy Captain Alberto P. Corti, press director for the junta in power. These principles and procedures had been approved by General Videla, Admiral Emilio Eduardo Massera, and Air Force Brigadier General Orlando Ramón Agosti on behalf of the armed forces and the junta that now controlled the government.

Key words in the instructions to the mass media editors and writers indicate that they are to report to a citizenry that will be regimented and regulated without benefit of any constitutional concepts of press and speech freedom. Fundamental values include "order" and "hierarchy." Newspapers are no longer to be concerned primarily with chronicling the major events of each day but with trying to change the social values of Argentines. How editors could determine which persons are qualified to express opinions on controversial topics is not explained. The newspapers and broadcasting stations apparently were so stunned by the simplistic moralistic crusade assigned to them in the gathering and processing of news that none of them even attempted to discuss the regulation in print or on the air.

By emphasizing business, health, and sports news, the Buenos Aires daily *Clarín,* tabloid in format and written in readable, concise Spanish, had in the 1970s become the largest-circulation newspaper in Argentina. In 1977 *Clarín* had a Sunday circulation of 586,000 and a weekday circulation of 387,000. The prestigious *La Prensa,* read by most of the nation's civic leaders, had a Sunday circulation of 205,000 and a weekday circulation of 189,000, and *La Nación* had circulations approximately the same as *La Prensa's.* With circumspection and moderation, *Clarín* editorially supported the policies of former President Arturo Frondizi (1958–1962) until the military seizure of power in 1966, and again from 1973 to the coming into power of General Videla in 1976. Concerned with its own self-preservation, *Clarín* then began to give editorial support to the new military government, ignoring some of the most arbitrary abuses of traditional constitutional political rights.

On April 22, 1976, *Clarín* printed a full-page story on the prepublication censorship of the Videla government and on the so-called self-censorship that Argentine newspapers and broadcasting stations reportedly had just agreed to in meetings with the government's public information administrators. An announcement on paper without any letterhead or government agency identification on it was distributed to editors representing all the mass media, at the presidential palace. It read:

> As of today, April 22, 1976, it is forbidden to inform, comment, or make reference to subjects related to subversive incidents, the appearance of bodies, and the death of subversive elements and of members of the armed and security forces in these incidents, unless they are reported to the media by a responsible official source. This restriction includes victims of kidnappings and missing persons.[47]

During 1976, 1977, and 1978, thousands of persons connected in various ways with guerrilla warfare, or with political extremists and the security forces engaging them in violent confrontation, have simply disappeared without adequate public records as to their whereabouts. In December 1977 the Council on Hemispheric Affairs in New York and Amnesty International each compared political prisoners as a proportion of population, and ranked Argentina and Cuba as detaining one for each twelve-hundred citizens as contrasted with Chile's one in two thousand, even though Chile had received a far more negative press portrayal in the United States.[48]

Peter C. Stuart, a reporter for the *Christian Science Monitor,* in a lengthy report on Argentina for *The New Leader* in 1978, stated that 5,000 Argentines had vanished since the Videla government went into office in 1976. Stuart felt that the annual rate of inflation of 340 percent for 1975 intensified general unrest and yielded, in 1976, political killings by Marxist guerrillas and their right-wing counterparts from the Argentine Anti-Communist Alliance at the rate of two per day. This terrorism was suppressed by the Videla government during 1977 by government actions equally as harsh and arbitrary.[49]

News of violence and related dictatorial government actions and programs could not be reported except for the government's own censored official reports. When journalists challenged the restrictions, the generals responded quickly. During 1977, five provincial newspapers were suspended for various periods for violating the ban on freely reporting about violence. And twenty-one Argentine editors and reporters vanished during that same year.

In April 1977 the government arrested Robert Cox, the British editor of the English-language Buenos Aires daily *Buenos Aires Herald* for publishing stories about subversive activities independent of the official government reports. After the prominent Florida daily, the *Miami Herald,* circulated news of the arrest throughout the hemisphere, Cox was released with the warning that repetition of such independent reporting might bring him eight years in prison.[50] Cox had written the only editorials in Argentina at that time demanding that right-wing killers be brought to justice along with left-wing terrorists.

Government threats against editors left their mark on what most Argentines could and could not read and hear. The front page of a Sunday edition of *La Nación* late in 1977 was dominated by accounts of activities of members of the ruling junta, taking up three of the page's seven stories. One sample: a routine communique issued jointly from President Videla and the president of Gabon about trade, with accompanying photo. Another front-page story was the illustrated coverage of the observance of the "Day Saluting Federal Police."[51]

A government report in 1978 that the annual rate of inflation for 1977 of 347 percent had been reduced to a projected 170 percent for 1978 was portrayed by the mass media of Argentina as an outstanding accomplishment of the government. Missing were commentaries that pay increases were much smaller than either the rise in prices or the recurring currency devaluation.

During 1978 the most widely viewed advertisement, on billboards and on television, was adapted from a government poster. It portrayed Argentina shaped like a beefsteak on a plate between a knife and fork. The slogan accompanying it read "Let's unite and we will not become a morsel for subversion." The mass media, under severe restrictions on what they could report about public life, could not print or broadcast numerous examples of austerity and self-sacrifice that might help that very government campaign for unity.

Instead of improving the political atmosphere by freeing the mass media to report accurately and thereby perhaps regain some public confidence in the government, the Videla regime decided to rely on more sloganeering, expanding the poster plea for unity with other efforts that professional public relations consultants might devise. The Ministry of Foreign Relations hired the New York public relations firm of Burson-Marsteller to help improve the image of the Videla administration.[52]

The Madison Avenue agency spent the $1.2 million it received for operational expenses from the ministry on exhaustive studies, and concluded that it could design and carry out a wide-ranging program of image building in eight major foreign countries, but the Burson-Marsteller projects did not include programs within Argentina itself. The Argentine government was advised to invite leading newspaper and broadcasting editors and writers from the United States and from other major nations with free-press systems to Buenos Aires to visit with carefully selected Argentine government officials, who could explain the problems the government has in coping with the economic crisis and the threats of terrorists. By early 1979 few foreign journalists could be found to take part in the program.

During Argentina's past periods of press freedom, numerous professors from its universities and research institutes wrote bylined features for the major daily newspapers. But after the coming into power of the Videla government in 1976, more than 2,000 professors were dismissed from university faculties and almost 100 academic courses were suppressed.[53] *La Prensa, La Nación,* and other quality newspapers gave up their longtime practice of recruiting intellectuals to write columns, and even staff members of the nonpolitical Argentine Association of Physics became reluctant to write for a mass audience in a political atmosphere in which government officials might presume that challenging essays were violations of the law.

In one sphere of mass communication, however, the government eased restrictions. In June 1978 the ban was revoked against foreign news services distributing news about Argentina within Argentina. Harold K. Milks, former chief of the Associated Press for South America and a longtime correspondent in Buenos Aires before settling in Arizona, felt that the government's Telam and the privately operated Saporiti agency could not collect and circulate enough significant news of national interest to media throughout the republic, given the censorship with which Argentine news personnel have had to work. Even the foreign correspondents of agencies distributing national news within Argentina were warned to be circumspect in their work, though the only control the Videla government had over them presumably was expulsion from the nation.

Milks quoted the government's public information secretary, Rear Admiral Rubén Franco, instructing foreign correspondents on the meaning of their new permission to handle domestic Argentine news:

> Now it is you, more than the government, who are custodians of the precious gift of freedom of information. No extremism can be tolerated.[54]

No longer do federal government officials consider press freedom a guaranteed right under the constitution but rather a "precious gift."

Persecution of *La Opinión*

The Buenos Aires daily *La Opinión* had the same highly respected professional standards that the more internationally famous *La Prensa* and *La Nación* had also put into practice. Despite numerous warnings from several military commanders of the Videla government to censor itself more stringently, *La Opinión* managed to publish as many national stories about labor-management debates and negotiations, trade deficits, inflationary pressures, and even political violence as the police and Interior Ministry would permit.

On March 17, 1974, *La Opinión* broke the news that two staff writers for Buenos Aires station *Radio Ciudad* had been similarly employed in Germany in 1939 and that the station was airing prewar Nazi slogans. Other media knew about the broadcasts but remained silent because of the prominent position certain fascist generals held in the new Perón administration.

Several times during 1975 the government threatened editors of *La Opinión* with possible prison terms after the paper reported strikes by the General Federation of Labor.

The government closed *La Opinión* from February 14 to February 24, 1976, for reporting that members of Congress feared a breakdown of the constitutional system.[55]

Principal enemy of the newspaper in the government was General Carlos Suárez Masón, commander of the First Army and closely associated with the far right periodical *Cabildo,* which during 1976 featured articles reprinted from German publications of the Hitler era, including essays by Julius Streicher and Alfred Rosenberg. The general attended meetings at which a few officers told right-wing civilian audiences that they hoped the armed forces would prevent any Jewish influence in Argentine life. The publisher of *La Opinión,* Jacobo Timerman, was the only Jewish publisher of a major Argentine paper, and the special target of hatred of Suárez.

On April 15, 1977, although neither the attorney general's office nor the police had any charges against either the publisher or his newspaper, army officers and soldiers from General Suárez's command post arrested Timerman and took him to the La Plata First Army headquarters. Apparently neither the Ministry of the Army nor any other government entity knew of the arrest because the military police carrying it out did not even know Timerman's home address, which was on file with various government offices. The military group first arrested one of *La Opinión's* editors and forced him to give them the address, the Associated Press later learned.[56]

The twenty army military police who seized Timerman also arrested *La Opinión* news editor Enrique Jara on April 15, and questioned him daily about the fact that Jara had been born across the estuary in Uruguay. The editor, like his publisher, had been a longtime consistent critic of both leftist and rightist extremists and a known opponent of both Communists and Nazis. Unable to connect his Uruguayan birth to even one story sympathetic to leftists, the military released Jara on April 23.

The goal of General Suárez was bigger than mere intimidation. He wanted Timerman discredited or imprisoned. Argentina was not to have even one Jewish publisher. In addition, *La Opinión* had challenged the *Principles and Procedures* censorship guidelines, setting a dangerous example in the view of the Videla government. If the independent-minded paper were expropriated, other media would take heed and not challenge the censorship rules.

General Suárez had a team of auditors examine the financial records of *La Opinión* and finally found an item that could be made to seem serious enough to excuse expropriation. The paper had borrowed money from a bank owned by the Graiver family. The government had accused the Graivers of investing funds that had come from the Montonero guerrillas. No court hearing or conviction on the matter had taken place. But the general insisted that because the newspaper had borrowed from a Graiver bank, itself under suspicion of having received Montonero money, the paper also was involved.

With no more evidence than the accusation of General Suárez, the government took title and possession of *La Opinión* on May 24, 1977, and installed an army colonel as its editor. The action was termed "expropriation" but legally that implies compensation to a private owner when a government forces the sale of anything to itself. No money was ever offered or paid to Timerman, making the "expropriation" a confiscation. Once the paper itself became a mouthpiece for a faction of the army, its customary readers dropped it, shrinking its circulation.

On November 11, 1977, President Videla issued a decree stripping Timerman of his citizenship, property, and civil rights. Without a court trial and with no witnesses or any evidence, the government declared Timerman guilty of violating the "Act of Institutional Responsibility." On October 14, 1977, in a secret session, a military court had found no evidence against Timerman, but that court finding was kept from the Argentine media, which indirectly learned about it later when the Associated Press confirmed that the October 14 court session had taken place.[57]

After an inquiry from U.S. Secretary of State Cyrus Vance as to why the Argentine government imprisoned Timerman without any specific charges or court trial, President Videla had the army move Timerman from the La Plata prison to the Villa Devoto jail in Buenos Aires. Inquiries from many publishers throughout the Western Hemisphere who knew Timerman personally from meetings of the Inter-American Press Association continued to embarrass or annoy the Argentine foreign ministry. This pressure from abroad brought about the transfer of Timerman from jail to house arrest in his own home.

James Neilson, assistant editor of the *Buenos Aires Herald,* wrote a special seven-page report on Timerman and *La Opinión* distributed by the Inter-American Press Association to all IAPA members in November 1978.

On September 25, 1979, Timerman was expelled from Argentina into exile in Israel, after the Argentine Supreme Court ordered his release, ending 29 months of imprisonment without a conviction. *La Opinión* remained a government newspaper.[58]

Controlled Sources of News

On November 15, 1978, Army Captain Héctor de Pirro, director of the presidential press office, distributed to representatives of all the mass media gathered at the presidential palace a report on the government's Water and Electric Power Corporation, which had sent a technical mission to the Soviet Union. Argentina had signed a contract under which the Soviet government would provide technical assistance for a hydroelectric plant on the Paraná River.[59]

Inasmuch as the Videla government had often tried to justify its censorship and curtailment of civil rights on grounds that the action was based on anti-Communist commitments of the junta, the Argentine contract with the Soviet Union seemed newsworthy. Did the action signify official distinction between domestic anti-Communist policies and foreign policies? Would Argentine-USSR trade be expanded? Such questions went unanswered.

Professional journalism's practices would have required reporters to attempt to get numerous questions about the contract with the Soviet Union answered at the Ministry of Foreign Relations or at other government offices. With the highly centralized control of official sources for news of the government, no such following up occurred.

During 1979 and 1980 news stories about Argentine government policies were never more than mildly critical. In March 1981 General Roberto Viola replaced Videla as president for a three-year term. Viola had the same media policies.

References

Alexander, Robert J. *The Perón Era* (New York: Columbia University Press, 1951).

Alisky, Marvin. "Argentina: News Services," in John C. Merrill, Carter R. Bryan, and Marvin Alisky, *The Foreign Press,* 2nd ed. (Baton Rouge: Louisiana State University Press, 1970).

Alisky, Marvin and Paul R. Hoopes. "Argentina's Provincial Dailies Reflect Neutralism of Mass Media in Country's Political Crisis," *Journalism Quarterly* 45 (Spring 1968): 95–98.

Associated Press correspondents. "Human Rights Violations in South America," *Arizona Republic,* Dec. 17, 1978, p. 26-A.

Baily, Samuel L. "Argentina: Reconciliation with the Peronists," *Current History* 60 (December 1965): 356, 369.

Banco Central. *Presupuesto General de la Administración Nacional para el Ejercicio 1948* (Buenos Aires: Banco Central de la República Argentina, 1949).

Barager, Joseph R. "Argentina: A Country Divided," in Martin C. Needler, ed., *Political Systems of Latin America,* 2nd ed. (New York: Van Nostrand Reinhold, 1970).

_____, ed. *Why Perón Came to Power* (New York: Alfred A. Knopf, 1968).

Blanksten, George I. *Perón's Argentina* (Chicago: University of Chicago Press, 1953).

Bradford, S. E. *The Battle for Buenos Aires* (New York: Harcourt, Brace, 1943).

Cohen, Alvin. "Revolution in Argentina?" *Current History* 62 (November 1967): 283–90.

Del Carril, Bonifacio. *Buenos Aires Frente al País* (Buenos Aires: Editores Emecé, 1944).

Easum, Donald B. *"La Prensa* and Freedom of the Press in Argentina," *Journalism Quarterly* 28 (Spring 1951): 229–30.

Flores, María. *The Woman with the Whip: Eva Perón* (Garden City, N.Y.: Doubleday, 1952).

Gainza Paz, Alberto. *Education and Journalism in the Struggle for Freedom* (Evanston, Ill.: Northwestern University, 1951).

_____. "Freedom of the Press Committee," *Proceedings of the Inter-American Press Association* (New York: IAPA, 1955), pp. 49–51.

Gardner, Mary A. "The Argentine Press Since Perón," *Journalism Quarterly* 37 (Summer 1960): 426–30.

Greenup, Ruth and Leonard. *Revolution before Breakfast: Argentina, 1941–1946* (Chapel Hill, N.C.: University of North Carolina Press, 1947).

Hoopes, Paul R. "Content Analysis of News in Three Argentine Dailies," *Journalism Quarterly* 43 (Autumn 1966): 536–37.

Huergo, María C. "The Argentina Press: Beginnings and Growth," *Journalism Quarterly* 16 (September 1939): 258–60.

Ingrey, Norman. "Rival Argentine Newspapers Mark Dates of Centennials," *Christian Science Monitor,* Oct. 18, 1969, p. 7.

Instituto Nacional de Estadística y Censos. *Instituto Nacional de Estadística y Censos* (Buenos Aires: INDEC, March 1978).

Inter-American Development Bank. *Economic and Social Progress in Latin America* (Washington, D.C.: IADB, 1977).

International Press Institute. *The Flow of News* (Zurich, Switzerland: IPI, 1953), pp. 87–100.

Johnson, Kenneth F. "Argentina" in Richard F. Staar, ed. *1978 Yearbook on International Communist Affairs* (Stanford, Calif.: Hoover Institution Press, 1978), pp. 330–31.

Josephs, Ray. *Argentina Diary* (New York: Random House, 1944).

_____. *Latin America: Continent in Crisis* (New York: Random House, 1948).

La Prensa editors. Correspondence to Marvin Alisky of September 2, 1977, and November 17, 1978.

_____. *Defense of Freedom* (New York: John Day Company, 1952).

Lernoux, Penny. "Systematic Persecution Said to Sap Strength of Argentina's Universities," *Chronicle of Higher Education* 12 (Dec. 11, 1978): 5.

Levene, Ricardo. *A History of Argentina* (Chapel Hill, N.C.: University of North Carolina Press, 1937).

MacDonald, Austin F. *Latin American Politics and Government,* 2nd ed. (New York: Thomas Y. Crowell, 1954).

Merrill, John C. "U.S. Panel Names World's Ten Leading Quality Dailies," *Journalism Quarterly* 41 (Autumn 1964): 568–72.

Milks, Harold K. "Argentina Strikes," *Arizona Republic,* June 8, 1978, p. 16-B.

Ministerio de Justicia. "Decreto 630," *Boletín Oficial,* Sept. 3, 1974, p. 7.

Neilson, James. "La Opinión," *Inter-American Press Association,* Nov. 1978, pp. 1–7.

Organization of American States. *América en Cifras 1972—Situación Demográfica* (Washington, D.C.: OAS, 1973).

Perón, Eva. *La Razón de Mi Vida* (Buenos Aires: Ediciones Peuser, 1951).

Perón, Juan D. *Conducción Política* (Buenos Aires: Escuela Superior Peronista, 1951).

Pierce, Robert N. *Keeping the Flame* (New York: Hastings House, 1979).

Radio Belgrano. Staff members interviewed for NBC Radio Network by Marvin Alisky in Buenos Aires, August 1949.

Rodríguez, Carlos J. *Yrigoyen: Su Revolución Política y Social* (Buenos Aires: Facultad de Derecho, 1943).

Rowe, Leo S. *The Federal System of the Argentine Republic* (Washington, D.C.: Carnegie Institution, 1921).

Schneider, Ronald M. "Argentina: Terrorism and Police Violence," *Collier's Year Book 1977* (New York: Macmillan, 1977), pp. 140–41.

Scobie, James R. *Argentina: A City and a Nation* (New York: Oxford University Press, 1971).

Snow, Peter. *Political Forces in Argentina* (Boston: Allyn and Bacon, 1971).

Staar, Richard F., ed. *1978 Yearbook on International Communist Affairs* (Stanford, Calif.: Hoover Institution Press, 1978).

Stuart, Peter C. "The Cost of Life in Argentina," *New Leader,* Apr. 24, 1978, pp. 14–16.

United States Department of State. *White Paper on Argentina* (Washington, D.C.: Department of State, 1945).

Whitaker, Arthur P. *The United States and Argentina* (Cambridge, Mass.: Harvard University Press, 1954).

Yooll, Andrew Graham. *The Press in Argentina 1973–78* (London: Index Press, 1979).

Newspapers and Periodicals: *Buenos Aires Herald,* Buenos Aires; *Clarín,* Buenos Aires; *El Caudillo,* Buenos Aires; *La Nación,* Buenos Aires; *La Opinión,* Buenos Aires; *La Prensa,* Buenos Aires; *La Razón,* Buenos Aires; *Latin American Digest,* Tempe; *London Economist,* London, England; *Mayoría,* Buenos Aires; *Miami Herald; New York Times; Primera Plana,* Buenos Aires; *Times of the Americas,* Washington, D.C.; *Veritas,* Buenos Aires.

10

Uruguay and Chile: From Freedom to Censorship

FOR most of this century, until the 1970s, two republics in Latin America enjoyed constitutional democracy and freedom of the press. Then, economic and political crises curtailed political liberties in general and freedom of the press and broadcasting in particular in both Uruguay and Chile.

URUGUAY

Fallen Utopia

Beginning with reforms in 1904, Uruguay evolved the most open society in Latin America for almost seven decades. A constitutional democracy, its two traditional highly competitive political parties maintained honest elections. Without military revolution, Uruguay early in the century voted for reforms that yielded Latin America's first welfare state. Press freedom flourished and with the coming of radio in the 1920s, that freedom extended to broadcasting.

During two periods of time, Uruguay attempted the Swiss concept of a plural presidency to obviate any possibility of a dictatorial chief executive. A pastoral land whose wealth came from agriculture and ranching, Uruguay spent itself into bankruptcy providing cradle-to-the-grave welfare for all its citizens. The economic disaster engendered the loss of political democracy and press freedom.

Wedged between two giant neighbors, Brazil and Argentina, Uruguay's land area of 72,172 square miles seems small, for it equals half the size of Arizona or less than England and Scotland combined. Entirely within the temperate zone, its level terrain has made land communication and transportation among all its cities and towns and the countryside easy to achieve.

Divided into nineteen departments (provinces) for administrative purposes, Uruguay remains demographically a huge head on a tiny body. More than half its entire population of 2.8 million, or some 1.5 million, live within the urban sprawl of greater metropolitan Montevideo, its capital. With an annual population increase of less than 1.2 percent, its population total has remained almost stable for several years.[1]

Most Uruguayans are of Spanish, Italian, or Portuguese descent. No Indian or other minority groups await integration into the national way of life, for almost all Uruguayans are already Spanish-speaking possessors of the national culture. With 92 percent adult literacy, Uruguay has long led the other Latin American nations in that category and in the percentages of its school-age children in primary and secondary schools.[2]

Until the Marxist urban guerrillas, the Tupamaros, unleashed violence into daily public life, during 1969 to 1972, civilian government excluded the military and police from policy formulation.

Six major daily newspapers of Montevideo sell approximately 430,000 copies each day, whereas eighteen provincial dailies have a circulation of 112,000.[3] With 1.8 million radios in daily use, even in highly literate Uruguay broadcast news remains the chief mass communication medium. The four television stations of Montevideo have repeater transmitters and provincial affiliates reaching the citizens of every neighborhood in the nation.

Batlle: Modernizer of Uruguay

José Batlle, whose father had been president of Uruguay from 1868 to 1872, studied law, then became a journalist and political reformer. On June 16, 1886, he founded the Montevideo daily newspaper *El Día,* which became the leading paper of the republic during most of the twentieth century.[4] It was the editorial voice of the traditionally liberal Colorado party, which remained the majority party in Congress from 1865 to 1959 and which controlled the presidency during those ninety-three years.[5]

The conservative Blanco or National party and the Colorado party go back to 1836 when Liberals and Conservatives fought a military battle at Carpintería, then organized to institutionalize their political differences in elections.

Batlle was elected president of Uruguay for two terms, 1903–1907 and 1911–1915, but he dominated public life from 1903 until his death in 1929.

A 1905 measure in Congress for a divorce law giving women full equality in terms of property rights was championed by Batlle for two years in news stories and editorials in *El Día* until it became law in 1907.

Batlle lent his prestige both as chief executive and as head of the Colorado party to his social reforms. He also had his newspaper *El Día* steadily campaign for a maximum workday of eight hours, overtime pay, and collective bargaining for unions, all of which became laws in 1915, earlier than in other Latin American republics.[6]

Politically and journalistically, Batlle pushed his Colorado majority in Congress to enact social reform laws. In 1912 the government established the State Insurance Bank that later evolved a social security system, and a Home Mortgage Bank. A 1915 law created the government monopoly for electric power and telephone service at subsidized low rates. Government banks expanded rural credit. Another Batlle law created the National Administration for the Port of Montevideo and the nation's port facilities.[7]

Batlle's greatest efforts went into the Constitution of 1919 that peacefully separated church and state, created woman suffrage in municipal and provincial (departmental) elections, and substituted for a one-man chief executive a plural presidency, a popularly elected National Council of Administration of nine members, with the majority party holding six seats and the minority party three. In addition, a president was elected to coordinate and carry out foreign policy. This two-headed executive apex, designed to prevent dictatorship, broke down in March 1933 under the economic depression that found unemployment soaring and the plural presidency stalled in inaction. President Gabriel Terra's mild coup dissolved the National Council, and the Constitution of 1934 restored the single presidency.

Batllismo, the Batlle philosophy urging a plural presidency, had brought on rival factions within the Colorado party. The *Lema* law permitted each faction to run a presidential candidate, then pool the faction votes for a single party total. In 1951 the Colorados had three factions and the Blancos had two. The demand was revived to try Batlle's dream of a plural presidency, but this time without the extra chief executive, simply substituting a National Council of Government for the president.

The longtime Blanco leader, Luis Herrera, decided to endorse the plan and leading Colorado and Blanco editorial voices found themselves for once on the same side. The Montevideo dailies, *El Día* and *Acción* for the Colorados, and *El Debate* and *El País* for the Blancos, each campaigned for the collegiate presidency. Voters endorsed a new constitution in December 1951, and in March 1952 a National Council of Government replaced the chief executive, thanks in part to strong newspaper campaigning.[8]

In 1958 the Blancos became the majority party as the plural presidency continued to struggle with shrinking export earnings from wool, beef, veal, and wheat, and as the welfare state benefits continued to expand. Uruguayan government employees could retire at age fifty-five, and citizens enjoyed almost free medical care and hospitalization. The unionized work force carried out more than 700 work stoppages and strikes a year during the 1950s, as pay increases and price rises chased each other in a spiral of inflation. With the 1953 cost-of-living index at a base of 100, the 1965 index zoomed to 2,395. The inaction of the plural presidency again became a mass media target and in 1966 voters ended it again, restoring a chief executive system to begin five-year terms in March 1967. President Gestido died after a few months in office and his term was served out by Vice-President Jorge Pacheco.

Carlos Manini Ríos, publisher of the Montevideo daily newspapers *La Mañana* and *El Diario,* served Gestido and Pacheco successively as minister of education, director of planning and the budget, and then head of the Bank of the Republic.[9]

The inflation rate for 1967 zoomed to 136 percent, as Uruguayans witnessed their purchasing power evaporating. With a total work force of 810,000, more than one-fourth worked for the government under laws that permitted no reduction of employees. Some 250,000 Uruguayans had retired under full social security pensions, some of them only forty-five years of age. The economic and political systems were strained to their very foundations.

Luis Batlle, nephew of the great José Batlle, in 1948 founded the Montevideo daily *Acción,* which his son Jorge Batlle edited and published throughout the 1960s, warning of the need to regain an economic foundation for the republic. *El País, Debate,* and *El Plata,* supporting the Blancos, each touched on part of the crises, but none of the newspapers could foresee the bankruptcy that awaited the economy. During July and August of 1967, a strike by newspaper employees for a 76 percent wage increase shut down all of the republic's newspapers except the Communist party daily, *El Popular,* and the non-political tabloid *Extra.*[10] The leading broadcasting station *Radio Carve,* owned by the Fontaina family that operates television station Channel 10, expanded its news programs because of the strike and then for several years continued to air numerous and lengthy news reports.

Head of the company for both stations, Raúl Fontaina, had served as president of the Inter-American Association of Broadcasters.

During this period, *Radio Espectador* also became a station emphasizing news programs, under the direction of Hugo Fernández, Jr. His father, Hugo Fernández Artucio, former editor of *El Día,* served with distinction as the republic's best known and leading editor for twenty-five years.

Also from 1967 on, *Radio Sarandí, Radio Oriental,* and *Radio Ariel* each increased their news coverage with half-hour and one-hour round-ups, in addition to their five-minute reports every hour.

Erosion of Democracy

Beginning in 1969, until suppressed by the military and the police in 1972, the Marxist guerrillas of the National Liberation movement, known as Tupamaros, engaged in hit-and-run warfare aimed at the overthrow of the government and the establishment of a Communist regime. Combined with an ailing economy, the periodic breakdown of law and order led in 1973 to the curtailment of constitutional democracy and freedom for the mass media.

Organized by a Marxist who left the Socialist party, Raúl Sendic, the Tupamaros in 1967 released a clandestine bulletin saying they had placed themselves "outside the law. . . . The hour of rebellion has definitively sounded for us. . . ."[11] In 1969 these guerrillas began a series of political kidnappings of Uruguayan officials, foreign diplomats, and traditional party leaders.

In July 1969, when the far left intellectual magazine *Marcha,* highly esteemed in academic circles in Uruguay, ran an editorial sympathetic to the guerrillas as protestors of the unsolved economic crisis, President Pacheco broke the tradition of press freedom, under emergency power to curb the violence, and had police confiscate that week's edition.[12]

During July and August 1970, the Tupamaros attracted attention to their struggle to overthrow the government by kidnapping a Brazilian diplomat, a U.S. technical advisor, a U.S. agricultural expert, and the British ambassador to Uruguay. When the Communist Party of

Uruguay (Partido Comunista del Uruguay, or PCU) daily newspaper, *El Popular,* reported on these kidnappings and related bank robberies and arson attacks by the Tupamaros in sympathetic detail, the government suspended five issues of that paper. When the conservative or Blanco daily, *El Debate,* published details of the government's inability to stop the Tupamaro raids, the Ministry of the Interior and the police intervened and confiscated that paper's offending issues.[13] Seventy years of press freedom had now been compromised by a political and economic crisis.

In November 1970 the daily *Acción* published a Tupamaro "Manifesto to Public Opinion" and the government imposed a twenty-four-hour suspension on the paper. In the same issue, *Acción* reported that the Tupamaros had successfully taken $1.2 million from the government's Discount and Savings Bank.[14]

In February 1971 the government suspended the leftist daily *Ya* for reporting in detail on successful guerrilla activities.

As economist Eric N. Baklanoff observed, the Uruguayan government for years had built a highly subsidized, high-cost urban industrial sector and elaborate welfare state by draining resources from the agricultural sector upon which the economy depended.[15] Uruguay took on high standards of living without having the national means to pay for them. Now in the 1970s, the economy struggled with bankruptcy, and political alienation spread enough to frighten a constitutionally elected government when faced with the Tupamaro warfare.

In May 1971, after several more kidnappings of prominent Uruguayans, a presidential decree restricted news coverage of the Tupamaros to the information provided by official sources. The Cuban news agency, *Prensa Latina,* defied that decree and continued to report all Tupamaro activities from Marxist sources, and therefore, on June 17, 1971, was ordered to suspend operations in Montevideo.[16]

In the November 1971 elections, for the first time the two major parties, Colorados and Blancos, received less than 91 percent of the total vote. A Broad Front (Frente Amplio or FA) provided a coalition for the Communist, Socialist, and Christian Democratic parties, and won 18 percent of the vote.[17] Colorado candidate Juan Bordaberry won and was inaugurated as president of Uruguay on March 1, 1972, for a five-year term. Some fifteen months later he curtailed Uruguay's traditional constitutional democracy by imposing press censorship in an attempt to end an era of violence.

In April 1972 the Tupamaros sought to "raise the level of struggle" by kidnapping and killing several more prominent Uruguayans. In Congress, despite delays and debates by the FA members, the Colorado and Blanco factions voted for a "Declaration of Internal War" against the Tupamaros. Soon police uncovered more than 200 hideouts and arrested 2,500 guerrillas and sympathizers. Sendic and other Tupamaro leaders who had escaped from prison in 1971 were recaptured by September 1972.

Under a limited state of siege law, the Security Measures Act, enacted in June 1969, the president and his minister of the interior continued to have the power to selectively censor if they could claim a danger to national security. On September 28, 1972, the government brought charges against a pro-Communist daily newspaper, *Ultima Hora,* for publishing fictional reports that encouraged violence. A court found the newspaper guilty.[18]

Tupamaros kidnapped José Pereyra González, the editor of the daily *El Día,* in October 1972 and released him a week later, after the paper published a detailed story about the event.[19] The government agreed that several such detailed reports had been necessary in order to secure the release of the editor.

Strikes and demonstrations had choked off any growth in industrial production. Walkouts by doctors and health workers made some hospitals inoperative. In February the leaders of the armed forces called for increased employment, land reform, a campaign against corruption, and wiser spending to reduce inflation, which had been eroding the purchasing power of almost everyone. On March 22, 1973, the armed forces issued a communique condemning the politicians for failure to help the president with national reconstruction and charging that the Tupamaros had tried to destroy the base of Uruguayan nationality.[20] Senator Enrique Erro and other Broad Front members in the Congress used their congressional immunity to continue to defend the Tupamaros and to attack the politics of the armed forces and of the administration.

Backed by the armed forces, civilian President Bordaberry staged a coup on June 27, 1973, which curtailed constitutional democracy and political freedom. He suspended Congress and the political parties, and also imposed censorship on all the mass media, ending almost seventy years of democracy. Bordaberry blamed Marxist-led violence, numerous acts of sedition, a chaotic Congress, and a bankrupt economy for the imposing of a military-backed government.[21]

The Communist party's daily, *El Popular,* and all other far-leftist newspapers and magazines, including those of the Socialist party and of the coalition Broad Front, were suspended for several days at a time whenever they challenged the government's authority or published stories not approved by the censors. *El Popular* was suspended from mid-September to mid-October for its editorial attacks on the coup in Chile that ousted the Marxist government of Salvador Allende, and the magazine *Marcha* received a similar suspension at that same time period for the same reason.[22] In December all Marxist and far left publications were banned.

Censored Media

In 1976, in place of a popular election, the Council of State, acting in behalf of the suspended Congress, elected a Colorado civilian, Aparicio Méndez, as president of Uruguay for a five-year term to September 1981. As the dailies *El Espectador* and *El País* observed carefully, not much political discussion or debate preceded this election.[23]

By 1978 Montevideo's eleven dailies had shrunk to six. The sick economy worked against periodicals as much as did the restrictions of censorship. In 1973 the leftist *Ultima Hora* was suspended for ignoring the censors but *BP Color* took bankruptcy after advertising revenues plunged.[24]

Commercial radio stations began in Uruguay in 1924 and the government's *Radio Sodre* began in 1930. Commercial television stations Channels 10, 4, and 12, and their repeater transmitters covering the republic, came in 1956. The government's Channel 5 also carries commercials.[25]

Even though cigarette commercials have accounted for large advertising revenues for television, Uruguayan stations had the courage from 1967 to 1978 to air discussions by scientists warning of health hazards from smoking. Despite threats from cigarette sponsors that they would curtail their television advertising, they did not.

Since June 1973, when the government instituted formal censorship, all television and radio stations have aired news programs that follow government restrictions. However, *Radio Carve* displayed special skill in reporting up to the limits set by the government, broadcasting in 1977 and 1978 comments on the economy by leaders of the suspended Colorado and Blanco political parties.

El País has demonstrated its own ability to work as close to the limits as allowed by censors. In an interview with President Aparicio Méndez in 1976, the paper got him to affirm the necessity to revive political parties once national security was made safe.[26]

Once the military leaders decided that Juan Bordaberry would leave office in 1976 and that the Council of State would elect a new chief executive, special leeway was given to the daily *El Día* to criticize him. On its editorial page for June 13, 1976, that paper charged that Bordaberry's arbitrary attitude and intolerance of opposition political parties was as "totalitarian as that of the Marxists."

CHILE

Multiparty Democracy Era

From 1891 to 1925, the so-called parliamentary era prevailed, in which a strong Congress overshadowed a weaker presidency, spawning a multiparty system in which the Conservative, Liberal, Radical and other parties, grew through their voices in the legislative branch.[27] The Constitution of 1925 reestablished a strong presidency, with the Congress being able to check or modify the chief executive's policies. A military leader, Carlos Ibáñez, established a dictatorship from 1927 to 1930. Military coups created a "Socialist Republic" in 1931 and ended it in 1932. Then coalition politics allowed civilian democracy to function until 1973, when a military government came to power.

Chile's 1977 population totaled 10.5 million, with some 3.5 million in the greater Santiago area. Almost no Indians or non-Spanish-speaking minorities impede universal communication, with Chileans being either of European origin or *mestizo,* and 90 percent of them literate.[28]

Chile in 1978 had 3.7 million radios in daily use, tuned to 150 radio stations, 29 of which are in Santiago. Though privately owned commercial outlets, they and their networks are guided by government censors. The three television stations in Santiago (Channels 4, 9, and 13) are owned by Valparaíso Catholic University, the University of Chile, and Santiago Catholic University, but the national network of 23 stations, covering the republic long before the 1973 military government took power, was owned by the government. The five Santiago daily newspapers account for 500,000 of the total 900,000 total circulation in the republic.[29]

A 1963 survey found that 86 percent of the adults read a daily newspaper and better than 90 percent listened to radio news every day.[30] In 1980 Chile had 3 million television receivers.

Even before the advent of the military government's censorship in 1973, one must not assume that the era of democracy was completely free of governmental guidance or attempted interference with the basically independent mass media.

One of the Santiago daily newspapers, *La Nación,* for decades had been owned and operated by the government itself, and therefore was required to support whatever administration happened to be in power, whether conservative, moderate, or liberal.

Gabriel González Videla was elected president of Chile in 1946 with support from various leftist groups, including the Communists. He even had Communists holding three cabinet posts but after a few months ejected them from the government. In 1951 he had Congress enact the Law for the Defense of Democracy, giving the president authority to arrest persons accused of menacing democracy.[31] González Videla interpreted that to mean closing off official news sources to hostile radical publications during crises. That law was revoked in 1957.

President Carlos Ibáñez during his 1952–1958 term became upset with the satirical political criticism of radio programs based on the humor magazine *Topaze.*[32] His cabinet ministers brought pressure to bear on advertisers for that series.

On July 11, 1956, the Chilean congress enacted a law creating a Register of Journalists (Registro de Periodistas), in which every editor and reporter, including broadcasting journalists, had to register with the government, join the professional level College of Journalists, and adhere to a code of ethics administered by a National Council.[33]

This 1956 law phased out of the profession of journalism anyone without a secondary and preparatory school education and legally opened the door for government-encouraged fines for potentially libelous or simply undocumented controversial stories.

In 1960 President Jorge Alessandri had enacted Law 425: Rectification of the Abuses of Publicity.[34] This empowered the attorney general and the minister of the interior to run a rectification if a government official could prove factual errors in a story about his entity in a hearing before the National Press Council. Before his term of office ended in 1964, President Alessandri had several rectifications printed in *El Siglo,* newspaper of the Communist party, and in *Ultima Hora,* newspaper of the Socialist party.

In 1963 President Alessandri's Minister of Justice, Enrique Ortuzar, drafted a law he dubbed the "Abuse of Publicity Act," but which critics soon termed the "Muzzle Act." The minister had been the target of frequent extreme attacks from the leftist newspaper *Clarín,* which prompted his action. As enacted by Congress in January

1964, the Law on Norms of Written and Oral Publicity dealt with various mass communication topics ranging from pornography to libel.[35] Title I required that, except for technical and foreign language publications, owners and administrators of newspapers, magazines, radio, and television stations must be Chilean citizens.

Title III provided prison terms and heavy fines for publishing out-of-context, distorted, or false versions of official statements or documents, or defamation through malice.

The Christian Democratic party's candidate, Eduardo Frei, in September 1964 won the presidential election with 56 percent of the popular vote, for the term November 1964 to November 1970. In August 1967 President Frei had Congress reduce the 1964 Publicity Abuses Act to a tame statute against pornography, with the potential threats to traditional press freedom removed.[36]

Frei's administration itself, however, was not free from an attempt to guide or control a bloc of newspapers. His government in September 1966 attempted to purchase a chain of five daily newspapers in four southern cities belonging to the Southern Journalistic Society (Sociedad Periodística del Sur, or SOPESUR). SOPESUR expressed the political views of the conservative National party, the 1965 merger of the Conservative and traditional Liberal parties. After vigorous protests by the Inter-American Press Association and by various Chilean groups, the government backed away from the purchase.[37] The papers were *La Patria* of Concepción, *El Diario Austral* and *El Gong* of Temuco, *El Correo* of Valdivia, and *La Prensa* of Osorno.

Also by November 1966, the Radical party and the National party complained that the advertising business from government agencies, such as the national airline LAN, had been withdrawn from the conservative daily *El Diario Ilustrado,* forcing it into bankruptcy.

In 1967 the Christian Democratic party's prominent leaders purchased controlling stock in the Zig-Zag Publishing Corporation, which was publishing the news magazine *7 Días,* the general interest magazine *Vea,* the leading women's magazine *Eva,* and the magazine of political cartoons *Topaze.* The Catholic Archdiocese of Santiago became a 14 percent junior partner with the Christian Democrats (PDC), insuring numerous periodicals sympathetic to PDC's Eduardo Frei, president of the republic.[38]

Also in 1967 Radomiro Tomic, who would become the PDC candidate for president in 1970, bought *Desfile,* a news magazine that supported the party. Three other PDC leaders bought the Orbe News Service, which distributed national news to Chilean newspapers and broadcasting stations.

During the Frei presidency (1964–1970), as during the Alessandri presidency (1958–1964) and for seventy years prior to that, the most prestigious and influential daily newspaper in the nation remained *El Mercurio* of Santiago, which supported the traditional Liberal party until it merged with the Conservative party to form the National party. *Mercurio* then supported the National party until military censorship in 1974 intervened. *Mercurio* was founded in 1827 in nearby Valparaíso, where it continued to maintain an edition. Its publisher, the Edwards family, also publishes two afternoon Santiago newspapers, not as famous or nationally read as the morning *Mercurio, Ultimas Noticias,* and the tabloid *La Segunda.* In surveys, various media specialists and scholars have rated *El Mercurio* one of the leading dailies of the world.[39]

Frei and his PDC administration, therefore, received editorial criticism from the National party's *El Mercurio,* the Communist party daily *El Siglo,* the Socialist party daily *Ultima Hora,* the generalized leftist daily *Clarín,* and the Radical party's daily *Tercera.* The government's own daily *La Nación* naturally supported the administration.

In October 1969 General Roberto Viaux publicly protested in the mass media to President Frei that beginning copper miners earned higher salaries than army colonels with twenty-five years of service. Viaux then led protests by various army units, prompting the president to retire him from the service and to censor press reports of army revolts. Under a state of siege decree, the government on October 17 confiscated editions of *El Mercurio, La Segunda,* and *Ultimas Noticias,* and arrested *Segunda* editor Mario Carneyro on charges of violating national security. On October 23 the censorship of news about the aborted rebellion was lifted.

Near the end of his term, President Frei also clashed with a foreign newspaper, barring Malcolm W. Browne of the *New York Times* from covering the September 1970 election. Browne, a Pulitzer-Prize winner based in Buenos Aires, had written articles about land seizures by Marxist-led squatters. Frei was concerned about what use the Marxist coalition candidate, Salvador Allende, was making of such stories.[40]

The Allende Era

In the September 1970 election, Popular Unity, a coalition of the Communist and Socialist parties plus the Radical and three smaller leftist parties, had Marxist Salvador Allende as presidential candidate. With 36 percent of the popular vote, Allende had a 1.4 percent plurali-

204

ty over his opponents and the Chilean Congress, sitting as an electoral college, declared him president of the republic. For the first time in Latin American history, a popularly elected Marxist headed a government pledged to change the pluralistic political system to a Marxist one. No armed revolution had occurred, and the Congress and the nation remained deeply divided among leftist, centrist, and rightist groups. As expropriations proceeded for one-third of the privately owned businesses and industries, pressures mounted.

Allende had the editorial support of the Socialist daily *Ultima Hora,* the Communist daily *El Siglo,* the generalized leftist daily *Clarín,* the government-owned *La Nación,* and some of the provincial press. Some forty radio stations were identified with the Marxist coalition as supporting the government, as were two of the Santiago television stations and their provincial affiliates.[41] He was able to name his own director for Quimantu, the government's publishing corporation, to issue books supporting his administration. Some 5 million books on Marxist economics and politics were sold during two years of the Allende presidency.[42]

Allende was inaugurated as president of Chile on November 3 and one week later on November 10 stated that a study had begun of the possible nationalization of the conservative daily *El Mercurio.* To lessen government pressures on the paper, Agustín Edwards on November 11 resigned as *Mercurio* board chairman, being replaced by politically neutral Fernando Leniz. During the three years Allende was president, the leftist daily *Clarín,* with 250,000 circulation, became the largest circulating newspaper. Government news sources became belligerent to *El Mercurio* reporters, and its circulation trailed that of *Clarín.*

On January 13, 1971, agents of the Internal Tax Service occupied the business offices of *Mercurio* as the government began lengthy and detailed inspection of the newspaper's records, looking for tax violations.

After exploring formats for news programs over station *Radio Corporación,* owned by the Socialist party, the government in 1971 increased the variety and quantity of its own special broadcasts. Broadcasting laws allowed the president to link all radio stations into a national emergency network for government crisis reports.

Chile by 1971 had left, right, and center reports competing for attention in all the mass media.

On May 17, 1971, the government froze advertising rates and sales prices for all newspapers and magazines, and at the same time increased the salaries of all publication employees by 50 percent. A majority of the newspapers announced that they might have to close, and the next month Minister of Economy Pedro Vuskovic announced the end to the freeze on advertising rates.[43] Newspapers throughout Latin America and the Inter-American Press Association had protested the restriction on revenues as a danger to the continuance of the press.

In September 1971 United Press International carried a story from Colombia reporting members of the Chilean government had distributed arms to Colombian guerrillas. On September 15, 1971, President Allende closed UPI's operations in Chile, allowing the news service to resume its work two weeks later.[44]

At the same time, *El Mercurio* reported that government pressures on advertisers had reduced its advertising revenue more than 50 percent.

An anti-Marxist women's street protest in early December 1971 was extensively covered by *Radio Balmaceda* in Santiago, prompting the government to declare a state of emergency decree, and to take the broadcasting station off the air for 24 hours. On December 11, for reporting on violence and unrest, *Radio Balmaceda* received a forty-eight-hour suspension, and *Radio Agricultura* and *Radio Cooperativa* received warnings not to air such broadcasts or they would also face suspensions.[45]

In June 1972 the Chamber of Deputies and the Senate voted to accept charges against Allende's Interior Minister Hernán del Canto for refusing to allow police to arrest leftists who seized private farms and factories to force an acceleration of the government's nationalization program. When the conservative daily *La Segunda* published the congressional charges, its editor, Mario Carneyro, was jailed on June 21 on charges of breaching state security.[46] The Court of Appeals later ordered the editor released.

Allende's proposals to replace the two-chamber Congress with a people's assembly intensified the civil strife of 1972 and 1973, culminating in August 1973 in strikes by truck and bus drivers paralyzing the nation's transportation industry. News of these events found the government and many of the mass media colliding.

In June 1973, when the government filed criminal charges against *El Mercurio* for running a political advertisement referring to the Allende administration as "illegitimate," the newspaper had to suspend operations for six days.[47]

Also that June the Interior Ministry closed *Radio Agricultura* for reporting on violence in the copper mining areas, lifting the suspension after one week. *Radio Yungay* refused to carry all the government's special network news and was shut down indefinitely. One of the refused news reports was from *Puro Chile,* a Communist party Santiago tabloid.

During August 1973 strikes closed a majority of the factories, railroad traffic from Santiago to the south ended, and truck drivers brought much of the trucking industry to a halt. The annual rate of inflation approached 1,000 percent. By September the economy had nearly collapsed. On September 11, 1973, the armed forces ousted the Allende government and a junta designated General Augusto Pinochet as president of Chile.

Military Government Censorship

The military government in September 1973 closed the Communist daily *El Siglo,* the Communist tabloid *Puro Chile,* the Socialist *Ultima Hora,* the leftist daily *Clarín,* the paper of the People's Republic of China *Combate,* and all other Marxist publications.[48]

In October 1970, the Christian Democratic party had established the Santiago daily newspaper *La Prensa.* The military censors suspended this paper for a few issues and then let it revive. Although the Christian Democratic party itself was not suspended by the government until March 12, 1977, the PDC leaders decided to suspend *Prensa* voluntarily on March 4, 1974, after almost six months of daily disputes with censors over critical editorials and news stories going beyond limits imposed by the government.

Allende's decree of December 27, 1970, ordering all Chilean radio stations to devote at least 40 percent of their music on the air to Chilean songs was cancelled on September 15, 1973, giving the military government one of its rare public approval messages by the Association of Broadcasters, who presumed the end of the musical restriction meant other broadcasting freedoms, which were not forthcoming.

From October 1973 to April 1974, correspondents for foreign news services, networks, newspapers, and magazines were sending out daily lengthy reports on arrests and government crackdowns on the supporters of the Allende regime, but the Chilean media were under restrictions whereby they could not report many of the same details. As the leftist and other criticism from abroad intensified, the junta dropped its studies of how to ease censorship. Its Media Commission, which was formed to propose looser guidelines for the press, disbanded in mid-1974.

Leopoldo Linares, correspondent for the Venezuelan daily *El*

Nacional of Caracas, surveyed the Chilean government-media situation for the latter part of 1977. He found that the censors could rely on self-censorship by Chilean editors of stories that could set off public alarm or violent demonstrations.[49] If news editors did not seek consultation from the censors on highly controversial stories, then the government could act under the National Security Decree of December 12, 1975, which authorized the junta to suspend newspaper editions or radio-television broadcasts creating public panic.

Inasmuch as the most positive actions of the government since 1973 were to reduce the runaway inflation rate, almost any story about the cost of living went unchallenged. The inflation rate of 1,000 percent in 1973 was reduced to 375 percent in 1974, 340 percent in 1975, 174 percent in 1976, and 31 percent in 1980.

In June 1978 the daily *El Mercurio* and the news magazine *Ercilla* were permitted to publish an interview with Alamiro Guzmán, a Marxist leader of the Mine Workers Union.[50] The government was trying to end demands from the AFL-CIO in the United States to ease restrictions on Chilean unions. Threatened with an economic boycott by the AFL-CIO, in early 1979 the Chilean Minister of Labor granted unions collective bargaining, limited strike rights and the right to have dues checkoff procedures. Media coverage of these activities was to be phased in gradually.[51]

Orlando Letelier, Chilean ambassador to the United States under President Allende, was killed in Washington as an exile in September 1976. On February 14, 1979, a federal court in Washington convicted two anti-Castro Cubans of his murder. The weekly news magazine *Qué Pasa,* published in Santiago by Emilio Sanfuentes, reported in detail the accusations of columnist Jack Anderson and of other U.S. critics of the Chilean military government that Chilean rightists were also involved. *Qué Pasa* ran two pages of accusations from articles by Robert Woodward of the *Washington Post* and from Jack Anderson against the former Chilean secret service, DINA.[52] That edition of the Chilean magazine was the most extensively critical of the military government the censors had permitted to be published.

The same magazine in July 1978 also ran a lengthy interview with Carlos Paul, president of the National Press Association, in which he pointed out that criticism in the newspapers would be unable to oust the government and therefore more press freedom was justified.[53] The plea was not answered nor did the daily censorship end or lessen.

In 1979 and 1980 two antigovernment news magazines, *Hoy* and *Mensaje,* in Santiago, were permitted to publish mild criticism of the government. And the press in general was allowed to publish details critical of the Pinochet government in stories about the conviction of two anti-Castro Cubans for the 1976 killing of Allende supporter and former ambassador, Orlando Letelier, in Washington.[54] These were exceptions to the general censorship.

For decades, the government operated the daily *La Nación,* assuring its support of whatever administration was in office. The Pinochet regime allowed it to expire with the overthrow of Allende in 1973. As a successor, the government established *El Cronista* as one of the five major dailies of the republic in 1975. In addition to censorship, the government has its own newspaper voice.[55]

References

Alisky, Marvin. *Uruguay: A Contemporary Survey* (New York: Praeger, 1969).
_____. "Uruguay" in Richard F. Starr, ed., *1974 Yearbook on International Communist Affairs* (Stanford, Calif.: Hoover Institution Press, 1974), pp. 372–77.
_____. "Uruguay Prizes its Print, Broadcast Press," *Quill* 55 (Oct. 1967): 32–34.
_____. "Uruguay's Utopian Broadcasting," *Journal of Broadcasting* 13 (Summer 1969): 277–83.
Baklanoff, Eric N. "Pathology of Uruguay's Welfare State," *Mississippi Valley Journal of Business and Economics* 2 (Spring 1967): 65–67.
Burnett, Ben G. *Political Groups in Chile* (Austin: University of Texas Press, 1970).
Carter, Roy E., Jr. and Orlando Sepulveda. "Some Patterns of Mass Media in Santiago de Chile," *Journalism Quarterly* 41 (Spring 1964): 216–24.
Editor and Publisher. *Editor & Publisher International Yearbook 1978* (New York: Editor & Publisher, 1978), pp. III-41–III-48.
Ehrmann, Hans. "Letter from Chile," *Performance* (May–June 1973): 99–101.
Fagen, Patricia. "The Media in Allende's Chile," *Journal of Communication* 25 (Winter 1974): 59–70.
Fasano, Federico. *Paren las Rotativas* (Montevideo, Uruguay: Editorial Octubre, 1973).
Fitzgibbon, Russell H. *Uruguay: Portrait of a Democracy* (New Brunswick, N.J. Rutgers University Press, 1954).
Gil, Federico G. *The Political System of Chile* (Boston, Mass.: Houghton Mifflin, 1966).
Handleman, Howard. "Uruguayan Journal," *Worldview* (October 1977): 16–17.
Hanson, Simon G. *Utopia in Uruguay* (New York: Oxford University Press, 1938).
Houseman, Martin. "Chile's CD's Taking Over Publications," *Overseas Press Bulletin* 11 (Nov. 18, 1967): 1–2.
Inter-American Development Bank. "Chile Statistical Profile," *Economic and Social Progress in Latin America: 1977 Report* (Washington, D.C.: IADB, 1977), pp. 182–83.
Inter-American Press Association. "Allende Eases Pressures After Protests by the Press," *IAPA News,* July 1971, pp. 1–2.
International Press Institute. "Abuse of Publicity Act Divides Chilean Journalists," *IPI Report* (Zurich), Apr. 1964, pp. 11–12.
Knudson, Jerry. "The Chilean Press Since Allende," (Paper at International Communication Division, Association for Education in Journalism, Houston, Texas, August 1979).
Krause, Charles A. "Chileans Relax Amid Improving Outlook for Rights," *Washington Post,* Mar. 19, 1979.
Linares, Leopoldo. "Chile: Four Years Later," *Atlas World Press Review* 27 (February 1978): 21–22.

Marbut, Frederick B. "Chile Has Law to Enforce Code of Ethics," *Quill* 48 (April 1960): 15–17.

Matas, Raúl. "Chile on the Air," *Américas* 7 (October 1955): 6–9.

Merrill, John C. *The Elite Press: Great Newspapers of the World* (New York: Pitman, 1968).

Ministerio de Hacienda. *IV Censo de Población* (Montevideo, Uruguay: Dirección General de Estadística y Censos, 1969), Part I, pp. 3–29.

OPI, Uruguay. *Organización de la Prensa del Interior 1977* (Montevideo, Uruguay: OPI, 1977), pp. 7–12.

Pierce, Robert N. "Lights Out in Santiago," *Quill* 62 (January 1974): 17–21.

_____. *Keeping the Flame* (New York: Hastings House, 1979).

Redding, David G. "The Economic Decline of Uruguay," *Inter-American Economic Affairs* 21 (Spring 1967): 55–72.

Stanley, Diane. "The Press in Chile: The Rectification Law," *Nieman Reports* 15 (January 1961): 27–31.

Taylor, Philip B. *Government and Politics of Uruguay* (New Orleans: Tulane University Political Science Studies, 1960).

United States Information Agency. *Mass Media in Chile* (Washington, D.C.: U.S.I.A., 1977).

Vanger, Milton I. "Uruguay Introduces Government by Committee," *American Political Science Review* 48 (June 1954): 510–15.

Weinstein, Martin. *Uruguay: The Politics of Failure* (Westport, Conn.: Greenwood Publishers, 1975).

Newspapers and Periodicals: *Acción*, Montevideo; *Diario de las Américas*, Miami, Florida; *Editor & Publisher*; *El Día*, Montevideo; *El Espectador*, Montevideo; *El Mercurio*, Santiago; *El País*, Montevideo; *La Mañana*, Montevideo; *La Nación*, Santiago; *Latin America Political Report*, London, England; *Los Angeles Times*; *New York Times*; *Qué Pasa*, Santiago; *United Press International*, Santiago.

11

Censored Central America

IN Central America the popularly elected democracy of Costa Rica for decades has enjoyed press freedom for its newspapers, magazines, and broadcasting stations. The other republics of Central America, plus Panama, have, by contrast, suffered censorship.

GUATEMALA

Most of Guatemala's political history has found dictator generals ruling the republic. When constitutionally elected civilian President Julio Méndez Montenegro served his full 1966–1970 term of office and in 1970 turned the office over to his popularly elected successor, he became only the third such president of Guatemala to do so in the history of the republic.

Crowded into its national territory of only 42,000 square miles, Guatemala's 1977 population of 6 million was overwhelmingly Indian, with a ruling mestizo minority, and an adult illiteracy rate of 75 percent—a percentage estimated by news editors and educators.[1] The six daily newspapers of Guatemala City, with a total circulation of 205,000, serve the entire nation since none of the provincial cities maintains a daily newspaper.[2] Thanks to widespread distribution of battery-operated transistor radios, radio constitutes the principal medium of mass communication, with the newspaper readership concentrated among the upper class and the government bureaucracy. Some forty-seven radios per 1,000 population are in daily use.

Of the ninety-four radio stations in Guatemala, all but eight have been privately owned since the 1940s, and as of 1978, sixty-nine of these stations carried news programs called "Radioperiódicos" or radio newspapers.[3] Each such news program is owned by its producers who gather, write, and air the news; sell advertising time; and then purchase the air time for the newscasts from each station. This system facilitates the government's ability to purchase, bribe, or subsidize most of the broadcast news.[4]

One of the daily newspapers in Guatemala City, *Diario de Centro América,* founded in 1880 as a commercial publication, was acquired in 1931 by the government as the official journal of record and serves that function plus that of a medium of some general news. Its content comes directly from government sources and the selection of news is determined by its official editors.

The leading daily of the republic, *El Imparcial,* strives to report as much objective news of national life as possible, but through the years has suffered longer periods of censorship than of relative independence.

From Dictatorship to the Arbenz Era

Guatemala has suffered some long dictatorships, complete with press censorship. President Manuel Estrada Cabrera ruled for twenty-two years, from 1898 to 1920. General Jorge Ubico's dictatorship, with press censorship and no civil rights, lasted fourteen years, from 1930 into 1944. Then a socialist reformer, Juan José Arévalo, was popularly elected for a six-year term, from March 1945 to March 1951. Then a more militant leftist, pro-Marxist Jacobo Arbenz, was elected president for the 1951–1956 term, but was ousted by the armed forces in mid-1954, initiating an era of military presidents with conservative governments.

During the Arbenz presidency, the Communists controlled the Guatemalan Labor party, the Guatemalan Federation of Labor, the Ministry of Education, and the government's radio station and network, station TGW, which had more commercial revenue than competing private stations. TGW and its affiliates received news of government policies, programs, actions, and laws ahead of the private stations, allowing it to become the dominant mass medium in the nation.[5]

Because of the high degree of illiteracy and the small newspaper readership, the Arbenz administration permitted *El Imparcial* to run some critical stories about the government. Clemente Marroquín

Rojas, who had founded the daily *La Hora* in 1920, had suspended his paper from 1931 to 1944 during the Ubico dictatorship. *La Hora* also was able to report some news critical of the Arbenz government. When *La Hora* editorially demanded that Guatemala invade Belize in 1948, President Arévalo closed the paper for six weeks.[6] As a conservative, Marroquín had fewer pressures on his paper after the Arbenz ouster. *La Hora's* editorials have not been consistent, attacking at various times the United States, Communists, the church, the banks, tourists, and leftist reformers.

Before the ouster of Arbenz, station TGW was utilizing news from TASS, the Soviet Union's news service, as its chief source. The news from Western news services in the newspapers reached fewer Guatemalans.

After the presidencies of military leaders Carlos Castillo Armas, Miguel Ydígoras, and Enrique Peralta from 1954 to 1966, Guatemala finally had a popularly elected civilian government. The Constitution of 1965 added the office of vice-president to the government. Earlier constitutions had been suspicious of having such a position in which a leader might be tempted to oust a chief executive to succeed to his position. The 1965 Constitution also gave the president the authority to restrict individual rights, including freedom of the press, similar to the earlier Law of Public Order restrictions.[7]

From Civilian Back to Military Rule

Professor of law Julio Méndez Montenegro was inaugurated as president of the republic on July 1, 1966, and served his full four-year term. His vice-president was Clemente Marroquín Rojas, who also continued as publisher of the daily *La Hora.* The paper editorially attacked the president, who was more progressive or liberal than the vice-president.[8]

Prensa Libre, another Guatemala daily, founded in 1951, during the early Méndez Montenegro administration also enjoyed the freedom to criticize or run stories the government considered negative. Its criticism remained mild, for the publisher and editors agreed with the attempted tax and other reforms of the government.

In 1968 the era of violence in public life engulfed Guatemala. Marxist guerrillas and right-wing forces both began killing prominent Guatemalans and foreigners. The rightist White Hand groups and the Marxist Armed Revolutionary Forces (Fuerzas Armadas Revolucionarios or FAR) were copied by other groups. Even the Archbishop of Guatemala was kidnapped until ransom was paid.

President Méndez Montenegro issued a state of siege decree in March 1968, so that periodically he could suspend civil rights or invoke censorship of the press and broadcasting. Before he left office in July 1970, he did censor stories involving the search for FAR leader Marco Antonio Yon Sosa, a FAR leader killed by the army in a battle on May 16, 1970, in northern Guatemala.[9]

A conservative military leader, Colonel Carlos Arana won the 1970 election and served as president from 1970 to 1974. He mobilized the army and police to suppress the guerrilla warfare, and utilized press censorship often when stories involved maneuvers against the rebel groups.

The daily *La Nación* was established in February 1970, and early in its operations carried considerable news about the conservative Democratic Institutions Party and the liberal Christian Democratic Party. By the mid-1970s, it had become politically neutral, but provided good coverage of the nation's economic and social activities. During the Arana presidency, it sometimes practiced self-censorship on sensitive national security measures as the government battled to end guerrilla activities.

From July through October 1970, all of the Guatemalan newspapers and radio news programs reported the political assassination of 107 persons, the majority of them leftists. Then on November 12, 1970, President Arana decreed press censorship as the army moved in force against the guerrillas.

From 1970 to 1974, however, the press was allowed to report most of the controversies over land ownership and land use, as well as the token agrarian reform programs and their problems.[10]

General K. Eugenio Laugerud García was elected president in 1974 for the 1974–1978 term. Violence in public life had ended by 1974, and the government encouraged self-censorship among news editors in return for access to official news sources. The Laugerud administration promoted news of the National Front Against Violence, a group of lawyers, students, and labor leaders.[11]

A 1976 earthquake, which killed 23,000 people, tended to draw the government and the mass media together in a campaign for national reconstruction of thousands of homes and businesses.

As political scientist Caesar D. Sereseres pointed out in 1976, Guatemala's highest-ranking military leaders had become better educated in dealing with the public. Their courses at the Center for

Military Studies included public relations. Most generals and colonels had been required to study public administration at the Center.[12]

General Romeo Lucas García, elected president of Guatemala in 1978, reflected this improved skill of government administrators in guiding the mass media. During 1978 the emphasis shifted to self-censorship for editors, with relatively few government pressures actually applied.

The September 15 issue of *Prensa Libre* and the September 16 issue of *La Nación* typified the news emphasis of all Guatemalan papers during 1978. Both editions were filled with stories about the problems of the Somoza government in Nicaragua fighting Sandinista guerrillas, plus a roundup of world news. However, both papers had very few stories about the government of Guatemala except for routine announcements.

In 1979, with the defeat of the Somoza government by the Sandinistas in Nicaragua, guerrilla activity in Guatemala increased, further intensifying press censorship. Self-censorship gave way to government-imposed restrictions as Guatemalan guerrillas received aid from Nicaragua, Costa Rica, Panama, and Cuba.

HONDURAS

Honduras had a population estimated in 1979 at 3 million, with 75 percent adult illiteracy. Two of the four daily newspapers in the capital of Tegucigalpa, *El Día* and *El Cronista,* account for 42,000 of the republic's meager total of 100,000 daily newspaper circulation, including two dailies operating in the chief provincial city of San Pedro Sula.[13] These six newspapers are read mainly by government bureaucrats and the tiny upper class. Most Hondurans listen to two or more of the 124 radio stations blanketing the nation, or watch television in the few urban centers. Broadcasting consists mainly of entertainment, with radio news usually little more than headline and bulletin summaries.

From Two-Party Politics to Dictatorship

The sixteen-year dictatorship of Tiburcio Carías, from 1932 to 1949, like most of the governments before it, institutionalized press censorship and a political system that was generally lacking civil rights.[14] From 1949 to 1971, the Liberal party and the National or Conservative party did struggle for dominance, giving the nation both competing parties and rival newspapers. The Liberal party owned one Tegucigalpa daily, *El Pueblo,* and the National party owned another Tegucigalpa daily, *El Nacional.*

From 1957 to 1963, the Liberal party reformer, Ramón Villeda Morales, as president, permitted the press to criticize his government.

In August 1962, for example, the conservative *El Nacional* attacked the administration with a front page story claiming that Villeda was indignant that priests opposed Communist groups and those sympathetic to Fidel Castro. Nothing factual in the editorial disguised as a news story confirmed the charge.[15]

Frequently, *El Nacional* would feature as news stories editorials against the Villeda administration, against the Liberal party, or against its newspaper *El Pueblo.* The level of journalism was unprofessional but Honduras did enjoy a period of press freedom in which the government did not attempt to curtail political criticism.

During the 1950s and 1960s, the daily owned by the Liberal party, *El Pueblo,* exercised no higher level of reporting or editing than did *El Nacional. Pueblo* frequently referred to the National party leaders of the present or past as an "alliance of tyrants" who practiced political gangsterism. In one August 1962 issue, *Pueblo* asserted that a former National party minister of education believed that democracy was an ally of communism. In the same issue, *Pueblo* ran an editorial entitled "Dictionary of the Infamy of the National Party," which accused the opposition party of circulating lies.[16]

In the 1970s, when military dictatorship first forced both parties to merge and then to become meaningless, the dailies *Nacional* and *Pueblo* expired.

During the era of press freedom, the daily *El Día* remained consistently anti-Communist and anti-Castro, whereas the daily *El Cronista* editorially went leftward and supported Castro's Cuba and Communist nations in general. However, neither of these two papers supported—or opposed—their own government.[17]

Military Rule

On October 3, 1963, near the end of Villeda's term, and just ten days before a scheduled presidential election, Colonel Oswaldo López Arellano and the military leaders of the republic ousted the civilian government. López Arellano declared himself president. In 1965 a fraudulent election chose a constituent assembly to draft a new constitution. The asembly declared itself the Congress and proceeded to "elect" López Arellano to a full six-year term as president, over the objections of the Liberal party.

In 1971, as his term was ending, López Arellano devised a scheme whereby he remained commander of the armed forces while Ramón E. Cruz, a civilian from the National party, would be elected president, with both political parties sharing the same number of seats in the Congress as a national unity plan. In December 1972 Cruz was ousted by the military for not following orders, and the republic returned to the uncomplicated dictatorship of Colonel López Arellano, with both political parties impotent and inactive.[18] Press censorship prevailed though few Hondurans were affected by the newspapers and the competing party journalism already had died.

In 1975 widespread bribery charges and corruption began to multiply against López Arellano after United Brands officials disclosed in the U.S. press that $1.25 million had been paid so that the Honduran government would reduce taxes on bananas.[19] *Wall Street Journal* stories of April and May circulated among the military leaders, who ousted López and installed Colonel Juan Melgar as president. Press censorship was eased so that the Honduran papers and the radio newscasts could discredit the López Arellano regime and justify the new Melgar administration. During much of 1977, Melgar's government allowed press freedom.

On August 8, 1978, military leaders ousted President Melgar for failing to improve the economy and for failing to get the hostile neighboring republic of El Salvador to cooperate in rebuilding the Central American Common Market.[20] Government guidance of the press returned. The leading radio station HRN and its network of affiliates set the pattern for the other radio stations by cutting back news to an emphasis on sports, agricultural trends, and news of the entertainment world, with brief bulletins on government activities. Serialized daily dramas or soap operas still capture large radio audiences, as do musical programs.

President Policampo Paz García and his junta spoke vaguely of elections in the 1980s as they kept government news sources under control, releasing to the media as little controversial news as possible.

In September 1978 a front page announcement in the San Pedro Sula daily *La Prensa* pointed out that it was now the largest newspaper in Honduras, with a circulation of 46,477 certified by the Audit Bureau of Circulation of Chicago.[21]

EL SALVADOR

Crowded into only 8,200 square miles of national territory, El Salvador's population, estimated at 4.5 million in 1978, remains half illiterate.[22] Three of its five daily newspapers—*El Diario de Hoy, La Prensa Gráfica,* and *El Mundo*—account for 217,000 of its total newspaper circulation of 260,000, and these papers were owned by progovernment activists of the National Conciliation party (Partido de Conciliación Nacional or PCN).[23] The other two papers as well as the radio and television newscasts comply with progovernment policies.

After the overthrow of the 13-year dictatorship of General Maximiliano Hernández Martínez (1931–1944), some efforts were made for a more democratic government. The only genuine reformer, President Oscar Osorio (1950–1955), abided by press freedom. In 1955 Colonel José Lemus, as president, restored press censorhip. Since 1961 every chief executive had been an army colonel from the dominant PCN, representing the military, the large landowners, and other conservative groups.

In the 1977 elections the traditional opposition Christian Democratic party formed a coalition with other center-left groups as the National Opposition Union (UNO), but again the PCN candidate, Colonel Carlos Romero, was elected president for the 1977–1982 term. Guerrilla activity against the government in 1977 and 1978 found the government preventing such news from being used by the media.[24]

Since 1970 the government has transmitted for five or more hours a day on each of the two television channels courses for the public schools, stressing vocational and secondary courses.[25]

In October 1979 President Romero was ousted. During 1980 a ruling coalition junta subdued guerrilla attacks and maintained press censorship. With Cuban and Soviet weapons, the Democratic Revolutionary Front continued its warfare, forcing the government to censor news for national security.

NICARAGUA

From 1937 to mid-1979 the Somoza family dominated Nicaragua, which had the form of a two-party government but not the substance. From 1950 to 1979 an opposition daily newspaper, *La Prensa,* alternating between being censored by the government and being able to criticize public life, served as a periodic escape valve for opposition frustrations.

After the ouster of the Somoza government in July 1979, a coalition administration began the slow process toward press freedom amid the uncertainties of a provisional government. A constitution remained to be drafted and future elections remained undefined. For forty-three years, Nicaragua had lived with press censorship, with limited exceptions. National experience with press freedom had been absent.

On August 17, 1979, the five-person ruling junta announced a "Press Freedom Law" that warned the media not to publish stories against the recently victorious revolutionary government nor ones favorable to the ousted Somoza forces. The junta seized the Somoza-owned daily *Novedades* and since August 1979 has published its own daily, *Barricada,* from the Novedades plant.

Some 2.4 million Nicaraguans live in a national area of 50,000 square miles, with an adult illiteracy rate officially listed at 55 percent but actually more than 65 percent. Newspaper circulations have remained small, whereas nine out of ten households utilize radio for news headlines.

Era of Token Press Freedom

After governing Nicaragua for two decades, General Anastasio Somoza, Sr., was assassinated in September 1956. His younger son, General Anastasio Somoza, Jr., became commander of the armed forces, the National Guard, and his older son, Luis Somoza, became president of the republic after the Somoza party, the Liberal party, closed ranks for an election against a Conservative party challenger.[26]

Under Luis Somoza, pressures on the mass media were reduced. The University of Nicaragua and the Fulbright Commission contracted to open a school of journalism and social sciences loosely tied to the National University, with me as founding director, in 1960. At the time, the late Pedro J. Chamorro, publisher and editor of the Managua daily *La Prensa,* was able to run critical news stories and editorials daily, attacking government policies directly, which it had not been able to do under the late general.[27]

With Smith-Mundt funds, the Fulbright Commission permitted me to hire Horacio Ruíz, managing editor of *La Prensa,* and Gustavo Montalbán, its city editor, as part-time faculty to emphasize objective news reporting and responsible editorial criticism. Another *La Prensa* editor, Pablo Antonio Cuadra, became our journalism school dean. In

1961, when the school spawned a new generation of investigatory reporters for radio and for *La Prensa,* the minister of education pressured the National University into withdrawing the school's affiliation. Then the new Catholic University of the Jesuits promptly accepted the journalism school as one of its entities.

During the 1960s, the Somoza family owned the Managua daily *Novedades.* The other four dailies then functioning also politically supported the government. The U.S. Ambassador to Nicaragua, Thomas E. Whelan, had received a political appointment to that post in 1951 and served for ten years. By the time he was replaced in 1961, he had been accustomed to issuing periodic statements for the newspapers and radio endorsing Somoza government policies.[28] Whelan's severe criticism of opponents of the Somozas often became major stories in the Nicaraguan press and on radio and television.

In 1960 President Luis Somoza, feeling secure in his control over news sources, had the minister of public education, René Schick, allow our journalism and social sciences school to conduct the first full-scale, professional-level public opinion poll among a cross section of the population.[29] The survey measured fatalism versus faith in modern technology. We submitted a questionnaire of twenty-one questions to the Ministry of the Interior, which rejected six of them for political overtones. We found a strong tendency for Nicaraguans to be fatalistic, with only 30 percent believing that human nature can be changed or that modern science can better living conditions for most people in a traditional society.

By 1961 government censors were stationed at *Radio Mundial,* the station with the largest audiences for news in the republic, after that station had consistently quoted critical editorials and stories from *La Prensa.* In a nation where only 100,000 daily newspapers were circulating, most Nicaraguans were getting their news from *Radio Mundial, Radio Reloj, Radio Darío,* or *Radio 590.* Since 1962 none of these stations have been free of censorship. When Channels 6 and 8 expanded into networks, their news departments were headed by public relations officers of the government, even though the television system was a mixed private-public corporation.

Radio Noticias in 1960 expanded its independent news coverage, airing many stories daily that were critical of the government. Finally censors ended that practice after stories began to detail clashes between police and students and the operation of leftist guerrillas in the mountains beyond army patrols.[30]

Radio station X, owned by the Somoza family, for decades served as the model of optimistic radio news broadcasting, barely mentioning disasters (until the 1972 earthquake) unless they were foreign in nature.

Tighter Controls

Censorship of the press and broadcasting varied from strict to token after the administration of Luis Somoza ended in 1963. Former Education Minister René Schick was elected president and served until his death in August 1966, when Minister of the Interior Lorenzo Guerrero became acting president until the end of the term in 1967.

In 1967 the constitution was amended, changing the presidential term from four to five years, and General Anastasio Somoza, Jr., was elected for the 1967–1972 term. To lessen criticism from within the republic and abroad, the dominant Liberal party amended the constitution so that from 1972 to 1974 a plural executive, a triumvirate, officially headed the government, with two Liberal party supporters of the Somozas and one opposition Conservative party member making up the apex of the executive branch. The presidential term was lengthened to six years.

From 1972 to 1974 General Somoza pointed to the interim triumvirate to lessen criticism of his family's continuation in office, but he continued to govern Nicaragua as National Guard commander. In September 1974 he was elected to a six-year presidential term.

Up until his ouster in July 1979, Somoza would point periodically to the lone opposition daily newspaper, La Prensa, to those who criticized his censorship of broadcasting and control of the other newspapers.

During July and August 1973, La Prensa continued its daily attacks on the head of the government's housing bank, Fausto Zelaya. This time the newspaper was doing the Somoza government a favor by exposing irregularities in earthquake salvage that had delayed payments for destroyed workers' housing damaged in the December 1972 earthquake.[31] The newspaper series actually forced some resignations from the housing bank's top level of administrators.

In December 1974 Marxist-led guerrillas of the Sandinista movement, dedicated to the ouster of the Somoza government, kidnapped in Managua the Nicaraguan foreign minister, the republic's ambassadors to the United States and to the United Nations, the mayor of Managua, and some other prominent Nicaraguans at a reception. The government had to release twenty-six Sandinista political prisoners into exile to gain the release of these prominent citizens, and full uncensored coverage of the event had to appear in all of the Nicaraguan newspapers and on all the radio and television stations.[32]

On January 10, 1978, unidentified killers assassinated Pedro J. Chamorro, publisher of *La Prensa,* the longtime symbol of all Nicaraguan journalists trying to practice their profession in defiance of government censorship and pressures. Chamorro had been jailed for brief periods on and off since the 1950s after *La Prensa* had become strongly critical of the government in editorials and stories. His death brought demands from the Inter-American Press Association, of which he was a board member, for the Somoza government to capture those responsible.[33]

The Somoza government claimed that Chamorro's opposition had helped better its image. But the anger over his death aroused not only the Sandinistas, but Chamorro's own Conservative party, whose only common bond with the Marxists had been opposition to the Somoza government. Both groups blamed the government for Chamorro's death.

Throughout 1978 Sandinista guerrillas maintained a state of insurrection against the National Guard and the government, which managed to locate the unlicensed station, *Radio Sandinista,* and close it September 14.

The killing of the *La Prensa* publisher became a big factor in increasing United States pressure on the Nicaraguan government to negotiate with the Conservative party and leftist opponents. A team of mediators from the United States, Guatemala, and the Dominican Republic tried to arrange a 1979 plebiscite on Somoza's resigning.

On February 8, 1979, the United States ended military and economic aid programs in Nicaragua to pressure Somoza into reconsidering a popular vote on a new government in 1979. Still he refused.

La Prensa continued publishing critical stories about the government until March 1979, when civil war erupted. Battles continued until Somoza resigned in July. On July 20 a coalition junta took power in Managua. It promised press freedom in the future. Radio news headlines continued to be Nicaragua's main source of news.

Radio Católica emphasized church, religious, and social problems not stated in political terms. *Radio Managua* and other non-Somoza stations continued to use air time for popular music, dramas, comedy, sports events, and meager news reports that met the guidelines of caution.

In December 1976, the government had inaugurated *Radio Nacional,* a 100,000-watt station reaching listeners throughout the republic. In 1978 and 1979 it featured agricultural news and many vocational courses on agriculture, ranching, fishing, and skilled trades. Its news programs had been prepared by the Somoza government, and after July 20, 1979, by the coalition junta's administration.

For the latter half of 1979, the junta's *Radio Sandino* pro-Marxist news programs were carried by all other Nicaraguan broadcasting stations. Nongovernment news could be found principally in the daily *La Prensa*. In 1980 twenty ardent supporters of the government resigned from *La Prensa* to publish their own daily, *El Diario Nuevo*, which joined with the Sandinista daily *Barricada* in emphasizing uncritical, enthusiastic coverage of the government. The Sandinista regime pressured *La Prensa* not to criticize the government.

CONTRASTS

Democratic Costa Rica's Press Freedom

Contrasting sharply with the other Central American republics, Costa Rica practices genuine democracy and enjoys complete press freedom. Its 2 million citizens have achieved 90 percent adult literacy and hold honest elections in which the political "outs" can and do oust the party in power.

Since 1889, abridgement of representative government and of press freedom has occurred only from 1917 to 1919 and again during the 1948 civil war. Former President Rafael Calderón (1940–1944) and President Teodoro Picado (1944–1948) teamed with Communist supporters to pressure the unicameral Congress to cancel the results of the 1948 election, won by Otilio Ulate, leader of the conservative National Union party (PUN). Liberals under José Figueres joined Ulate to form a citizens' army to defeat the small military police force that Costa Rica maintains in lieu of armed forces. Ulate served his elected term.

The constitution provides for a four-year term and a former chief executive must wait two terms before running again. Figueres founded the liberal National Liberation party (PLN) and won the presidency after Ulate. Then followed a PUN victory in 1958, a PLN victory in 1962, then a PUN victory in 1966. By then the conservatives had absorbed the National Republican party and the PUN now stood for National Unification party.

Then in 1970 Figueres won a second term as the PLN candidate. In 1974, Daniel Oduber of the PLN won the presidency, breaking the pattern of the opposition party ousting the incumbent party.[34]

In 1978 the "outs" ousted the incumbent party again, but the veteran National Unification party was not the victor, but rather the new similar sounding National Unity, a coalition representing many of the other opponents of the PLN. Rodrigo Carazo, in winning the presidency and defeating the PLN, again emphasized the genuinely democratic system.

Through the years, the daily *La República* editorially supported the PLN, and the rival San José daily *La Nación* editorially supported the PUN or Unification party. Former Costa Rican President Otilio Ulate owned two dailies, *Diario de Costa Rica* and *La Hora*, which after his death in October 1973 became editorially more independent of the conservative political groups. In general, Costa Rican newspapers have tended to publish considerable detailed information about all the political groups and most of the major political leaders.

Costa Rica's two radio networks and forty-two radio stations and four television stations also have been free of government interference.[35]

In 1970 the National College of Journalists was established by law and all practicing news personnel were required to have a secondary education and apprentice training. In 1978, at the October annual conference of the Inter-American Press Association, this professional group's director, Carlos Mora, reported that in no way could the government use the requirement for professional preparation as a means of censoring the news.

The National Council of Churches of the United States maintains the Latin America headquarters for its adult literacy agency, Alfalit, in San José because of the media freedom there which cannot be paralleled elsewhere in Central America.

From August 1978 to August 1979, San José station *Radio Reloj* increased its news about neighboring Nicaragua because of censorship across the border. The station also has reported often on government pressures on the mass media of Panama, Costa Rica's other neighbor.

Pressured Panama

Before the military coup of October 1968, in which General Omar Torrijos ousted civilian President Arnulfo Arias, Panama's press and broadcasting were usually free of government censorship but often under the influence of bribery. Beginning in 1968 the government imposed censorship on the press and began selecting the news editors of the privately owned media under decree power.

In 1970 the military government of Torrijos had the courts and the

National Bank intervene because of tax irregularities in the newspapers owned by the Arias family, the Spanish-language and English-
language editions of *Panama America, Crítica,* and *La Hora.* In addition, the government foreclosed on two other papers, *El Mundo* and *El
Día.*[36]

The 1972 constitution, which gave Torrijos a six-year term as
Chief of Government, did not basically change the situation.[37] The
election in 1978 of a civilian president, Aristídes Royo, whose authority
was backed by the armed forces of Torrijos, continued government
restrictions and guidelines for the press. On September 27, 1979,
President Royo ordered all privately owned radio stations to carry only
news from government stations. Panama Canal press coverage was
under government control.[38]

References

Alisky, Marvin. "Central American Radio," *Quarterly of Film, Radio, and Television* 10
    (Fall 1955): 59–61.
_____. "Public Opinion Under Dictatorship in Nicaragua," *Nieman Reports* 16 (April
    1962): 12–14.
_____. "Radio in Guatemala," *Radio Daily-Television Daily* 66 (June 24, 1954): 6–7.
_____. "Our Man in Managua," *The Reporter* 23 (Dec. 22, 1960): 26–27.
_____. "The End of Nicaragua's Radio Freedom," *Journal of Broadcasting* 5 (Fall 1961):
    311–14.
Denton, Charles F. "Costa Rica: A Democratic Revolution" in Howard J. Wiarda and
    Harvey F. Kline, eds., *Latin American Politics and Development* (Boston, Mass.:
    Houghton Mifflin, 1979), pp. 347–49.
Editor and Publisher. *Editor & Publisher International Yearbook 1978* (New York: Editor
    & Publisher, 1978), pp. III-43–III-44.
Gardner, Mary A. *The Press of Guatemala* (Minneapolis, Minn.: Association for Educa-
    tion in Journalism Monograph 18, 1971).
_____. "The Press of Honduras," *Journalism Quarterly* 40 (Winter 1963): 75–82.
Guatemala, Asamblea Nacional. *Ley de Emisión del Pensamiento* (Guatemala: Decreto 24
    de la Asamblea Nacional, 1956).
Inter-American Press Association. "Chamorro Assassination Shakes Somoza Dynasty,"
    IAPA News, February 1979, p. 1.
Kinzer, Steven. "El Salvador," *New Republic* 177 (Sept. 3, 1977): 15–17.
_____. "Nicaragua: Universal Revolt," *Atlantic* 243 (February 1979): 4–17.
Martin, Everett G. "At United Brands, Fight for Control Came after Honduran Payoff,"
    Wall Street Journal, May 7, 1975, p. 1.
McDonald, Ronald H. "El Salvador: High Cost of Growth" in H. J. Wiarda and H. F.
    Kline, eds., *Latin American Politics and Development* (Boston: Houghton Mifflin,
    1979), pp. 388–89.
Melville, Thomas and Marjorie. *Guatemala: The Politics of Land Ownership* (New York:
    Free Press, 1971).
Ministerio de Economía de Guatemala. *Estadísticas Sociales* (Guatemala: Dirección
    General de Estadística, 1977).
Morris, James A. "Honduras: A Unique Case?" in H. J. Wiarda and H. F. Kline, eds.,
    Latin American Politics and Development (Boston: Houghton Mifflin, 1979), pp.
    346–57.

Organization of American States. *Constitution of the Republic of Guatemala 1965* (Washington, D.C.: Pan American Union, 1966).

Pierce, Robert N. "Costa Rica's Contemporary Media Show High Popular Participation," *Journalism Quarterly* 47 (Fall 1970): 544–52.

Ropp, Steve C. "Panama's Domestic Structure and the Canal" in H. J. Wiarda and H. F. Kline, eds., *Latin American Politics and Development* (Boston: Houghton Mifflin, 1979), pp. 482–92.

Sereseres, Caesar D. "The Guatemala Armed Forces" (Paper at Latin American Studies Association, Atlanta, Georgia, March 1976).

Walker, Thomas W. "Nicaragua: The Somoza Family Regime," in H. J. Wiarda and H. F. Kline, eds., *Latin American Politics and Development* (Boston: Houghton Mifflin, 1979), pp. 316–31.

Newspapers and Periodicals: *El Diario de Hoy*, San Salvador; *El Imparcial*, Guatemala City; *La Prensa*, Managua, Nicaragua; *La Prensa*, San Pedro Sula, Honduras; *La Prensa Gráfica*, San Salvador; *Latin America*, London, England; *Phoenix Gazette;* *Times of the Americas*, Washington, D.C.; *Wall Street Journal.*

12

Various Voices

THE three categories of mass media systems in Latin America are highly generalized and each nation contains some exceptions to its classification of being free, censored, or guided. Even without formal censorship since 1978, Brazil in 1979 had newspapers with less freedom than the press of Mexico, where control mechanisms insure widespread proestablishment reporting but also permit a variety of right-wing and left-wing criticism of the government.

Cuba's Communist government requires the conformity of all mass media. Within Marxist guidelines, however, newspapers can publish limited criticism of local government, as the national government seeks to direct criticism away from itself.[1]

In Chile, censorship has prevailed, yet two opposition magazines were published during 1978, 1979, and 1980, and the press has been allowed to publish antigovernment details of the conviction of two killers of former ambassador Orlando Letelier, who had been in the Allende administration. Such stories have been directly critical of the Pinochet government. Press circulation totaled 1,600,000 during the presidency of Christian Democrat Eduardo Frei (1964–1970), decreased to 1,400,000 during the presidency of Marxist Salvador Allende (1970–1973), and by 1978 had decreased to under 900,000. Prospects for the press in the 1980s seemed negative since a proposed new constitution would permit press censorship even though an elected civilian government might return to power.[2]

The exact degree of press leeway to report on public life independent of government guidance changes in most of the Latin American nations after major economic or political crises. This volume was written in 1978 and 1979 and cannot reflect basic political changes coming after early 1980.

Peru's state of flux is a case in point. In mid-1978, the government's policy of assigning each newspaper to a distinct group of workers representing a sector of the economy was ended. By early 1979 government guidance had been marred by several instances of censorship of news magazines. As Peru tried to prepare for a shift to elected civilian government for the 1980s, a multiparty political system revived that required many different viewpoints be published. However, such a system implied increased instability in the governments that might come to power. Such governments tend to pressure the press.

Licensing Journalists

Can a nation require that those practicing journalism be better educated to upgrade the quality of reporting, without restricting freedom of the press? In Costa Rica, since 1970, the law requires reporters to have a secondary education and membership in the professional Association (Colegio) of Journalists. These requirements have not hampered that republic's independent reporting of government and politics.

Jerry Knudson has studied the Collegiate (Colegiado) System in Bolivia, which began in 1972, requiring all journalists to be licensed so that their profession could be upgraded into trained, full-time work.[3] In interviews with the Association of Journalists of La Paz President Alberto Nathes Zuazo, with Bolivia's leading writer, Augusto Céspedes, as well as with publishers, editors, and reporters, Knudson found that the Collegiate System upgraded the requirements for practicing journalism.

Before 1972 Bolivians in news work often wrote part-time for fees, and subsisted on bribes (*coimas*) and by holding down two other regular jobs while reporting or editing. With the requirement that only those with a Colegio license can work on newspapers, the Statute for Professionalization of the Journalist, enacted on May 9, 1972, set educational requirements.[4]

Under this law, Bolivians with ten years of experience could obtain the permit and title of "Professional Journalist." Reporters and editors with seven years experience could obtain the title by presenting a thesis. Those entering the profession after 1977 would have to be graduates of Bolivia's only university journalism program, at the Universidad Católica Boliviana.

Every reporter and editor in Bolivia must now be inscribed in the

National Register of Professional Journalists, administered by the government's Ministry of Information and Sports. In 1980 as Bolivia, despite elections, failed to return to civilian government from military rule, the future of the registry as a control mechanism remained uncertain.

In Costa Rica and Chile, a Colegio for journalists exists to upgrade educational requirements, but in each case, the program is administered by the journalism profession itself and not as a government register of control. In Venezuela in 1972 a Law of the Exercise of Journalism was promulgated that required that those entering the profession must first obtain a university degree in journalism.

In Ecuador a 1968 Law of Professional Defense of the Journalist permits those with ten years of experience to be inscribed in the National Union of Journalists, and those with five years of experience to receive a course of instruction from the Ministry of Education. This law anticipated the eventual closing of the field to those without training, but that has not followed. The same law prohibits authorities from requiring reporters to reveal confidential news sources or from being dismissed because of opinions written in articles.[5] But in practice, these guarantees have not been enforced in recent years by the military governments of President Guillermo Rodríguez Lara (1971–1976) and President Alfredo Póveda (1976–1979). As Ecuador in 1979 returned to elected civilian government, the future of such a law remained in doubt.

As various associations of news personnel and governments in Latin America continue to consider the upgrading of the profession of journalism through systems of licensing based on educational requirements or experience, the key to press freedom will center in whether such registries are administered by the professional groups themselves or by the government.

Self-Help

As John S. Nichols has pointed out, in 1970 thirteen leading Latin American daily newspapers pooled their resources to establish LATIN, a regional news agency for Latin America.[6] A decade later, LATIN was serving newspapers in every Latin American republic except Cuba. The publishers and editors themselves, some in nations with censorship, some in nations with guidance and pressures, and a few in nations with press freedom, found that professional dedication to improving their newspapers began with self-help. By purchasing a news service, organized by and for Latin American news editors, they improved the quality and quantity of the stories received daily. In addition to LATIN, Mexico's Latin American Information Service or Servicio Informativo Latinoamericano (SILA) since 1976 has served increasing numbers of newspapers in Latin America.[7]

The biggest morale booster among Latin American publishers, editors, and reporters struggling for independence of operations and against government censorship or pressures and guidance has been the Inter-American Press Association. The IAPA was founded in embryonic form in a Pan American Congress of Journalists in April 1926 in Washington, D.C., under the auspices of the Pan American Union. The IAPA organized into its present form in 1950, and has been holding annual assemblies ever since.[8] A key element of the IAPA is its Freedom of the Press Committee. Every year the IAPA alerts all the media in the hemisphere about those Latin American governments imposing the most severe censorship and restrictions. IAPA members send protests to the offending governments, some of which are concerned enough about a positive foreign image to ease restrictions.

Mary A. Gardner has been the leading scholar of IAPA activities through the years. She found the IAPA alert throughout the 1950s and 1960s to press restrictions by Perón in Argentina, Batista then Castro in Cuba, Trujillo in the Dominican Republic, Paz in Bolivia, and whoever else in Latin America placed hurdles in the path of press freedom.[9] The IAPA vigilance continued through the 1970s.

Professor Gardner found the IAPA working among all of the newspaper publishers of the hemisphere for adoption of a journalistic code of ethics to inhibit the widespread practice in most of the Latin American republics of the acceptance of bribes for favorable news coverage of government officials. Given the income of the average working reporter or editor, and given the inflation rates of recent decades, the IAPA was not able to devise any effective means for inhibiting the widespread use of bribes.

The IAPA helped the newspapers of Latin America take a big step toward improved professional journalism when it created in 1954 the Office of Certified Circulation (OCC). With independent auditors from New York, the OCC can guarantee the reliability of circulation claims by publishers. This helped increase advertising from the United States, Canada, Western Europe, and Japan in the leading newspapers and magazines of Latin America. The OCC circulation figures encourage advertisers to spend more in the reputable publications of Latin America that can guarantee the size of their circulations. By 1960 the OCC had become independent of the IAPA, operating as a solvent and successful independent hemisphere-wide agency.[10]

Since its organization in 1953, the Inter-American Broadcasters

Association (Asociación Interamericana de Radiodifusión or AIR), has striven for similar upgrading of Latin American broadcasting, but has not had the organizational coordination or political impact among Latin American governments achieved by the IAPA.[11]

Multinational Advertising

As *Advertising Age* surveys have shown, the bulk of billings and income of multinational advertising agencies in Latin America have centered in four republics: Brazil, Mexico, Venezuela, and Argentina.[12] In the first three of these nations, the increasing advertising revenues have contributed to the upgrading of the production of the major newspapers, network television, and radio broadcasting. Multinational agencies account for more than half the billings and income from advertising for the mass media in these four countries.

In addition to multinational agencies advertising products aimed at the middle and upper classes in Latin America, considerable multinational advertising also involves consumer goods aimed at the low-income majority of the population in most of the republics. While the impoverished sectors have little to spend, their aggregate disposable income makes them a meaningful market for low-priced goods, especially for radio advertising. The Peruvian Ministry of Labor, reporting on the city slums, noted that Peruvian shanty dwellers spend most of their income on food and clothing, spending almost none of it on housing.[13]

A marketing study in São Paulo, Brazil, showed that 67 percent of the consumer market reached by media advertisers consisted of individuals with less than $500 annual per capita income. Yet 85 percent of their purchases of appliances and even television receivers were financed through installment credit, prompted by radio and television commercials.[14]

In 1977 multinational advertising in Latin America went into radio and television for 65 percent of the total advertising agency billings. Advertising executives recognized that more Latin Americans were in daily contact with radio, and in the urban centers with television, than with daily newspapers.[15]

Within an atmosphere of political democracy in Venezuela from 1976 to 1979, radio and television executives attempted to formulate a national broadcasting policy for their industry independent of the government. This was done for advertising standards, news coverage, public relations, and public service.[16]

In Venezuela, Colombia, Costa Rica, Mexico, the Dominican Republic, Peru, and Brazil, the content of advertising remains uncensored, as long as no direct political messages are inserted. Even in countries with censorship—Argentina, Chile, Uruguay, Paraguay, Guatemala, El Salvador, Honduras, Nicaragua, Panama—the gray areas of public service announcements on radio often go uncensored, even when involving questions about public life that cannot be raised in the news stories on the air or in the newspapers. Such questions relate, for example, to waiting periods for service at public health clinics, lack of openings for new students at schools and instructions for getting on the waiting list, difficulties in getting a bank loan, or problems in public transportation.

Government Newspapers

In Nicaragua the government newspapers set the editorial policies for all the mass media.

As we noted in the chapters on Mexico, as well as imposing government control mechanisms ranging from allocation of newsprint to investments in television networks, the Mexican government itself owns and operates one of the Mexico City dailies, *El Nacional*. In addition a government corporation, SOMEX, owns controlling stock in the chain of thirty-seven García Valseca daily newspapers.[17]

In Cuba the daily newspapers are owned by the Communist party rather than the government, insuring uniform support for the government. In Brazil the centralized authority of the military government insures its power in public life without the need for the government to invest in newspapers or even to exercise formal censorship. In Panama the government has woven its investments throughout the corporations publishing the newspapers, with no clear public record of the extent of that control other than the censored or guided printed editions of the papers themselves. In Peru the government continued to designate the executive publishers of the expropriated newspapers while attempting to make each daily into a voice for a specific workers society, a plan that in mid-1978 went into limbo until the return of an elected civilian government. In 1980 newspaper ownership returned to private companies.

In Chile we have a case of overkill. The Pinochet government since 1973 has maintained press and broadcasting censorship. Before 1973 Santiago had thirteen dailies, but in 1979, only five. As Professor Knudson points out, the government itself operates one of these five dailies.[18]

For decades the Chilean government owned and operated the daily *La Nación.* Whatever administration was in office—whether Radical, Conservative, Christian Democratic, or Communist-Socialist Popular Unity parties—*Nación* supported it editorially. This daily expired with the 1973 ousting of Allende. With its 600 employees out of work, the government created the daily *La Patria* and gave it to the Association of Journalists (Colegio de Periodistas), which could not keep it going financially.

On September 8, 1975, the government, with funds from its official government *Boletín,* established *El Cronista* as a regular Santiago daily newspaper.

Silvia Pinto, editor of *El Cronista,* reports a circulation of 35,000, which means that most Chileans buy the other Santiago dailies or the provincial press. Miss Pinto, a 1961 graduate of the University of Chile, worked for *Nación* and served the government as a press attaché in Buenos Aires. In addition to being editor, she is president of the corporation that publishes *Cronista,* with 60 percent of its shares held by the government and 40 percent by private investors or other entities. As vice-president of the Colegio, she also serves as a buffer between that group and the military government.[19]

The lack of success of *Cronista* illustrates the poor prospect for most dictatorships in trying to compete with professional privately owned dailies, even when those dailies must support the government.

Government Broadcasting

As our studies of individual countries have shown, Latin America has shifted from its early era of almost universally privately owned broadcasting into an era in the 1970s of substantial government investment and control of television and radio stations.

With the advent of the Communist government in Cuba in 1961, it comes as no surprise that all radio and television stations and networks are owned by the government. However, in Colombia, traditionally a constitutional democracy emphasizing a private sector more than a public sector, the 1970s did bring a surprise when all television stations and the two video networks were taken over and operated by the Ministry of Communications.[20] Colombia's government-media pattern has remained inconsistent, inasmuch as its radio stations and networks have been privately owned in the main, and the government has refrained from press censorship in general. Yet in response to guerrilla attacks on government installations in 1978, a presidential decree did authorize the prohibition in Colombia of news about such violence. In February 1979 the emergency statute was ended.

In Argentina, despite the censorship of the first Perón era from 1943 to 1955, and the military government restrictions from 1966 to 1973, it was not until October 1973 that the government expropriated the privately owned television stations of Buenos Aires for nonpayment of back taxes. Similarly, the government acquired television stations in Mar del Plata and in Mendoza, giving it direct control of video news in the major metropolitan areas.[21]

In Peru, in November 1971, the government gained control of broadcast news by purchasing 51 percent of the stock in all privately owned television stations and 25 percent of the stock in all privately owned radio stations. The government's own *Radio Nacional* network for years has attracted the largest audiences for news programs, obviating the need for the government to purchase a majority of the stock in the radio stations that are still privately owned.

In Mexico a 1969 law requires every radio and television station to provide 12.5 percent of its daily air time for public service announcements or other programming from the government.[22] In addition, since 1937 every radio station in Mexico must hook up to a special network Sunday nights for the government's "National Hour." To further insure government impact in broadcasting, in the 1970s, the Mexican government invested directly in television stations and networks. In Mexico City the government owns and operates Channel 8 and Channel 13 as commercial outlets, competing with the privately owned channels for advertising revenue. Channel 8 operates its own network of five affiliated stations in three states, and Channel 13 has a network of twenty-six affiliates in twenty-three states. In addition, the government's holding corporation, Televisa, provides a management entity coexisting with the Telesistema of privately owned Channels 2, 4, and 5 and their respective networks.

In Nicaragua in 1980 the government firmly controlled all broadcasting activities.

IAPA's Warnings and Hopes

In March 1979 the Freedom of the Press Committee of the Inter-American Press Association updated the government-press status in the various Latin American nations.[23]

The IAPA warned that even though Mexico had press freedom, the newsprint authority PIPSA had been restricting supplies of paper to the antigovernment daily *El Norte* in Monterrey, a major critic of the establishment.

In Argentina, in addition to formal censorship, the government had forced Argentine dailies to limit importation of newsprint and to purchase large quantities of paper from a mill partly owned by the government and financed by government banks. In addition, the Argentine government in 1978 raised taxes on newsprint as an additional control mechanism over the press.

In both Bolivia and Ecuador, the governments in 1978 suspended press censorship to prepare these two nations for the transition from a military to a popularly elected civilian government, but many standby regulations could guide official news sources and restrict editors in time of crisis.

In Brazil the government ended press censorship in 1978 and permitted limited air time for the opposition MDB party candidates for Congress on radio and television to equal air time for the government's ARENA majority party. Yet full political freedom had not returned to public life and editors felt the pressure to engage in some self-restraint in attacking the government's policies.

In Central America the IAPA found full press freedom only in Costa Rica. Government measures were taken against critical reporters in Guatemala, Honduras, El Salvador, and Nicaragua.

Press freedom continued in Colombia and Venezuela. Press freedom with minor government guidelines prevailed in the Dominican Republic.

Press censorship continued in Haiti, Panama, Paraguay, Chile, and Uruguay. In Guayana, the government controlled the news through official news sources, being selective in the release of details about the economy and the political system.

In Cuba the complete conformity of the Communist state continued. The media served the government. One Cuban journalist, Alfredo Izaguirre Riva, who had been a reporter for *El Crisol* until 1959, was released from prison after twenty years and was allowed to leave Cuba in time to attend the spring 1979 meeting of the IAPA Board of Directors. However, news personnel were not among the few hundred political prisoners released in 1978.

In Peru the suspension of ten news magazines for several weeks in early 1979 provoked severe IAPA criticism. The government indicated it would try to avoid further censorship. In mid-1978 the government ended its plan of assigning expropriated newspapers to workers societies representing different trades and vocations and allowed employees of the newspapers and former publishers to purchase stock in the dailies. This action was part of an easing of governmental guidance during the transitional period back to elected civilian government planned for 1980.

As of 1979 in Latin America, three republics enjoyed complete press freedom, seven republics had relative press freedom with varying degrees of governmental guidance, and eleven republics suffered press censorship or control of the news through official news sources. Even though there was no formal censorship in eleven of the twenty-one republics, the press and broadcasting serving a majority of Latin Americans had to function under some government pressures.

In the hands of autocratic government leaders, media controls may fend off political opponents. For reformers in office, media controls may mean greater mass support for their reforms. Yet despite government and political pressures from the right and from the left, thousands of Latin American journalists and broadcasters continue to try to perform their jobs with professional autonomy. They continue to resist government interference, for their mission is not partisan propaganda but to inform citizens about the public life of their nations. They believe the biblical promise: "Ye shall know the truth and the truth shall make you free."

Of the journalists, broadcasters, politicians, and government leaders who believe in the people's right to know about the public life of their nation, one could say in Spanish: "Comunicar es educar y educar es redimir." That means, "To communicate is to educate, and to educate is to redeem."

References

Argudin, Alfonso. "Mexican Press Influence," *Journalism Quarterly* 24 (Winter 1947): 135–38.

Bechtos, Ramona. "Advertising in Brazil," *Advertising Age* (March 1973): 10–11.

Colombia. Ministerio de Comunicaciones. *Memoria al Congreso Nacional 1978* (Bogotá: Congreso Nacional, 1978).

Cunningham, W. H., R. M. Moore, and I. C. M. Cunningham. "Urban Markets: São Paulo Experience," *Journal of Marketing* 38 (April 1974): 2–12.

Domínguez, Jorge I. *Cuba: Order and Revolution* (Cambridge, Mass.: Harvard University Press, 1978).

Fejes, Fred. "Multinational Advertising Agencies and Latin America" (Paper at Latin American Studies Association, Pittsburgh, Pennsylvania, April 1979).

Gardner, Mary A. "Central and South America Mass Communication: Selected Information Sources," *Journal of Broadcasting* 22 (Spring 1978): 196–216.

_____. *The Inter-American Press Association* (Austin: University of Texas Press, 1967).

Hester, Albert L. and Richard R. Cole, eds. *Mass Communication in Mexico* (Brookings, S.D.: South Dakota State University, for Association for Education in Journalism, 1975).

Inter-American Broadcasters Association. "IABA Will Work for American Solidarity," *Boletín de la AIR* (Mexico City), 1 (January 1954): 1–4.

International Press Institute. *Government Pressures on the Press* (Zurich, Switzerland: IPI, 1955).

Knudson, Jerry. "Flame of Freedom Is Dim in Chile," *Philadelphia Inquirer,* Feb. 27, 1979, p. 11-A.

_____. Licensing News: The Bolivian Experience" (Paper at International Communication Division of Association for Education in Journalism, Seattle, Washington, August 1978).

Merrill, John C. and Harold A. Fisher. *The World's Great Dailies* (New York: Hastings House, 1980).

Mexico, Secretaría de Comunicaciones y Transportes. "Acuerdo: 12.5 de Tiempo al Estado," *Diario Oficial,* June 27, 1969, Sect. I.

Nichols, John S. "LATIN: Latin American Regional News Agency" (Paper at International Communication Division of Association for Education in Journalism, San Diego, California, August 1974).

_____. "LATIN," *Gazette* 21 (1975): 170–81.

Salinas, Raquel. *Communication Policies: The Case of Latin America* (Stockholm, Sweden: Institute of Latin American Studies of Sweden, 1978).

Ruíz Eldredge, Alberto. "Nuevos Conceptos para la Información," *Opiniones Latino-americanas,* August 1978, pp. 46–48

Terraza Ayala, Oscar. *Consideraciones Sobre la Necesidad del Colegio de Periodistas de Bolivia* (Cochabama, Bolivia: 1973).

Uslar Pietri, Arturo. "Tarea de Periodistas," *Opiniones Latinoamericanas,* August 1978, pp. 44–45.

Newspapers and Periodicals: *El Cronista,* Santiago, Chile; *El Diario,* La Paz, Bolivia; *Excelsior,* Mexico City; *La Prensa,* Buenos Aires; *La Nación,* Santiago, Chile; *Times of the Americas,* Washington, D.C.; *U.S.–Mexico Border Cities Association,* El Paso, Texas.

Notes

CHAPTER 1

1. William L. Rivers, Susan Miller, and Oscar Gandy, "Government and the Media," in Steven Chaffee, ed., *Political Communication* (Beverly Hills, Calif.: Sage Publications, 1975), pp. 218–19.

2. John C. Merrill, *The Imperative of Freedom: A Philosophy of Journalistic Autonomy* (New York: Hastings House, 1974), pp. 33–43.

3. John E. Fagg, *Latin America: A General History* (New York: Macmillan, 1963), pp. 129, 153, 207.

4. James W. Wilkie, ed., *Statistical Abstract of Latin America 1978* (Los Angeles: UCLA Latin American Center, 1978), pp. 74–85; some recent data compiled from Latin American entries throughout *Collier's Year Book 1978* (New York: Macmillan, 1978).

5. Inter-American Statistical Institute, *América en Cifras* (Washington, D.C.: Organization of American States, 1975), pp. iii-iv.

6. *United Nations Statistical Yearbook 1978* (New York: United Nations, 1978), Supplement Report tables K-2 to L-2.

7. Marvin Alisky, "Central American Radio," *Quarterly of Film, Radio and Television* (Berkeley: University of California Press), 10 (Fall 1955): 51–63.

8. Robert S. Drysdale and Robert G. Myers, "Continuity and Change: Peruvian Education," in Abraham F. Lowenthal, ed., *The Peruvian Experiment* (Princeton, N.J.: Princeton University Press, 1975), pp. 254–301.

9. Merrill, *Journalistic Autonomy,* pp. 23–43; for a broad overview, Heinz-Dietrich Fisher and John C. Merrill, eds., *International Communication* (New York: Hastings House, 1970): 49 essays on communication restrictions and freedoms in various nations.

10. Harold L. Cross, *The People's Right to Know* (New York: Columbia University Press, 1953), pp. 3–11.

11. Edward González, *Cuba under Castro: The Limits of Charisma* (Boston: Houghton Mifflin Company, 1974), pp. 146–67, 217–36.

12. Marvin Alisky, "Peru's Government-Press Relations," *Journalism Quarterly* 53 (Winter 1976): 661–65.

13. Louis Barron, ed., *The Americas: Worldmark Encyclopedia of the Nations,* vol. 3 (New York: Harper and Row, 1971).

14. "Cadena," *Memoria de SOMEX* (México, D. F.: SOMEX, 1972), p. 38.

15. Marvin Alisky, "Early Mexican Broadcasting," *Hispanic American Historical Review* 34 (November 1954): 515–26.

16. Clifton Neita, "The Daily Gleaner's Lonely Battle," *Wall Street Journal,* Mar. 19, 1979, p. 22. For an overview of the English speaking areas of the Caribbean, see John A. Lent, "Commonwealth Caribbean Mass Media: Historical, Cultural, Economic, and Political Aspects" (Ph.D. diss., University of Iowa, 1972).

17. John T. McNelly and Julio Molina, "Communication, Stratification and International Affairs Information in a Developing Urban Society," *Journalism Quarterly* 49 (Summer 1972): 316–26, 339.

18. Robert W. Desmond, *The Press and World Affairs* (New York: D. Appleton-Century, 1937), pp. 65–68.

19. Joe Alex Morris, Jr., *Hora de Cierre a Cada Minuto* (Buenos Aires: Ediciones Gure, 1959), pp. 110–18.

20. Reports in the Mexico City daily *Excelsior*, July 22 and 23, 1976.

21. "The UNESCO fight," *IAPA News*, October–November 1976, pp. 1–2.

22. "Angles of Vision, Treatments Differ in Reporting a Story," *Washington Post*, Nov. 17, 1978, p. 21-A; "UNESCO May Shelve News Code," *New York Times*, Nov. 15, 1978, p. 2; "Putting UNESCO on Notice," *Wall Street Journal*, Oct. 26, 1976, p. 22. For an overview, Jeffrey St. John, "The Third World and the Free Enterprise Press," *Policy Review* 2, no. 2 (1978): 59–70.

23. Marvin Alisky, "Argentina: News Services," in John C. Merrill, Carter R. Bryan, and Marvin Alisky, *The Foreign Press*, 2nd ed. (Baton Rouge: Louisiana State University Press, 1970), p. 201.

24. *Memoria de la Sociedad Mexicana de Crédito Industrial* (México, D.F.: SOMEX, 1973), pp. ii-iii.

25. Edgardo Reis, correspondent for *O Globo*, interview in Washington, D.C., Nov. 16, 1978.

26. Harry B. Murkland, "Editors' Blind Spot," *Américas* 1 (May 1949): 12–14.

27. "Economics: Industry," *Brazil Today* (Brazilian Embassy, Washington, D.C.) 4 (Mar. 8, 1979): 1–2.

28. Marvin Alisky, "U.S. News Coverage of Latin America," *Proceedings of the Arizona Latin American Conference of 1975* (Tempe: ASU Center for Latin American Studies, Paper No. 2, 1976), pp. 2–7.

29. "36 Journalists Reported Working," *Miami Herald*, Dec. 1, 1973, p. 4-A; "A Statement from the President," *Bulletin of the Overseas Press Club of America*, Apr. 1, 1973, p. 2; Henry S. Ackerman, "Correspondents South of the Border," *Inter-American Press Association Fund*, Mar. 4, 1971, pp. 1–6.

30. Don Huth, "World Services: By Satellite, Landline," *AP World* 29 (Summer 1971): 12.

31. R. J. Cappon, "Personnel," *Report of the General News Editor of the AP*, Summer 1971, p. 12.

32. Albert L. Hester, "The News from Latin America, Via a World News Agency," *Gazette* 20, no. 2 (1974): 85–92.

33. Albert L. Hester, "Foreign News on U.S. Television: Seeing through a Glass Darkly, or Not at All" (Paper presented at the 10th Conference of the International Association for Mass Communication Research, at Leicester, England, September 1976).

34. Jerry Knudson, "Whatever Became of the Pursuit of Happiness: The U.S. Press and Social Revolution in Latin America" (Paper presented at the International Communications Division, Conference of the Association for Education in Journalism, at San Diego, California, August 1974).

35. Jerry Knudson, *The Press and the Bolivian National Revolution* (Minneapolis, Minn.: Association for Education in Journalism Monographs, no. 31, 1973), p. 2.

36. Ibid., p. 34.

37. Ibid., pp. 43–48.

38. Curtis D. MacDougall, *The Press and Its Problems* (Dubuque, Iowa: William C. Brown, 1964), pp. 42–94; Samuel DePalma, "Freedom of the Press, an International Issue," *U.S. Department of State Bulletin*, Nov. 14, 1949, pp. 724–40; William E. Hocking, *Freedom of the Press* (Chicago: University of Chicago Press, 1947), pp. 200–227.

39. Kenneth F. Johnson, "Scholarly Images of Latin American Political Democracy in 1975," *Latin American Research Review* 11 (Summer 1976): 127–37.

40. For the classic overview contrasting freedom to obtain news in democracies and dictatorships see Herbert Brucker, *Freedom of Information* (New York: Macmillan, 1949), 307 pp.

41. Fred P. Graham, *Press Freedoms under Pressure* (New York: Twentieth Century Fund, 1972), pp. 65–81.

42. August 17, 1954, press conference of President Figueres, "El Presidente," *Diario de Costa Rica,* Aug. 18, 1954.

43. "Noticias," *Radio El Espectador* broadcast in Montevideo, July 5, 1967.

44. "Ornés Warns of Dangers," *IAPA Updater,* Mar. 1, 1979, p. 2.

45. Merrill, *Journalistic Autonomy,* p. 45.

46. Data from *World Development Report 1978* (Washington, D.C.: World Bank, 1978).

47. UNESCO, ed., *World Communications: A 200-Country Survey of the Press, Radio, Television, and Film* (Paris: UNESCO, 1975), pp. ix-x.

48. United States Information Agency, *A Study of Media Habits in El Salvador, Honduras, and Panama* (Washington, D.C.: USIA, 1970).

49. Richard R. Martin, John T. McNelly, and Fausto Izcaray, "Is Media Exposure Unidimensional?" *Journalism Quarterly* 53 (Winter 1976): 619–25; John T. McNelly, "Mass Communication and Family Planning," *The Organization of Family Planning Programs* (Washington, D.C.: Smithsonian Institution Interdisciplinary Communications Program, Monograph 8, 1976), pp. 149–82; McNelly, "International News for the Third World Masses?" *Journal of Communication* 26 (Spring 1979).

50. John T. McNelly and Julio Molina, "Communication, Stratification and International Affairs Information in a Developing Urban Society," *Journalism Quarterly* 49 (Summer 1972): 316–26, 339.

51. Wilbur Schramm, *Mass Media and National Development* (Stanford, Calif.: Stanford University Press, 1964).

52. Ted Morello, "Journalism School beside the Andes," *Quill* 43 (July 1955): 10, 14–15.

53. Raymond B. Nixon, "UNESCO's Program in Journalism," *Editor & Publisher,* May 7, 1960, p. 27.

54. *EL Comercio,* Mar. 29, 1960; *El Telégrafo* of Guayaquil, Apr. 1, 1960.

55. "Latin Journalists Will Participate in Exchange," *Times of the Americas,* Feb. 28, 1979, p. 2.

56. Jack M. McLeod, Ramona R. Rush, and Karl H. Friederich, "Mass Media Exposure and Political Knowledge in Quito, Ecuador" (Paper at International Communications Division, Association for Education in Journalism conference, Boulder, Colorado, August 1967).

CHAPTER 2

1. "Extermina al Aventurerismo el Registro a la Oposición," *Excelsior,* Dec. 12, 1978, pp. 1, 15.

2. L. Vincent Padgett, *The Mexican Political System,* 2nd ed. (Boston: Houghton Mifflin, 1976), pp. 76, 92, 106; Martin C. Needler, *Politics and Society in Mexico* (Albuquerque: University of New Mexico Press, 1971), pp. 1–38.

3. James W. Wilkie, *The Mexican Revolution: Federal Expenditure and Social Change Since 1910,* 2nd ed. (Berkeley: University of California Press, 1970), pp. xxi-xxxi.

4. Stanley R. Ross, *Is the Mexican Revolution Dead?* 2nd ed. (Philadelphia: Temple University Press, 1975), pp. 3–34.

5. For overviews of the Mexican political system see Frederick C. Turner, *The Dynamic of Mexican Nationalism* (Chapel Hill: University of North Carolina Press, 1968); Victor Alba, *The Mexicans* (New York: Praeger, 1967); Kenneth M. Coleman, *Diffuse Support in Mexico: The Potential for Crisis* (Beverly Hills, Calif.: Sage Publications, Comparative Politics Series, vol. 5, 1976); Kenneth F. Johnson, *Mexican Democracy: A Critical View* (Boston: Allyn and Bacon, 1971); and Robert E. Scott, *Mexican Government in Transition,* 2nd ed. (Urbana, Ill.: University of Illinois Press, 1959).

6. Susan Kaufman Purcell, *Public Policy and Private Profits: A Mexican Case Study* (Berkeley: University of California Press, 1975), documents the priorities.

7. Inter-American Development Bank, *Economic and Social Progress in Latin*

America 1977 Report (Washington, D.C.: IADB, 1977), pp. 137, 170, 303; James W. Wilkie, ed., *Statistical Abstract of Latin America 1977* 18 (1977):82–83.

8. Marvin Alisky, "Mexico Versus Malthus: National Trends," *Current History* 66 (May 1974): 200–203, 227–30; Dirección General de Estadística, *IX Censo General 1970* 1 (1973): 14–16.

9. "Periódicos," *Medios Publicitarios Mexicanos,* Aug.–Oct. 1976 and Feb.–Apr. 1977 quarterly reports; Marvin Alisky, "Mexico's Rural Radio," *Quarterly of Film, Radio and Television* 9 (Summer 1954): 405–17.

10. Pablo González Casanova, *Democracy in Mexico* (New York: Oxford University Press, 1970), pp. 88–89; *Editor & Publisher International Yearbook 1978* (New York: Editor & Publisher, 1978).

11. Evelyn P. Stevens, *Protest and Response in Mexico* (Cambridge, Mass.: MIT Press, 1974), p. 30.

12. Guillermo Montaño, "La Otra Cara de la Luna," *Siempre* 64 (Nov. 25, 1964): 77, 86.

13. *Excelsior,* Apr. 27 and 28, 1972.

14. Photograph on the cover of *Tiempo* for Dec. 31, 1973. The story emphasizing the misery appeared on pp. 14–16.

15. Leonard Cárdenas, Jr., "Contemporary Problems of Local Government in Mexico," *Western Political Quarterly* 18 (December 1965): 858–65.

16. Bernard Rubin, "Secrecy, Security, and Traditions of Freedom of Information," in Otto Lerbinger and Albert J. Sullivan, eds., *Information, Influence and Communication* (New York: Basic Books, 1965), pp. 136–75; Luis Castaño, "El Desarrollo de los Medios de Información en la América Latina y Crisis de la Libertad de Expresión," *Ciencias Políticas y Sociales* 8 (April–June 1962): 291–306.

17. Ifigenia Martínez de Navarrete, *La Distribución del Ingreso y el Desarrollo Económico de México* (México, D.F.: Instituto de Investigaciones Económicas, Universidad Nacional Autónoma de México, 1960), pp. 70–75.

18. Padgett, *Mexican Political System,* pp. 68–69.

19. Johnson, *Mexican Democracy,* pp. 67–76.

20. Roderic Ai Camp, *Mexican Political Biographies, 1935–1975* (Tucson: University of Arizona Press, 1976), 468 pp.; Marvin Alisky, *Who's Who in Mexican Government* (Tempe: Arizona State University Center for Latin American Studies, 1969), pp. 1–64.

21. Marvin Alisky, *The Governors of Mexico* (El Paso: Texas Western Press Monographs of UTEP, 1965), pp. 1–32.

22. William L. Rivers, Susan Miller, and Oscar Gandy, "Government and the Media," in Steven Chaffee, ed., *Political Communication* (Beverly Hills, Calif.: Sage Publications, 1975), pp. 217–36; see also Ben H. Bagdikian, *The Effete Conspiracy, and Other Crimes of the Press* (New York: Harper and Row, 1972); Douglas Cater, *The Fourth Branch of Government* (Boston: Houghton Mifflin, 1959); Bernard Cohen, *The Press and Foreign Policy* (Princeton, N.J.: Princeton University Press, 1963); and E. G. Krasnow and L. L. Longley, *The Politics of Broadcast Regulation* (New York: St. Martin's Press, 1973).

23. Richard R. Cole, "Mexico and the Foreign Press," *Quill* 58 (January 1970): 18–19.

24. James Davis, "The Press and the President in Mexico," *Inter-American Press Association Special Report,* June 1971, pp. 2–4.

25. "S. A." stands for "Sociedad Anónima," which translates as "Corporation" or "Incorporated." For a view of PIPSA in the 1950s and 1960s, see Alisky, "Mexico," in John C. Merrill, Carter R. Bryan, and Marvin Alisky, *The Foreign Press,* 2nd ed. (Baton Rouge: Louisiana State University Press, 1970), p. 181.

26. Ricardo Ampudia, editor of the Mexico City magazine *Hoy,* interviewed by Marvin Alisky at Stanford University, Oct. 10, 1978, about the newsprint tax.

27. Calvin P. Blair, "Nacional Financiera," in Raymond Vernon, ed., *Public Policy and Private Enterprise in Mexico* (Cambridge, Mass.: Harvard University Press, 1964), p. 214.

28. Productora e Importadora de Papel, *Papel para Imprimir Periódico* (México, D.F.: PIPSA, 1978), pp. 2–4.

29. Laura Nogales, director of sales for PIPSA, interviewed by Marvin Alisky, Mexico City, Oct. 26, 1978.

30. José Taladrid, director general of PIPSA, interviewed by Marvin Alisky, Mexico City, Oct. 27, 1978. Administrators of Papel Túxtepec newsprint production corporation interviewed by Marvin Alisky, Mexico City, Oct. 24 and 25, 1978.

31. "Reajuste en el Suministro y Alza del Papel," *Excelsior,* Sept. 18, 1973, pp. 1, 19.

32. "Pérdidas por Millones Dejó el Incendio de PIPSA," *El Heraldo,* May 4, 1976, pp. 1, 11 A.

33. Consuelo Medal, *El Periodista Como Orientador Social* (México, D.F.: Escuela Nacional de Ciencias Políticas y Sociales, UNAM, 1965), pp. 95–97.

34. "Consejo de la PIPSA," *Tiempo,* May 9, 1960, pp. 14–15.

35. Ronald Chilcote, *The Press in Latin America, Spain, and Portugal* (Stanford: Institute of Hispanic American and Luso-Brazilian Studies, 1963), pp. xii–xiii.

36. Personal telephone communication from members of the PIPSA Board to Marvin Alisky on Jan. 8, 1968.

37. Marvin Alisky, "Growth of Newspapers in Mexico's Provinces," *Journalism Quarterly* 37 (Winter 1960): 75–82, tells of the GV chain.

38. "Mexican Government Takes Over Newspaper Chain," *U.S.-Mexico Border Cities Association,* May 1972, p. 10; *Memoria de la Sociedad Mexicana de Crédito Industrial* (México, D.F.: SOMEX, 1973), pp. ii–iii.

39. John C. Merrill, *The Elite Press: Great Newspapers of the World* (New York: Pitman Publishing Company, 1968), pp. 240–47.

40. Armando Vargas, "The Coup at Excelsior," *Columbia Journalism Review* 15 (September–October 1976): 45–48.

41. Interview with seven former *Excelsior* editors and writers and with the former legal counsel staffers by Marvin Alisky in Mexico City, Aug. 14–21, 1977.

42. Marvin Alisky, "Mexico's 'Watergate' Investigations Oust Hundreds of High-Level Bureaucrats," *USA Today* 107 (January 1979): 11–12. Armando Vargas named the exact amount paid for a political publicity story before 1963. See Vargas, *Coup at Excelsior,* pp. 45–48.

43. Mary A. Gardner, *The Inter-American Press Association* (Austin: University of Texas Press, 1967), pp. 36, 44, 53, 76, 79–82, 84–85, 118–19, 134; Robert Bruce Underwood, "A Survey of Contemporary Newspapers of Mexico," (Ph.D. diss., University of Missouri, Columbia, 1965), pp. 90–118; E. H. Erlandson, "The Press in Mexico: Past, Present, and Future," *Journalism Quarterly* 41 (Spring 1964): 232–36; Alisky, "Mexico," in *Foreign Press,* pp. 182–83.

44. Emilio O. Rabasa interviewed by Marvin Alisky in Tubac, Arizona, on Oct. 24, 1974, anticipated some publishing activities in his postgovernment career.

45. Camp, *Mexican Political Biographies,* p. 338.

46. See also the front-page stories on this controversy in *Excelsior,* July 7, 1976.

47. "Periódicos," *Medios Publicitarios Mexicanos,* Aug.–Oct. 1976 and Feb.–Apr. 1977 quarterly issues.

48. Alisky, *USA Today,* pp. 11–12.

49. Jorge Orozco, 'Vestigios Sobre la Desparición," *El Imparcial,* May 22, 1967, pp. 1, 4. See the strong warning in "Tres Años de Cárcel: El Fraude Electoral," *El Imparcial,* June 28, 1967, p. 1.

50. See especially *El Imparcial* for Mar. 11, 1976, and for July 21, 1976.

51. *El Diario de Yucatán,* Nov. 26, 27, 28, 29, and 30, 1967.

52. Antonio Flores Ramírez, "Centralismo y Federalismo," *El Diario de Yucatán,* Mar. 3, 1978, p. 3; "Las Tendencias Regionalistas en Yucatán," *El Diario de Yucatán,* Mar. 2 and 3, 1978, pp. 3, 7.

53. "Ríos Camarena Freedom Denied by Miami Judge," *The News* (English language daily, Mexico City), July 23, 1977; similar stories on the same date in *Excelsior,*

Novedades, El Sol, and *El Heraldo.*

54. "Mexico Ready for Ríos," *The News,* July 31, 1977, p. 32.

55. "Week in Review," *Novedades,* Mar. 17, 1978, p. 1.

56. *Excelsior,* Apr. 10 and 15, May 11, 17, 22, and 29, 1978.

57. *Novedades,* Mar. 30, Apr. 1 and 2, 1978.

58. *Novedades,* Apr. 30, 1978.

59. *Novedades,* June 2 and 7, 1978.

60. For more on the riots at the Plaza de Tlatelolco, see Padgett, *Mexican Political System,* pp. 54–55; Johnson, *Mexican Democracy,* pp. 148–64; Gilberto Balam, *Tlatelolco, Reflexiones de un Testigo* (México, D.F.: Editorial GB, 1969), pp. 4–26; *El Sol de México,* Aug. 28, 1968; *Excelsior,* Oct. 2 and 3, 1968.

61. *Excelsior,* Feb. 15, 1977, p. 1.

62. "With Friends Like These," *Latin America Political Report* 12 (June 23, 1978): 190.

63. George W. Grayson, "The Making of a Mexican President, 1976," *Current History* 71 (February 1976): 49–52, 83–84; summary of top news reports in *Times of the Americas,* Apr. 30, 1975, p. 2.

64. Octavio Paz, "Reconciliémonos con Nuestro Pasado," *Proceso* 2 (Oct. 9, 1978): 10–11.

65. Carlos Ramírez, "Nuestro Problema Es Político y Social, No Técnico," *Proceso* 2 (Oct. 23, 1978): 18–19.

66. One-eighth-page display advertisement, "Señor Presidente," *Excelsior,* July 26, 1978, p. 4-A.

67. James Nelson Goodsell, "New Forum for Mexico's Muffled Voice," *Christian Science Monitor,* Dec. 8, 1977, p. 25.

68. *El Sol de México,* Oct. 24, 1978.

69. *Excelsior,* Oct. 28, 1978.

70. *Una Más Uno,* Oct. 26, 1978; *La Prensa,* Oct. 27, 1978; *El Universal,* Oct. 30, 1978; *El Nacional,* Oct. 28, 1978; *El Día,* Oct. 28, 1978; and *El Sol de México,* Oct. 28, 1978.

CHAPTER 3

1. Marvin Alisky, "Radio and Television," in Helen Delpar, ed., *Encyclopedia of Latin America* (New York: McGraw-Hill, 1974), pp. 514–16; James W. Wilkie, *Statistical Abstract of Latin America 1978* 19 (1978): 114–58.

2. Secretaría de Programación y Presupuesto, Dirección General de Estadística, *Compendio Estadístico* (México, D.F.: Departamento de Censos, 1978), p. 43.

3. Cámara Nacional de la Industria de Radio y Televisión, *Anuario 1978* (México, D.F.: CIRT, 1978), pp. 2–4.

4. *Directorio de la CIRT* (México, D.F.: CIRT, 1978), p. 17.

5. Marvin Alisky, "Early Mexican Broadcasting," *Hispanic American Historical Review* 34 (November 1954): 514–26.

6. Cámara Nacional de la Industria de Radio y Televisión, *Disposiciones Legales en Materia de Radio y Televisión,* (México, D.F.: CIRT, 1976), pp. 7–39.

7. Art. 4, *Ley Federal de Radio y Televisión* (México, D.F.: Secretaría de Gobernación, 1960), pp. 7–8.

8. Ibid.

9. Marvin Alisky, "Radio's Role in Mexico," *Journalism Quarterly* 31 (Winter 1954): 66–72; Alisky, "Mexico's Rural Radio," *Quarterly of Film, Radio, and Television* 9 (Summer 1954): 405–17.

10. CIRT members interviewed by Marvin Alisky during June 1970.

11. Pablo G. Macías, *Octubre Sangriento en Morelia* (México, D.F.: Editorial Acasim, 1968), p. 92.

12. *Excelsior,* Mar. 18, 1942, p. 9.

13. Evelyn P. Stevens, *Protest and Response in Mexico* (Cambridge, Mass.: MIT Press, 1974), p. 54.

14. Carlos Untel, "The University as Sanctuary," *National Review* 30 (Aug. 18, 1978): 1024–25.

15. Art. 31, Sect. V, *Ley Federal de Radio y Televisión,* pp. 14–15.

16. Art. 34, ibid.

17. José Luís Fernández, *Derecho de la Radiodifusión* (México, D.F.: Academia de Derecho Radiofónico, 1960), p. 186.

18. "Comisión de Radiodifusión," *Disposiciones Legales,* p. 38.

19. *Reglamento de la Ley Federal de Radio y Televisión* (México, D.F.: Secretaría de Gobernación, Apr. 4, 1973), Art. 49–58.

20. Marión de Jagos, "Homenaje de Cineastas a Margarita López Portillo," *Mujeres* 10 (May 31, 1977): 8–10.

21. "Reglamento de las Estaciones Radiodifusoras Comerciales, Culturales, y de Experimentación Científica y Aficionados," *Diario Oficial,* May 20, 1942, Art. 114–15.

22. Chapter V, Sect. 2 of the Federal Electoral Law of 1973 paralleled the amended Article 62 of the Federal Law of Radio and Television of 1960.

23. "Reglamento de la CFE: Cuatro Horas de Radio y Tv al Més a Cada Partido," *El Nacional,* Oct. 25, 1978, pp. 1, 7; "No Debemos Confundir la Libertad de Expresión con el Derecho a la Información," *El Nacional,* Oct. 4, 1978, p. 5; *Ley Orgánica de la Administración Pública Federal* (México, D.F.: Secretaría de Gobernación, Dec. 29, 1976), p. 6.

24. "Acuerdo: 12.5 de Tiempo al Estado," *Diario Oficial,* June 27, 1969, Sect. I, reprinted in CIRT, *Disposiciones Legales,* pp. 36–37.

25. Ibid., *Reglamento,* 1973, Art. 51.

26. Marvin Alisky, "Mexico's National Hour on Radio," *Nieman Reports* 7 (October 1953): 17–18; R. C. Norris, "A History of La Hora Nacional: Government Broadcasting Via Privately Owned Radio Stations in Mexico," (Ph.D. diss., University of Michigan, Ann Arbor, Michigan, 1963); interviews with the then director of the "National Hour" and all Gobernación broadcasting, Luis M. Farías, Feb. 2 and July 15, 1962, in Mexico City, by Marvin Alisky.

27. Belden and Associates, *Radiómetro: El Auditorio de México* (México, D.F.: Editorial Acosta, 1952), Sect. 7.

28. Excerpted from the *Reglamento* of 1973.

29. Marvin Alisky, "Mexico's Population Pressures," *Current History* 72 (March 1977): 106–7.

30. Bernice Rodríguez González, administrator of the Project of Communications about Population of the National Population Council, interviewed in Mexico City by Marvin Alisky, Nov. 8, 1976.

31. Octavio Paz, *The Labyrinth of Solitude; Life and Thought in Mexico* (New York: Grove Press, 1961), pp. 31, 35–36; Evelyn P. Stevens, "Mexican Machismo," *Western Political Quarterly* 18 (December 1965): 848–57; Samuel Ramos, *Profile of Man and Culture in Mexico* (New York: McGraw-Hill, 1963), pp. 54–68.

32. Consejo Nacional de Población, *México Demográfico Breviario 1975* (México, D.F.: CONAPO, 1975), p. 12.

33. Alisky, "Mexico's Population Pressures," p. 106.

34. *El Nacional,* Oct. 2, 1976.

35. Marvin Alisky, "Mexico Versus Malthus: National Trends," *Current History* 66 (May 1974): 203.

36. International Research Associates, *El Videómetro de México* (México, D.F.: 1978), pp. 2, 4.

37. "Programación Nacional de Tv," *Tele-Guía,* Dec. 24, 1978, p. 2.

38. *New York Times,* Nov. 19, 1950.

39. "Comunicación," *Tiempo,* July 30, 1979, p. 7.

40. "Gobierno Azteca Tomará de Radio y Tv 12.5 por Ciento de Tiempo y Publicidad," *La Prensa,* Oct. 14, 1971, p. 6: "La Creatividad de Televisa," *El Nacional,* June 13, 1973, p. 12.

41. "24 Horas," *Tiempo,* Oct. 19, 1970.

42. Interviews by "24 Horas" staffers Rodolfo Coronado, Angel Cabrera, and Emilio Azcárraga, Jr., over XEW and XEW-TV on Sept. 7, 1970.

43. "Frente de la Adversidad," *Tiempo,* June 19, 1978, pp. 13–15.

44. "Tiempo en Radio y Tv Aumentó," *El Heraldo,* Dec. 3, 1976, p. 2-B; "Crecimiento Impresionante de Radiodifusión," *El Heraldo,* Dec. 1, 1978, p. 4-B.

45. Ibid.

46. Dennis T. Lowry, "Radio, TV and Literacy in Mexico," *Journal of Broadcasting* 14 (April 1970): 239–44.

CHAPTER 4

1. For overviews of the military-led revolution, see David Chaplin, ed., *Peruvian Nationalism: A Corporatist Revolution* (New Brunswick, N.J.: Transaction Books, 1976); Abraham F. Lowenthal, ed., *The Peruvian Experiment: Continuity and Change under Military Rule* (Princeton, N.J.: Princeton University Press, 1975).

2. Harry Kantor, *Ideología y Programa del Movimiento Aprista* (México, D.F.: Ediciones Humanismo, 1955), pp. 27–28.

3. *El Comercio,* Jan. 10 and 12, July 10, 12, 28, 29, Aug. 8, and Oct. 31, 1940.

4. David P. Werlich, *Peru: A Short History* (Carbondale, Ill.: Southern Illinois University Press, 1978), p. 9.

5. Robert S. Drysdale and Robert G. Myers, "Peruvian Education," in Lowenthal, *The Peruvian Experiment,* p. 258; estimate for 1978 from the Ministerio de Educación del Perú.

6. "Peru," *Editor & Publisher International Yearbook 1978* (New York: Editor & Publisher, 1978), p. III-47.

7. Paul L. Doughty, "Social Policy and Urban Growth in Lima," in Chaplin, *Peruvian Nationalism,* pp. 99–100.

8. Howard Handelman, *Struggle in the Andes: Peasant Political Mobilization in Peru* (Austin: University of Texas Press, 1975), pp. 219–29. For an overview of peasant mobilization, see F. LaMond Tullis, *Lord and Peasant in Peru* (Cambridge, Mass.: Harvard University Press, 1970).

9. The significance of the Aprista is woven throughout Frederick B. Pike, *The Modern History of Peru* (New York: Praeger, 1967); Víctor Raúl Haya de la Torre, *Pensamiento Político de Haya de la Torre* (Lima: APRA, 1961), 5 vols.

10. *El Comercio,* Aug. 1, Sept. 8 and 9, 1945.

11. *La Prensa,* Jan. 8 and 9, 1947.

12. Marvin Alisky, "The Peruvian Press and the Nixon Incident," *Journalism Quarterly* 32 (Fall 1958): 411–19.

13. *El Comercio,* July 6–16, 1958.

14. Marvin Alisky, "Peru," in Ben G. Burnett and Kenneth F. Johnson, eds., *Political Forces in Latin America* 2nd ed. (Belmont, Calif.: Wadsworth, 1970), pp. 381–82.

15. *Oiga,* Sept. 20, 1968, pp. 8–11.

16. Carlos A. Astiz, *Pressure Groups and Power Elites in Peruvian Politics* (Ithaca, N.Y.: Cornell University Press, 1969), p. 267.

17. Decreto 291-68-HC, Aug. 9, 1968, under authority granted the cabinet to refinance debt.

18. Marvin Alisky, *Peruvian Political Perspective* 2nd ed. (Tempe: Arizona State University Center for Latin American Studies, 1975), pp. 14–15.

19. George W. Grayson, "Peru's Revolutionary Government," *Current History* 65 (February 1973): 61–63, 87.

20. Arturo Cavero Calixto, *El Centro de Altos Estudios Militares* (Chorrillos: CAEM, 1971), pp. 1–2.

21. Luigi R. Einaudi and Alfred C. Stepan, *Latin American Institutional Development: Changing Military Perspectives in Peru and Brazil* (Santa Monica, Calif.: Rand Corporation, Apr. 1971), p. 12; Einaudi, *Revolution from Within? Military Rule in Peru Since 1968* (Santa Monica, Calif.: Rand Corporation, July 1971), pp. 1–15.

22. "Ley de la Libertad de la Prensa," *El Peruano* (official government organ), Jan. 9, 1970, p. 1.

23. José Graham Hurtado, *Filosofía de la Revolución Peruana* (Lima: Oficina Nacional de Información, 1971), pp. 2–4; *El Comercio*, Jan. 10 and 11, 1970.

24. *El Comercio*, Mar. 5, 1970; *La Prensa*, Mar. 10, 1970.

25. Marvin Alisky, "Government-Press Relations in Peru," *Journalism Quarterly* 53 (Winter 1976): 661–62.

26. *La Prensa*, Feb. 21, 1971.

27. David Collier, "Squatter Settlements and Policy Innovation in Peru," in Lowenthal, *The Peruvian Experiment*, pp. 155–59; Marvin Alisky, "Peru's SINAMOS, Governmental Agency for Coordinating Reforms," *Public Affairs Bulletin* 11, no. 1 (1972): 1–4.

28. Jorge Vargas Escalante, *Cuarenta Años de Radio en el Perú* (Lima: Editorial Vargas, 1944), pp. 124–27; "Inauguración de la O.A.X.," *La Prensa*, June 20, 1925, p. 1.

29. Marvin Alisky, "Broadcasting in Peru," *Journal of Broadcasting* 3 (1959): 120–27.

30. Ibid.

31. Ministerio de Transportes y Comunicaciones, "Ley General de Telecomunicaciones," *El Peruano*, Nov. 10, 1971, p. 1. All earlier broadcasting regulations had been codified in 1957 as the *Reglamento General de Telecomunicaciones* (Lima: Ministerio de Gobierno y Policía, 1957), 46 pp.

32. "Bajo el Control del Gobierno del Perú, Compañías de Radio y Televisión," *La Prensa*, Nov. 12, 1971, p. 1.

33. "Asume el Gobierno Peruano el Control para Importa Papel," *La Prensa*, Nov. 19, 1971, p. 1.

34. Mark O. Dickerson, "Peru Institutes Social Property as Part of Its 'Revolutionary Transformation,' " *Inter-American Economic Affairs* 29 (Fall 1975): 23–33.

35. Winthrop P. Carty, "Latin American Press Freedom under Attack," *Times of the Americas*, Dec. 10, 1975, p. 3; "Renuncia de la SIP," *Diario de las Américas*, July 29, 1974, p. 2.

36. Commission of Onis Priests, "Onis Speaks," *Ladoc* (Lima) 4 (November 1974): 36–37.

37. *La Prensa*, Dec. 15, 1974.

38. Decreto Supremo No. 04–75–TR, "Reglamento de las Asociaciones Civiles Propietaria de los Diarios de Distribución Nacional," *El Peruano*, July 1, 1975, p. 1–37.

39. Ibid.

40. *El Comercio*, July 4, 1975.

41. *La Prensa*, July 11, 1975.

42. *Expreso*, July 14, 1975.

43. *Ojo*, July 9, 1975.

44. *Ultima Hora*, July 9, 1975.

45. *Correo*, July 9, 1975.

46. *La Prensa*, July 13, 1975.

47. "Peru: No Change?" *Latin America* 9 (Aug. 1, 1975): 234.

48. *Expreso*, Aug. 17, 1975.

49. *Associated Press* reports from Lima of Aug. 30 and Sept. 3, 1975.

50. Decreto Supremo 2975 in *El Peruano*, Sept. 3, 1975; "Deportations Are Canceled by Peru," *Times of the Americas*, Sept. 17, 1975, p. 1; "Peru: Liberalisation," *Latin America* (London) 9 (Sept. 19, 1975): 290.

51. *Miami Herald*, Oct. 24, 1975.

52. Jonathan Kandell, "Peru's Economic Setbacks Erode Revolution's Image," *New York Times,* May 2, 1976, pp. 1, 22.

53. "Peru: No Comment," *Latin America* 10 (Aug. 27, 1976): 269.

54. *El Comercio,* Nov. 19, 1976.

55. "Peruvian Regime Loosening Up Its Tight Hold," *IAPA News,* December 1976–January 1977, pp. 1–2.

56. "Peruvian Papers Reappear but Restrictions Remain," *Times of the Americas,* Feb. 2, 1977, p. 4.

57. Dennis Gilbert, "Society, Politics and the Press: An Interpretation of the Peruvian Press Reform of 1974" (Paper presented at the national meeting of the Latin American Studies Association, Houston, Texas, Nov. 4, 1977), pp. 17–19.

58. Decreto 22244, "Ley de Prensa," *El Peruano,* July 21, 1978, reprinted in part in *La Prensa,* July 21, 1978, pp. 8–9.

59. Chapter III, Daily Newspapers, Art. 13–19.

60. "Peru Backs Off from Plan to Give Dailies to People," *IAPA News,* June–July 1978, pp. 1–2.

61. "Los Miró Quesada Rechazan la 'Solución' del Gobierno," *Oiga,* July 24, 1978.

62. "Corrupt Dealings," *Latin American Political Report* 12 (Dec. 8, 1978): 379.

63. "Peru Defers Constitution Guarantees," *Arizona Republic,* Jan. 6, 1979, p. 3.

CHAPTER 5

1. Fundação IBGE, *Sinopse Estatística do Brasil 1977* (Rio de Janeiro: Instituto Brasileiro de Geografia e Estatística, 1977), pp. 2–20.

2. Banco do Brasil, eds., "The Dynamic Growth of Industry in Brazil," *Brazilian Bulletin* (Brazilian Government Trade Bureau), 10, Nov. 1977, pp. 2–4.

3. Thomas E. Skidmore, "Politics and Economic Policy-Making in Authoritarian Brazil," in Alfred Stepan, ed., *Authoritarian Brazil* (New Haven: Yale University Press, 1973), pp. 3–4.

4. "Brazil: Industry," *Worldmark Encyclopedia of Nations,* 3 (New York: Harper and Row, 1971), 41; "Brazil: Balance of Payments and International Trade," *Economic and Social Progress in Latin America: 1977 Report* (Washington, D.C.: Inter-American Development Bank, 1977), pp. 179–80.

5. "Uma Linguagem Brasileira," *O Globo,* Nov. 14, 1978, p. 29.

6. "Brazil: Statistical Profile," *Economic and Social Progress in Latin America: 1977 Report,* pp. 170–71.

7. Robert A. Packenham, "Yankee Impressions and Brazilian Realities," *Wilson Quarterly* 2 (Autumn 1976): 65.

8. Ibid.

9. *Sinopse Estatística do Brasil 1977,* pp. 164, 169.

10. Ministério das Comunicações, Secretaría de Radiodifusão, *Diretorias Regionais* (Brasilia: MDC Conselho Nacional, 1979), pp. ii–iv.

11. Bimonthly reports on listener preferences, *Radiómetro* (Rio de Janeiro: Medio, 1978).

12. "Por Dentro da TV," *O Globo,* Nov. 14, 1978, p. 38; "Longametragem," *Rede Tupi,* July 1978, p. 2.

13. Marvin Alisky, "Early Mexican Broadcasting," *Hispanic American Historical Review* 34 (November 1954): 515–16; excerpts from correspondence of pioneer Argentine and Brazilian broadcasters in letter from Horacio Chaves Paz of Buenos Aires to Marvin Alisky, Mar. 29, 1970.

14. Mel Harris, "Brazilian Broadcasting" (Paper presented at the International Communication Association, Phoenix, Arizona, April 22, 1971), p. 4; Brasil, Ministério da Educação e Saúde, *A Radiodifusão Educativa No Brasil* (Rio de Janeiro: Serviço de Documentação, 1946), p. 17.

15. Marvin Alisky, "Mexico's National Hour," *Nieman Reports* 7 (October 1953): 17–18.

16. Useful background books on the first Vargas era include Karl Loewenstein, *Brazil under Vargas* (New York, 1942); John W. F. Dulles, *Vargas of Brazil: A Political Biography* (Austin, 1967); Alzira Vargas do Amaral Peixoto, *Getúlio Vargas, Meu Pai* (Rio de Janeiro, 1960); for pressures on Vargas limiting somewhat his dictatorial tendencies, see John D. Wirth, "Brazilian Economic Nationalism: Trade and Steel under Vargas," (Ph.D. diss., Stanford University, 1966); Thomas E. Skidmore, *Politics in Brazil, 1930–1964* (New York, 1967); Jordan Young, *The Brazil Revolution of 1930 and the Aftermath* (New Brunswick, N.J., 1967).

17. John W. F. Dulles, *Castello Branco: The Making of a Brazilian President* (College Station: Texas A&M University Press, 1978), pp. 65–69.

18. Barreto Leite Filho, "Campanha," *Diário de Noticias,* Mar. 25, 1945, p. 3.

19. Thomas E. Skidmore, *Politics in Brazil, 1930–1964* (New York: Oxford University Press, 1967), p. 141.

20. Glaucio Ary Dillon Soares, "The Political Sociology of Uneven Development in Brazil," in Irving Louis Horowitz, ed., *Revolution in Brazil: Politics and Society in a Developing Nation* (New York, 1964), pp. 164–95.

21. "Advertisements Used by Vargas," *Associated Press Review of Brazil,* Dec. 30, 1945, distributed on trunk wires as Dispatch A 101.

22. "Goulart: 2,400 Cruzeiros," *Estado de São Paulo,* Feb. 22, 1954, p. 1.

23. Ministry of Justice investigation of Vargas memoranda to the Banco do Brasil for *Ultima Hora* loans, 1957 packet, Centro de Documentação de História Contemporânea do Brasil, Instituto de Direito Público e Ciência Política, Fundação Getúlio Vargas, Rio de Janeiro.

24. "Passing of Carlos Lacera Lamented by Brazil's Press," *Times of the Americas,* June 8, 1977, p. 2.

25. Oliveiros S. Ferreira, "Uma Caracterização do Sistema," *O Estado de São Paulo,* Oct. 17, 1965, p. 4; "Brazil Overview," *Agence France Presse,* Apr. 2, 1964, distributed in English and in Spanish.

26. Banco do Brasil, *1963–1978 Cacex* (Brasília: Carteira de Comércio Exterior, 1978), 8-page pamphlet.

27. Jonathan P. Lane, "Functions of the Mass Media in Brazil's 1964 Crisis," *Journalism Quarterly* 44 (Summer 1967): 297–306.

28. Correspondence from Alceu Gandini, assistant publisher of *Estado,* to Marvin Alisky, Jan. 5, 1977.

29. Lane, *Mass Media in Brazil's 1964 Crisis,* p. 300; Conselho Nacional de Comunicações, "Direito," *Decreto 568 de 18–5–1963,* p. 1.

30. Ibid., p. 2.

31. "Unsold Biographies of Castro Returned in Brazil," *The News* (Mexico City), Aug. 2, 1964, p. 2.

32. *Jornal do Brasil,* Feb. 20, 1964, p. 1.

33. *Panfleto,* Mar. 2, 1964, p. 3.

34. *Ultima Hora,* Feb. 25, 1964, p. 1.

35. *Diário Carioca,* Feb. 26, 1964, pp. 1, 3.

36. *Novos Rumos,* Feb. 28, 1964, p. 5.

37. *Rede Globo,* Mar. 13, 1964, column 4, program listings.

38. *O Jornal,* Mar. 7, 1964, p. 5.

39. *O Jornal,* Mar. 14, 1964, p. 22.

40. *Estado de São Paulo,* Mar. 14, 1964, p. 20.

41. Dulles, *Castello Branco,* pp. 340–42.

42. Ibid., p. 369; Phyllis Parker, "Separate but Equal? U.S. Policy toward Brazil, 1961–1964" (Independent Research Project, Lyndon B. Johnson School of Public Affairs, University of Texas at Austin, May 1976), pp. 90–97.

43. Peter T. Johnson, "Academic Press Censorship under Military and Civilian

Regimes: The Argentine and Brazilian Cases, 1964–1975," *Luso-Brazilian Review* 12 (Summer 1978): 6–7.

44. "Artigo 50, que Permite Censura Prévia a Publicações e Podería Ser Abrandado," *Estado de São Paulo,* Oct. 24, 1978, p. 1.

45. Edgardo Reis, correspondent for *O Globo,* interviewed by Marvin Alisky in Washington, D.C., Nov. 16, 1978; audience rating chart for *Rede Globo TV* for July–Dec. 1976.

46. Popularly known as the Lei Falcão, "Lei No. 6.339," *Atos do Poder Legislativo* (Brasília: Atos Complementares, Julho de 1977), 4, pp. 15–16; "Regulamento dos Serviços de Radiodifusão," *Codigo Brasileiro de Telecomunicaç*ões (Brasília: Ministério das Comunicações, 1973), pp. 1884–85.

47. "Radiobrás," *Perfil Federal* (Brasília: Ministério das Comunicações, 1977), pp. 36–38.

48. "Debray's Book Banned by Brazil Minister," *Miami Herald,* Oct. 5, 1967, p. A 12.

49. "Police Bar Issue of Rio Newspaper," *New York Times,* Jan. 8, 1969, p. 7.

50. James Nelson Goodsell, "Brazil's Military Regime Tightens Press Muzzle," *Christian Science Monitor,* June 11, 1969, p. 12.

51. David F. Belnap, "How Brazil Muzzles the Press," *Los Angeles Times,* Aug. 2, 1969, p. 7.

52. Ibid.

53. "1971 is Designated by Brito as Year of Freedom of Information," *IAPA News,* January 1971, p. 1; "Head of Hemisphere Press Group Assails Brazilian Censorship," *New York Times,* Dec. 24, 1970.

54. William Montalbano, "Press Freedom in Brazil," *Miami Herald,* Feb. 11, 1971, p. 3-B.

55. "Newsman Expelled," *Agence France Presse,* North American Service, Feb. 9, 1971, dispatch 101.

56. John C. Merrill, *The Elite Press: Great Newspapers of the World* (New York: Pitman Publishing Company, 1968), pp. 128–31.

57. "Ministro adverte: Excessos," *Estado de São Paulo,* Sept. 1, 1972, p. 1.

58. "Brazilian Military Drops Trial of Editor," *The News* (Mexico City), Oct. 11, 1972, p. 8.

59. Nathan A. Haverstock, "Censorship in Brazil Baffling," *Times of the Americas,* Oct. 25, 1972, p. 10.

60. Mark J. Curran, "The 'Journalistic Page' of the Brazilian Popular Poet," *Revista Brasileira de Folclore,* Apr. 1972, pp. 3–4.

61. "Brazil: Increased Repression," *Latin America* (London) 7 (1973): 148.

62. "No Rio, Multas de Candidatos," *O Globo,* Nov. 16, 1978, p. 7; "A Decisão Eleitoral," *Veja,* Nov. 15, 1978, p. 15.

63. Georgie Anne Geyer, "Women Set New Political Tactics," *Phoenix Gazette,* Dec. 7, 1978, p. 7. (Column syndicated nationally by the *Los Angeles Times.*)

64. "Papa Condena Aborto e Defende Unidade Cristã," *O Globo,* Nov. 14, 1978, p. 16.

65. Alfred Stepan, *The Military in Politics: Changing Patterns in Brazil* (Princeton, N.J.: Princeton University Press, 1971), paperback reprint 1974, 314 pp.

66. Ibid., pp. 99–100.

67. *O Jornal,* Aug. 10, 1945, as translated in Stepan, *Brazilian Military in Politics,* p. 102.

68. *Estado de São Paulo,* Aug. 24, 1954, as translated in Stepan, *Brazilian Military in Politics,* p. 103.

69. *Jornal do Brasil,* Aug. 30, 1978, p. 19.

70. Ibid., Aug. 29, 1978, p. 4.

71. *Jornal da Tarde,*Oct. 6, 1978, p. 3. See also news stories in the same issue on pp. 1, 5, 7. See reports on the investigations in *O Estado de São Paulo* for Oct. 1, 4, 8, and 14, 1978.

72. "Sea of Mud," *Latin America Political Report* 12 (1978): 316.

73. *Folha de São Paulo,* Sept. 5, 1978, p. 6.
74. "Colégio Eleitoral em Brasília," *Manchete,* Oct. 28, 1978, p. 14.
75. *O Globo,* Sept. 6, 1978, p. 3.
76. "Brazilian Soap Opera Tops," *Arizona Republic,* Aug. 6, 1978, p. 30; "Astro's Highest Rating," *Associated Press,* daily Brazilian summary, Aug. 1, 1978.
77. Albert Fishlow, "Flying Down to Rio: Perspectives on U.S.-Brazil Relations," *Foreign Affairs,* 57 (Winter 1978–79): 401. For additional background, see Riordan Roett, ed., *Brazil in the Seventies* (Washington, D.C.: American Enterprise Institute, 1976), 118 pp.

CHAPTER 6

1. International Monetary Fund, *International Financial Statistics* (Washington, D.C.: IMF, Apr. 1978), table 79.
2. Venezuela, Dirección General de Estadística y Censos nacionales, *Indicadores Socioeconómicos y de Coyuntura* (Caracas: DGE, July 1978), no. 3, pp. 2–4.
3. Ibid.; Ministerio de Hacienda, "Introducción," *Memoria* (Caracas: Ministerio de Hacienda, Apr. 1978), pp. 2–17.
4. *Washington Post* correspondents, "Latin Americans Flocking to Miami on Spending Spree," *Arizona Republic,* Dec. 17, 1978, p. C-31.
5. "Venezuela," *Time* 64 (1955): 29; see also Leo B. Lott, "Venezuela," in Martin C. Needler, ed., *Political Systems of Latin America,* 2nd ed. (New York: Van Nostrand Reinhold, 1970), pp. 272–73.
6. Lott, "Venezuela," p. 274.
7. "Venezuela's Turnabout," *San Francisco Chronicle,* Dec. 6, 1978, p. 52; "Venezuelan Elections," *Associated Press,* Dec. 10, 1978, morning report.
8. Robert J. Alexander, *The Communist Party of Venezuela* (Stanford, Calif.: Hoover Institution Press, 1969), pp. xix, xxi.
9. Correspondence, Tad Szulc to Marvin Alisky, Jan. 2, 1959.
10. For party overviews, see Robert J. Alexander, *The Venezuelan Democratic Revolution: A Profile of the Regime of Rómulo Betancourt* (New Brunswick, N.J.: Rutgers University Press), and John D. Martz, *Acción Democrática: Evolution of a Modern Political Party in Venezuela* (Princeton, N.J.: Princeton University Press, 1966).
11. "Venezuela: A TV Blitz Produces an Upset," *Time* 112 (Dec. 18, 1978): 44–46.
12. "Venezuelan Left Tries to Introduce Some Ideas," *Times of the Americas,* Nov. 1, 1978, p. 5. Anticipating this growing use of radio and television to reduce internal isolation was former President Rómulo Bétancourt in his book *Venezuela's Oil* (London: George Allen and Unwin, 1978), in which he found that 65 percent of the national income was going to the top 20 percent of the population, though even poverty-level households were acquiring television sets.
13. "Venezuela: A TV Blitz," p. 46.
14. Monte Hayes, "Venezuela: Color Its People Determined," *Arizona Republic,* Dec. 10, 1978, p. M-7.
15. "Datos para la Iniciación de las Encuestas," *El Universal,* July 9, 1977, p. 3.
16. "Radio Continente News Director Given 5 Days," *Foreign Broadcast Information Service* 6 (Aug. 31, 1978): p. L-1.
17. *El Universal,* Dec. 29, 1978, and Jan. 15, 1979.
18. "Venezuela: All Change," *Latin America Political Report* 12 (Dec. 8, 1978): 1.
19. Pedro Penzini Fleury, "Peligro: Radio," *El Nacional,* Dec. 23, 1977; "Venezuela Closes Two Radio Shows," *Times of the Americas,* Jan. 4, 1978, p. 1.
20. "Múgica Names Communist Candidate in Venezuela," *Arizona Republic,* Sept. 14, 1977, p. 2.
21. "Venezuela's Well-Oiled Democracy: Film Production Industry," *Variety,* Apr. 6, 1977, pp. 64–66; Marianela Saleta, "Venezuela's Film Policy," *Variety,* Apr. 6, 1977, p. 66.
22. "Venezuela Cinema Digging into Govt.," *Variety,* Apr. 6, 1977, pp. 66–67.

CHAPTER 7

1. Harry Bernstein, *Venezuela and Colombia* (Englewood Cliffs, N.J.: Prentice-Hall, 1964), pp. 116–38.

2. Rafael Azula Barrera, *De la Revolución al Orden Nuevo* (Bogotá: Editorial Kelly, 1956), pp. 489–90.

3. Robert H. Dix, *Colombia: The Political Dimensions of Change* (New Haven: Yale University Press, 1967), pp. 10–12; John D. Martz, *Colombia: A Contemporary Survey* (Chapel Hill, N.C.: University of North Carolina Press, 1962), pp. 9–10.

4. "Colombia Basic Data," *Colombia Today* 13, no. 10 (1978): 6.

5. Dieter K. Zschock, "Inequality in Colombia," *Current History* 72 (February 1977): 68.

6. Ibid., pp. 72, 86.

7. *Editor & Publisher International Yearbook 1978* (New York: Editor & Publisher, 1978), pp. III-42–III-43.

8. Vernon L. Fluharty, *Dance of the Millions: Military Rule and Social Revolution in Colombia, 1930–1956* (Pittsburgh, Pa.: University of Pittsburgh Press, 1957), pp. 68–78.

9. Dix, *Colombia: Political Dimensions*, p. 209.

10. "Un Consejero de la Nación," *Semana*, Feb. 21, 1955, p. 15.

11. *El Siglo*, Oct. 21, 1940.

12. Austin F. MacDonald, *Latin American Politics and Government* (New York: Thomas Y. Crowell, 1949), pp. 387–88.

13. Germán Arciniegas, *The State of Latin America* (New York: Alfred A. Knopf, 1952), pp. 162–63.

14. Martz, *Colombia: Contemporary Survey*, pp. 49–51.

15. Fluharty, *Military Rule and Social Revolution in Colombia*, Chapters 6 and 7.

16. *The Times of London*, Apr. 12, 1948; *Chicago Tribune*, Apr. 11, 12, and 14, 1948; *New York Times*, Apr. 18, 1948; *La Prensa* (Buenos Aires), Apr. 18, 1948.

17. *El Tiempo*, Apr. 30, 1948.

18. *El Tiempo*, May 16, 1948; *El Relator* of Cali, May 17, 1948.

19. *Associated Press* interview with Secretary Marshall for April 13, 1948.

20. *El Colombiano*, June 29, 1948, front-page story.

21. Ibid.

22. *El Espectador*, July 18, 1948.

23. Richard Maullin, *Soldiers, Guerrillas, and Politics in Colombia* (Lexington, Mass.: Lexington Books, 1973), pp. 8, 14, 23–25.

24. Dix, *Colombia: Political Dimensions*, pp. 111–12.

25. David F. Belnap, "Colombia Regains Press Freedom," *Editor & Publisher* 90 (May 25, 1957); 11, 90.

26. Dix, *Colombia: Political Dimensions*, p. 118.

27. John C. Merrill, *The Elite Press: Great Newspapers of the World* (New York: Pitman Publishing Company, 1968), pp. 40, 51, 106.

28. *El Siglo*, Aug. 22, 1953, p. 1.

29. *Diario Oficial*, Aug. 22, 1953, p. 1.

30. *New York Times*, Mar. 7, 1954, p. 43.

31. *New York Times*, Mar. 3, 1955, p. 7.

32. *New York Times*, June 11, 1955, p. 3.

33. Martz, *Colombia: Contemporary Survey*, p. 205.

34. "Rojas Pinilla y la Libertad de Prensa," *Visión*, Oct. 14, 1955, p. 14.

35. Belnap, "Colombia Regains Press Freedom," pp. 11, 90.

36. *La Unidad*, Jan. 17, 1961, p. 1.

37. Maullin, *Soldiers, Guerrillas, and Politics in Colombia*, pp. 49, 135.

38. *El Tiempo*, Mar. 1, 1966; *La República*, June 11, 1968; *El Espectador*, Sept. 22, 1966; *El Siglo*, Mar. 8, 1968.

39. Ministerio de Comunicaciones, *Memoria al Congreso Nacional 1978* (Bogotá: Congreso Nacional, 1978), pp. 169, 181, 184.

40. Ibid., pp. 11–12.
41. Michael Scully, "Adventure in Inspiration," *Reader's Digest* 64 (September 1954): 25–28.
42. Dix, *Colombia: Political Dimensions*, p. 317.
43. "Colombia Pioneers in the Use of Radio for Rural Education," *Colombia Today*, July 1970, p. 4.
44. James W. Carty, Jr., "Colombia's El Campesino," *Grassroots Editor* 8 (September–October 1967): 20–21.
45. *United Press International* dispatch, July 25, 1970.
46. *New York Times,* Dec. 31, 1970.
47. *El Tiempo,* Mar. 1, 1971.
48. "López-Michelsen: Estricta Censura a la Radio," *Diario de las Américas,* Nov. 8, 1975, p. 1.
49. *El Tiempo,* Jan. 14, 1979.
50. Ibid.
51. "Government Lifts News Broadcasting Restrictions," *Foreign Broadcast Information Service* 6 (Feb. 12, 1979): F-3; "Colombia Charges Plot to Protect Subversives," *Times of the Americas,* Mar. 14, 1979, p. 16.

CHAPTER 8

1. Jorge I. Domínguez, *Cuba: Order and Revolution* (Cambridge, Mass.: Harvard University Press, 1978); Edward González, *Cuba under Castro: The Limits of Charisma* (Boston: Houghton Mifflin, 1974); Maurice Halperin, *The Rise and Decline of Fidel Castro* (Berkeley: University of California Press, 1972); and Jaime Suchlicki, ed., *Cuba, Castro, and Revolution* (Coral Gables, Fla.: University of Miami Press, 1972).
2. Domínguez, *Cuba: Order and Revolution*, p. 165.
3. Junta Central de Planificación, *Compendio Estadístico de Cuba* (Havana: Juceplan, 1975), pp. 117–227.
4. Richard Fagen, *The Transformation of Political Culture in Cuba* (Stanford, Calif.: Stanford University Press, 1969), pp. 2–16; Tad Szulc, "Cuban Television's One-Man Show," in Robert L. Shayon, ed., *The Eighth Art* (New York: Holt, Rinehart and Winston, 1962).
5. Maurice Halperin, *The Rise and Decline of Fidel Castro* (Berkeley: University of California Press, 1972), p. 230.
6. *Granma Weekly Review* (in English), May 9, 1971, p. 1.
7. Foreign Broadcast Information Service, *Trends in Communist Media* 6 (1978): 8–12; 6 (1978): pp. 3–7.
8. Foreign Broadcast Information Service, *Latin American Daily Report* 6 (Feb. 23, 1979): 3–7.
9. Leland H. Jenks, *Our Cuban Colony* (New York: Vanguard Press 1928), pp. 185, 269.
10. Domínguez, *Cuba: Order and Revolution*, pp. 103, 112–14, 193.
11. Carlos Márquez Sterling, *Historia de Cuba* (New York: Las Americas, 1969), pp. 543–73.
12. Marvin Alisky, "Havana Havoc: Too Many Dailies," *Nieman Reports* 10 (April 1956): 16–18.
13. Ibid.
14. Marvin Alisky, "Cuba Press: Censorship Replaces Bribery," *Nieman Reports* 11 (April 1957): 17–18.
15. Jerry W. Knudson, *Herbert L. Matthews and the Cuban Story* (Minneapolis, Minn.: Association for Education in Journalism Monograph 54, 1978), pp. 4–11.
16. Ibid.
17. Marvin Alisky, "Confused Cuba: Printers Who Edit—Government by Television," *Nieman Reports* 14 (April 1960): 12–14.

18. Domínguez, *Cuba: Order and Revolution*, pp. 206–8; *Revolución*, Oct. 19 and Nov. 23, 1959.

19. Lloyd A. Free, *Attitudes of the Cuban People Toward the Castro Regime* (Princeton, N.J.: Institute for International Social Research, 1960).

20. Michael Sewell, "Some Themes of Politico-Economic Socialization in Cuba's *Granma*," *South Eastern Latin Americanist* 21 (September 1977): 1–7.

21. Ibid.

22. González, *Cuba under Castro*, pp. 151–52.

23. James W. Carty, Jr., *Cuban Communications* (Bethany, West Va.: Bethany College, 1978), pp. 1–78.

24. Carty, "Cuban Communicators," *Caribbean Quarterly* 22 (December 1976): 59–67.

25. Ibid., p. 65.

26. Carty, "Castro Prefers Foreign Journalists," *Times of the Americas*, Oct. 4, 1978, p. 16.

27. Philip Terzian, "Cuba in Panavision," *Harper's* 258 (January 1979): 28–30.

28. Jon Nordheimer, "20 Years with Fidel," *New York Times Sunday Magazine*, Dec. 31, 1978, pp. 16, 28.

29. *Verde Olivo* 19 (Sept. 10, 1978).

30. Domínguez, *Cuba: Order and Revolution*, pp. 304–5.

31. *Granma*, Feb. 6, 1977, and Mar. 28, 1978.

32. *Palante*, Dec. 22, 1978, issue, 16 pp.

33. *Granma Weekly Review*, Feb. 26, 1978, pp. 1–3.

CHAPTER 9

1. John C. Merrill, *The Elite Press: Great Newspapers of the World* (New York: Pitman Publishing Company, 1968), pp. 11–17, 247–53; "Newspapers of the World," *The Times* (London), Mar. 2, 1965, p. 5; Alberto Gainza Paz, *Education and Journalism in the Struggle for Freedom* (Evanston, Ill.: Northwestern University, 1951), pp. 19–20.

2. Inter-American Development Bank, *Economic and Social Progress in Latin America* (Washington, D.C.: IADB, 1977), pp. 137–38; *América en Cifras 1972*—Situación Demográfica (Washington, D.C.: Organization of American States, 1973); Argentina, *Instituto Nacional de Estadística y Censos* (Buenos Aires: INDEC, Mar. 1978), pp. 2–47.

3. Leo S. Rowe, *The Federal System of the Argentine Republic* (Washington, D.C.: Carnegie Institution, 1921); Carlos J. Rodríguez, *Yrigoyen: Su Revolución Política y Social* (Buenos Aires: Facultad de Derecho, 1943); Ricardo Levene, *A History of Argentina* (Chapel Hill, N.C.: University of North Carolina Press, 1937).

4. Juan D. Perón, *Conducción Política* (Buenos Aires: Escuela Superior Peronista, 1951); James R. Scobie, *Argentina: A City and a Nation* (New York: Oxford University Press, 1971); Peter Snow, *Political Forces in Argentina* (Boston: Allyn and Bacon, 1971).

5. Interviews with Radio Belgrano staff members for NBC Radio Network by Marvin Alisky, Buenos Aires, during August 1949.

6. Austin F. MacDonald, *Latin American Politics and Government*, 2nd ed. (New York: Thomas Y. Crowell, 1954), pp. 77–82; the U.S. Department of State's *White Paper on Argentina* (Washington, D.C., 1945), documenting wartime influence of Germany, was quoted out of context in various Peronista publications to popularize the idea that the United States was involved in domestic Argentine politics.

7. See also George I. Blanksten, *Perón's Argentina* (Chicago: University of Chicago Press, 1953); Robert J. Alexander, *The Perón Era* (New York: Columbia University Press, 1951); S. E. Bradford, *The Battle for Buenos Aires* (New York: Harcourt, Brace, 1943); Bonifacio Del Carril, *Buenos Aires Frente al País* (Buenos Aires: Editores Emecé, 1944); Ruth and Leonard Greenup, *Revolution before Breakfast: Argentina, 1941–1946* (Chapel Hill, N.C.: University of North Carolina Press, 1947).

8. Joseph R. Barager, ed., *Why Perón Came to Power* (New York: Alfred A. Knopf, 1968), pp. 3, 15, 23.

9. Arthur P. Whitaker, *The United States and Argentina* (Cambridge: Harvard University Press, 1954), pp. 145–50.

10. Eva Perón, *La Razón de Mi Vida* (Buenos Aires: Ediciones Peuser, 1951), pp. 41–45; María Flores, *The Woman with the Whip: Eva Perón* (Garden City, N.Y.: Doubleday, 1952), pp. 71–83.

11. John C. Merrill, "U.S. Panel Names World's Ten Leading Quality Dailies," *Journalism Quarterly* 41 (Autumn 1964): 568–72; International Press Institute, *The Flow of the News* (Zurich: IPI, 1953), pp. 87–100.

12. Norman Ingrey, "Rival Argentine Newspapers Mark Dates of Centennials," *Christian Science Monitor,* Oct. 18, 1969, p. 7.

13. Donald B. Easum, "La Prensa and Freedom of the Press in Argentina," *Journalism Quarterly* 28 (Spring 1951): 229–30.

14. "El Presupuesto de la Propaganda," *La Prensa,* Jan. 7, 1948, p. 1; *Presupuesto General de la Administración Nacional para el Ejercicio 1948* (Buenos Aires: Banco Central de la República Argentina, 1949), pp. 270–75.

15. Easum, "La Prensa and Freedom of the Press," p. 232; Ray Josephs, *Argentina Diary* (New York: Random House, 1944), pp. 378–79; Ray Josephs, *Latin America: Continent in Crisis* (New York: Random House, 1948), pp. 370–73.

16. Editors of *La Prensa, Defense of Freedom* (New York: John Day Company, 1952), pp. 2–16.

17. *Código Penal* (Buenos Aires: Ministerio de Justicia, 1949), Sect. II, Art. 219.

18. *Defense of Freedom,* pp. 15–16; statements of Alberto Gainza Paz in "Freedom of the Press Committee," *Proceedings of the Inter-American Press Association* (New York: IAPA, 1955), pp. 49–51.

19. *New York Times,* Oct. 15, 1949, p. 4; Dec. 4, 1949, p. 1; Dec. 26, 1949, p. 18; Jan. 3, 1950, p. 14; Jan. 4, 1950, p. 22; and Jan. 11, 1950, p. 7.

20. María C. Huergo, "The Argentine Press: Beginnings and Growth," *Journalism Quarterly* 16 (September 1939): 258.

21. *La Prensa,* Feb. 20, 1950, p. 1; *New York Times,* Feb. 28, 1950, p. 18.

22. "La Prensa," *London Economist,* Mar. 10, 1951, p. 19; *La Prensa,* Mar. 5, 1950, p. 1.

23. "Violence against La Prensa Employees," *Associated Press* South American report, Feb. 28, 1951. Uncensored accounts were published across La Plata estuary in Uruguay by Montevideo dailies. See "La Situación en Buenos Aires," *El Día* (Montevideo), Feb. 28 and 29, 1951, pp. 1–2.

24. *Excelsior* (Mexico City), Mar. 27, 1951, p. 1.

25. Joseph R. Barager, "Argentina: A Country Divided," in Martin C. Needler, ed., *Political Systems of Latin America,* 2nd ed. (New York: Van Nostrand Reinhold, 1970), pp. 470–71.

26. See Paul R. Hoopes, "Content Analysis of News in Three Argentine Dailies," *Journalism Quarterly* 43 (Autumn 1966): 536–37.

27. Marvin Alisky and Paul R. Hoopes, "Argentina's Provincial Dailies Reflect Neutralism of Mass Media in Country's Political Crisis," *Journalism Quarterly* 45 (Spring 1968): 95–98.

28. Mary A. Gardner, "The Argentine Press since Perón," *Journalism Quarterly* 37 (Summer 1960): 426–30.

29. Ibid., p. 428; correspondence from editors of *La Prensa* to Marvin Alisky, Sept. 2, 1977, and Nov. 17, 1978.

30. Arthur P. Whitaker, "Argentina: Recovery from Perón," *Current History,* Apr. 1957, pp. 209–10; Samuel L. Baily, "Argentina: Reconciliation with the Peronists," *Current History* 60, (December 1965): 356, 369; Alvin Cohen, "Revolution in Argentina?" *Current History* 62 (November 1967): 283–90.

31. See the 46th anniversary edition of *Veritas* 46 (Dec. 15, 1976): 140 pp.

32. "Calma, Calma, Radicales," *Primera Plana* 5 (Aug. 1, 1967): 14–15.

33. Marvin Alisky, "Argentina: News Services," in John C. Merrill, Carter R. Bryan, and Marvin Alisky, *The Foreign Press,* 2nd ed. (Baton Rouge: Louisiana State University Press, 1970), p. 201.

34. Alisky and Hoopes, "Argentina's Provincial Dailies," p. 96; *La Prensa,* Aug. 26, 1967, p. 1; *La Razón,* Aug. 26, 1967, p. 1.

35. See Kenneth F. Johnson, "Argentina," in Richard F. Staar, ed., *1978 Yearbook on International Communist Affairs* (Stanford, Calif.: Hoover Institution Press, 1978), p. 331.

36. *La Prensa,* Oct. 10, 1973, pp. 1, 4.

37. Explanations from both editors and publishers in *Buenos Aires Herald,* Aug. 22, 1973; *La Prensa,* Aug. 23 and 29, 1973; *La Nación,* Aug. 25, 1973; and *La Razón,* Aug. 28, 1973.

38. *El Caudillo,* Mar. 17, 1974; *La Opinión,* Mar. 17, 1974.

39. *La Opinión,* Aug. 28 and Sept. 17, 1974.

40. Decreto 630, *Boletín Oficial,* Sept. 3, 1974, p. 7.

41. "Murder of Aramburu," *Latin American Digest* 5 (October 1970): 8–9.

42. *La Prensa,* Apr. 27 and 29, 1975.

43. *Mayoría,* Feb. 13 and 14, 1976.

44. *La Opinión,* Feb. 13, 1976.

45. Ronald M. Schneider, "Argentina: Terrorism and Police Violence," *Collier's Year Book 1977* (New York: Macmillan, 1977), pp. 140–41.

46. (Translated), "Principles and Procedures to Be Followed by Mass Communication Media," *Buenos Aires Herald,* Mar. 25, 1976, p. 2.

47. *Clarín,* Apr. 22, 1976.

48. Associated Press team of correspondents, "Human Rights Violations in South America," *Arizona Republic,* Dec. 17, 1978, p. 26-A.

49. Peter C. Stuart, "The Cost of Life in Argentina," *The New Leader,* Apr. 24, 1978, pp. 14–16.

50. "Editor's Arrest in Argentina Revives Fears for Free Press," *Miami Herald,* Apr. 30, 1977, p. 22-A. See "Clausura de La Opinión," *Excelsior* (Mexico City), Feb. 16, 1976, p. 6-A.

51. Stuart, "The Cost of Life in Argentina," p. 16.

52. "Madison Avenue to Improve Argentina's Image," *International Daily News,* May 31, 1978, p. 8.

53. Penny Lernoux, "Systematic Persecution Said to Sap Strength of Argentina's Universities," *The Chronicle of Higher Education* 12 (Dec. 11, 1978): 5.

54. Harold K. Milks, "Argentina Strikes," *Arizona Republic,* June 8, 1978, p. 16-B.

55. *Decreto 619,* Feb. 13, 1976.

56. "Argentine Summary," *Associated Press,* Apr. 18 and May 24, 1977.

57. "Timerman," *Times of the Americas,* Apr. 26, 1978.

58. Jacob Kovadloff, "Press Suppression in Argentina: The Timerman Case," *USA Today* 107 (September 1979): 30–32.

59. "Talks Being Held in Moscow for Signing Paraná Contract," *Telam* dispatch distributed by the Foreign Broadcast Information Service on November 16, 1978, *Daily Report,* 6, p. B-1.

60. Andrew Graham Yooll, *The Press in Argentina 1973–78* (London: Index Press, 1979), pp. 14–200.

CHAPTER 10

1. Ministerio de Hacienda, Dirección General de Estadística y Censos, *IV Censo de Población* (Montevideo; DGEC, 1969), Part I, pp. 3–29.

2. Ibid.

3. *Organización de la Prensa del Interior 1977* (Montevideo: OPI, 1977), pp. 7–12; "Uruguay," *Editor & Publisher International Yearbook 1978* (New York: Editor & Publisher, 1978), pp. III-47–III-48.

4. Russell H. Fitzgibbon, *Uruguay: Portrait of a Democracy* (New Brunswick, N.J.: Rutgers University Press, 1954), pp. 126–28.

5. See the overview in Philip B. Taylor, Jr., *Government and Politics of Uruguay* (New Orleans: Tulane University Political Science Studies, 1960), 285 pp.

6. Marvin Alisky, *Uruguay: A Contemporary Survey* (New York: Praeger, 1969), pp. 25–27.

7. Simon G. Hanson, *Utopia in Uruguay* (New York: Oxford University Press, 1938), pp. 19–25.

8. Milton I. Vanger, "Uruguay Introduces Government by Committee," *American Political Science Review* 48 (June 1954): 510.

9. *La Mañana,* Jan. 21, 1969.

10. Marvin Alisky, "Uruguay Prizes Its Print, Broadcast Press," *Quill* 55 (October 1967): 32–34.

11. Martin Weinstein, *Uruguay: The Politics of Failure* (Westport, Conn.: Greenwood Publishers, 1975), pp. 120–23.

12. *El Día,* July 12, 1969.

13. *United Press International* dispatch, June 26, 1970.

14. *Acción,* Nov. 17, 1970.

15. Eric N. Baklanoff, "Pathology of Uruguay's Welfare State," *Mississippi Valley Journal of Business and Economics* 2 (Spring 1967): 65–67; David G. Redding, "The Economic Decline of Uruguay," *Inter-American Economic Affairs* 21 (Spring 1967): 55–72.

16. *Diario de las Américas,* June 18, 1971.

17. Weinstein, *Uruguay: The Politics of Failure,* pp. 125–27.

18. *Los Angeles Times,* Sept. 29, 1972.

19. *El Día,* Oct. 30, 1972.

20. *El País,* Mar. 22, 1973.

21. *El País,* June 29, 1973.

22. Marvin Alisky, "Uruguay," in R. F. Staar, ed., *1974 Yearbook on International Communist Affairs* (Stanford, Calif.: Hoover Institution Press, 1974), p. 375.

23. *El Espectador* and *El País,* Sept. 23, 1976; Howard Handelman, "Uruguayan Journal," *Worldview,* October 1977, p. 16.

24. Federico Fasano, *Paren las Rotativas* (Montevideo: Editorial Octubre, 1973), pp. 30–38.

25. Marvin Alisky, "Uruguay's Utopian Broadcasting,"*Journal of Broadcasting* 13 (Summer 1969): 277–83.

26. *El País,* July 27, 1976.

27. Federico G. Gil, *The Political System of Chile* (Boston: Houghton Mifflin, 1966), pp. 47–70.

28. "Chile Statistical Profile," *Economic and Social Progress in Latin America: 1977 Report* (Washington, D.C.: Inter-American Development Bank, 1977), pp. 182–83.

29. *Editor & Publisher International Yearbook 1978,* pp. III-41, III-42; U.S. Information Agency, *Mass Media in Chile* (Washington, D.C.: USIA, 1977), p. 9.

30. Roy E. Carter, Jr., and Orlando Sepulveda, "Some Patterns of Mass Media Use in Santiago de Chile," *Journalism Quarterly* 41 (Spring 1964): 216–24.

31. Ben G. Burnett, *Political Groups in Chile* (Austin: University of Texas Press, 1970), p. 36.

32. Raúl Matas, "Chile on the Air," *Américas* 7 (October 1955): 6–9.

33. Frederick B. Marbut, "Chile Has Law to Enforce Code of Ethics," *Quill* 48 (April 1960): 15–17.

34. Diane Stanley, "The Press in Chile: The Rectification Law," *Nieman Reports* 15 (January 1961): 27–31.

35. "Abuse of Publicity Act Divides Chilean Journalists," *IPI Report* (International Press Institute, Zurich), Apr. 1964, pp. 11–12.

36. "Muzzle Law Modified by Chile Government," *Editor & Publisher,* Aug. 12, 1967, p. 32.

37. "IAPA, Chile at Odds Over Press Control," *Editor & Publisher,* Oct. 1, 1966, p. 32.

38. Martin Houseman, "Chile's CD's Taking Over Publications," *Overseas Press Bulletin* 11 (Nov. 18, 1967): 1–2.

39. John C. Merrill, *The Elite Press: Great Newspapers of the World* (New York: Pitman Publishing Company, 1968), pp. 38, 51, 106, 240.

40. "Chile Bars Times Reporter, Charging Hostile Articles," *New York Times,* Sept. 3, 1970, p. 9.

41. Patricia Fagen, "The Media in Allende's Chile," *Journal of Communication* 25 (Winter 1974): 59–70.

42. Hans Ehrmann, "Letter from Chile," *Performance,* May–June 1973, p. 99.

43. "Allende Eases Pressures After Protests by the Press," *IAPA News,* July 1971, pp. 1–2.

44. *United Press International* dispatch, Sept. 30, 1971.

45. *New York Times,* Dec. 12, 1971.

46. *El Mercurio,* June 22, 1972.

47. *Los Angeles Times,* July 2, 1973.

48. Robert N. Pierce, "Lights Out in Santiago," *Quill* 62 (January 1974): 17–21.

49. Leopoldo Linares, "Chile: Four Years Later," *Atlas World Press Review* 27 (February 1978): 21–22.

50. "Chile: Bearing the Cross," *Latin America Political Report* 12 (June 23, 1978): 191.

51. "Chile Will Restore Freedom to Unions," *Arizona Republic,* Jan. 4, 1979, p. 3.

52. "Exhoto a Chile: Versiones de la Prensa Norteamericana," *Qué Pasa* 5 (Mar. 2–8, 1978): 8–9.

53. "Carlos Paul: No Creo Que Los Diarios Boten Gobiernos," *Qué Pasa* 5 (July 13–19, 1978): 28–31.

54. Charles A. Krause, "Chileans Relax Amid Improving Outlook for Rights," *Washington Post,* Mar. 19, 1979.

55. Jerry Knudson, "The Chilean Press Since Allende" (Paper at International Communication Division, Association for Education in Journalism, Houston, Texas, August 1979).

CHAPTER 11

1. Ministerio de Economía, *Estadísticas Sociales* (Guatemala: Dirección General de Estadística, 1977), pp. 3–12.

2. *Editor & Publisher International Yearbook 1978* (New York: Editor & Publisher, 1978), pp. III-43–III-44.

3. Marvin Alisky, "Central American Radio," *Quarterly of Film, Radio and Television* 10 (Fall 1955): 59–61.

4. Mary A. Gardner, *The Press of Guatemala* (Minneapolis, Minn.: Association for Education in Journalism Monographs, 1971), pp. 12–14.

5. Marvin Alisky, "Radio in Guatemala," *Radio Daily–Television Daily* 66 (June 24, 1954): 6.

6. Gardner, *The Press of Guatemala,* pp. 21–23.

7. Organization of American States, *Constitution of the Republic of Guatemala 1965* (Washington, D.C.: Pan American Union, 1966), pp. 27–28; Guatemala, *Ley de Emisión del Pensamiento* (Guatemala: Decreto 24 de la Asamblea Nacional, 1956), p. 16.

8. Gardner, *The Press of Guatemala,* p. 24.

9. *El Imparcial,* May 17, 1970.

10. Thomas and Marjorie Melville, *Guatemala: The Politics of Land Ownership* (New York: Free Press, 1971) explains these problems.

11. "Guatemala," *Latin America* 10 (July 23, 1976): 29.

12. Caesar D. Sereseres, "The Guatemalan Armed Forces" (Paper presented at the annual meeting of the Latin American Studies Association in Atlanta, Georgia, March 26, 1976).

13. *Editor & Publisher Yearbook 1978,* p. III-44.

14. James A. Morris, "Honduras: A Unique Case?" in Howard J. Wiarda and Harvey F. Kline, eds., *Latin American Politics and Development* (Boston: Houghton Mifflin, 1979), pp. 347–49.

15. Mary A. Gardner, "The Press of Honduras," *Journalism Quarterly* 40 (Winter 1963): 75–82.

16. Ibid.

17. Ibid.

18. "Honduran Army Overthrows Cruz in Bloodless Coup," *Phoenix Gazette,* Dec. 4, 1972, p. 1.

19. "At United Brands, Fight for Control Came After Honduran Payoff," *Wall Street Journal,* May 7, 1975, p. 1.

20. *La Prensa* (San Pedro Sula), Aug. 9, 1978.

21. *La Prensa* (San Pedro Sula), Sept. 24, 1978.

22. Ronald H. McDonald, "El Salvador: The High Cost of Growth," in Wiarda and Kline, *Latin American Politics,* pp. 388–89.

23. *Editor & Publisher Yearbook 1978,* p. III-43.

24. Steven Kinzer, "El Salvador," *New Republic* 177 (Sept. 3, 1977): 15–17.

25. *El Diario de Hoy,* June 8, 1970; *La Prensa Gráfica,* May 16, 1977.

26. Thomas W. Walker, "Nicaragua: The Somoza Family Regime," in Wiarda and Kline, *Latin American Politics,* pp. 316–31.

27. Marvin Alisky, "La Prensa Leads the Fight Against Nicaragua Censorship," *Quill* 49 (March 1961): 15–16, 19.

28. Marvin Alisky, "Our Man in Managua," *The Reporter* 23 (Dec. 22, 1960): 26–27.

29. Marvin Alisky, "Public Opinion under Dictatorship in Nicaragua," *Nieman Reports* 16 (April 1962): 12–14.

30. Marvin Alisky, "The End of Nicaragua's Radio Freedom," *Journal of Broadcasting* 5 (Fall 1961): 311–14.

31. *La Prensa,* July 10–28 and Aug. 7–15, 1973.

32. Stephen Kinzer, "Nicaragua: Universal Revolt," *The Atlantic* 243 (February 1979): 4–17.

33. "Chamorro Assassination Shakes Somoza Dynasty," *IAPA News,* Feb. 1979, p. 1.

34. Charles F. Denton, "Costa Rica: A Democratic Revolution," in Wiarda and Kline, *Latin America Politics,* pp. 375–81.

35. Robert N. Pierce, "Costa Rica's Contemporary Media Show High Popular Participation," *Journalism Quarterly* 47 (Fall 1970): 544–52.

36. "Panama Regime Eyes Control of Press," *Times of the Americas,* Feb. 18, 1970, p. 4.

37. Steve C. Ropp, "Panama's Domestic Structure and the Canal," in Wiarda and Kline, *Latin American Politics,* pp. 482–92.

38. Associated Press, "Panama Threatens," *Arizona Republic,* Sept. 28, 1979, p. A-18.

CHAPTER 12

1. Jorge I. Domínguez, *Cuba: Order and Revolution* (Cambridge, Mass.: Harvard University Press, 1978), p. 304; *Granma,* Feb. 6, 1978.

2. Jerry Knudson, "Flame of Freedom Is Dim in Chile," *Philadelphia Inquirer,* Feb. 27, 1979, p. 11-A.

3. Jerry Knudson, "Licensing News: The Bolivian Experience" (Paper at the International Communication Division of the Association for Education in Journalism, Seattle, Washington, August 1978).

4. *El Diario,* May 10, 1972.

5. Oscar Terraza Ayala, *Consideraciones Sobre la Necesidad del Colegio de Periodistas de Bolivia* (Cochabama, 1973), pp. 12–13.

6. John S. Nichols, "LATIN: Latin American Regional News Agency" (Paper at the International Communication Division of the Association for Education in Journalism, San Diego, California, August 1974).

7. *Excelsior,* Jan. 7, 1976.

8. Mary A. Gardner, *The Inter-American Press Association* (Austin: University of Texas Press, 1967), pp. 3, 18, 25.

9. Ibid., pp. 47–58.

10. Ibid., pp. 65–70.

11. "IABA Will Work for American Solidarity," *Boletín de la AIR* (Mexico City) 1 (January 1954): 1.

12. Fred Fejes, "Multinational Advertising Agencies and Latin America" (Paper at Latin American Studies Association, Pittsburgh, Pennsylvania, Apr. 5, 1979), pp. 16–17.

13. "Slums of Lima," *Journal of Marketing* 32 (April 1968): 96–97.

14. W. H. Cunningham, R. M. Moore, and I. C. M. Cunningham, "Urban markets: The São Paulo Experience," *Journal of Marketing* 38 (April 1974): 2–12.

15. Fejes, "Multinational Latin American Advertising Agencies," pp. 23–24.

16. Raquel Salinas, *Communication Policies: The Case of Latin America* (Stockholm, Sweden: Institute of Latin American Studies of Sweden, 1978), Study No. 9.

17. "Mexican Government Takes Over Newspaper Chain," *U.S.-Mexico Border Cities Association,* May 1972, p. 10.

18. Jerry Knudson, "The Chilean Press Since Allende" (Paper at International Communication Division, Association for Education in Journalism, Houston, Texas, August 1979), pp. 2, 10–11.

19. Ibid.

20. Colombia, Ministerio de Comunicaciones, *Memoria al Congreso Nacional 1978* (Bogotá: Congreso Nacional, 1978), pp. 169–84.

21. *La Prensa,* Oct. 10, 1973.

22. "Acuerdo: 12.5 de Tiempo al Estado," *Diario Oficial,* June 27, 1969, Sect. I.

23. "1978 IAPA Report on Press Unduly Optimistic," *Times of the Americas,* Apr. 11, 1979, pp. 4, 6.

Index

259